Religion and Politics in Africa

Religion and Politics in Africa

JEFF HAYNES

EAST AFRICAN EDUCATIONAL PUBLISHERS LTD
Nairobi

ZED BOOKS
London & New Jersey

To Sue and Katy

Religion and Politics in Africa was first published in 1996 by
Zed Books Ltd, 7 Cynthia Street, London N1 9JF, UK, and
165 First Avenue, Atlantic Highlands, New Jersey 07716, USA

East African edition published in 1996 by East African Educational
Publishers Ltd, Mpaka Road, Woodvale Grove, Westlands,
PO Box 45314, Nairobi, Kenya

Copyright © Jeff Haynes, 1996

Cover designed by Andrew Corbett
Typeset in Monotype Baskerville by Lucy Morton, London SE12
Printed and bound in the United Kingdom
by Biddles Ltd, Guildford and King's Lynn

A catalogue record for this book is available from the British Library
US CIP data is available from the Library of Congress

ISBN 1 85649 391 1 (Hb)
ISBN 1 85649 392 x (Pb)

East African ISBN 9966 46 657 6

Contents

Introduction

This book provides an account of the ways in which politics and religious institutions and groups interact with states in contemporary Africa.[1] The emphasis is on Christianity, Islam and a variety of 'syncretistic'[2] religions. The book is both thematic and comparative, locating the role of religion in politics in Africa in historical, social and international context. The approach adopted is based upon comparison within and between African states. Such an analytical framework allows comparison and contrast of various religious and political factors, including the nature of the relationship between the African state and assorted religious actors, including 'mainstream' religious organizations,[3] on the one hand, and between popular religious groups[4] (including 'fundamentalist' sects), on the other. In short, the book is concerned with an examination of the roles of religion in politics in contemporary Africa with reference to the historical, especially colonial, past.

In this book I use the term 'religion' in two distinct yet related ways. First, in a material sense, it refers to religious establishments (that is, institutions and officials) as well as to religious and religio-political groups and movements whose *raisons d'être* are to be found within both religious and political concerns. Examples in a global context include the conservative Roman Catholic organization Opus Dei, and the Hindu-chauvinist Bharatiya Jana Party of India. Examples in an African context include a number of radical Islamist groups, including the Islamic Salvation Front of Algeria (FIS), the Islamic Party of Kenya, and Balukta of Tanzania. Second, in a spiritual sense, religion pertains to models of social and individual behaviour that help believers to organize their everyday lives. In this sense, religion is to do with the idea of transcendence – that is, it relates to supernatural realities; with

I

sacredness – that is, as a system of language and practice that organizes the world in terms of what is deemed holy; and with ultimacy – that is, it relates people to the ultimate conditions of existence.

A further concern of the book is to seek to locate Africa's religio-political groups – including 'fundamentalist' groups, which will be examined in Chapter 7 – within a comparative context that will allow us to place such groups in Africa in a wider, international context.

The Concerns and Structure of the Book

Before examining politics and religion in Africa in the contemporary period, an analysis of the colonial era is undertaken in order to place the independence decades in proper perspective. To this end, I argue in Chapter 1 that the roots of the contemporary relationship between religion and politics in Africa can be traced back to the period of European colonialism, which lasted from about 1880 to about 1960. During this time there was, by and large, a clear affinity between Christian missionaries and colonial administrators; this did not rest solely on their shared 'Christian-ness', as it were, but was also bolstered by their shared 'European-ness'. That is to say, even though Christian officials and missionaries may, on occasion, have been unhappy with certain aspects of colonial policy – such as European settlers' confis-cation of African land in the 'white highlands' of Kenya – there were generally many more points of agreement than disagreement between religious and secular colonial personnel. Both parties, religious and secular, were, after all, pursuing the same aim: to bring the benefits of European civilization (as they saw it), including the Christian God, to as many Africans as possible. During the early years of the twentieth century, however, many Africans left the mission churches to join the growing number of African independent churches because they were seen as more in tune with Africans' religious needs than the hierarchical, European-dominated mission churches.

A further factor consolidating ties between European Christian leaders and secular colonial personnel was the challenge of Islam. By the late nineteenth century, Islam was a highly significant religion in many parts of West, East and, to an extent, Central Africa. Political arrangements, often involving variants of the indirect rule pattern prom-ulgated by Lord Lugard in parts of British-controlled Africa, including Uganda and northern Nigeria, were particularly conducive to the forging of mutually beneficial arrangements between leaders of Muslim communities and colonial administrations. Christian religious personnel may have been unhappy with the forging of *modi operandi* with their Muslim rivals, but were generally forced to accept such where administrators deemed it expedient, especially in northern Nigeria which was strongly Muslim by the time of the arrival of the Europeans in the late nineteenth century. Yet, while Muslim empires – such as that of El Hadj Oumar in combating the French, and of the Hausa-Fulani in fighting the British – had been important for a time in preventing the full consolidation of European rule in Africa, by the early twentieth century Muslim community leaders and colonial administrators had by and large arrived at ways of working together whereby the former agreed to administer their communities' affairs on behalf of the latter in exchange for both pecuniary rewards and a range of political and religious freedoms. Of particular importance was the spread of modernizing forces – urbanization, Western education, governmental centralization, the growth of a money economy – which collectively helped to mould African Muslims' responses to European colonialism.

As Chapter 2 shows, the articulation of African nationalists' demands, both before and after World War II, largely in reaction to employment and other forms of discrimination that, as educated people, they especially resented, was a clear challenge to the mainstream Christian churches, which were strongly associated by many Africans with colonial rule. The main issue, in effect, was this: how should the mainstream church leaders – that is, the local European heads of the Catholic and Protestant churches – deal with a situation where, by the late 1950s, partly in response to developments elsewhere (such as in the Indian subcontinent where decolonization was a fact) material power appeared to be moving inexorably, and swiftly, from Europeans to Africans? The churches were initially opposed, then sceptical, and finally won round to the idea of African independence. As for the African nationalists, they were highly suspicious of the churches for reasons already mentioned, even though the churches themselves sought to Africanize their personnel as soon as possible once independence arrived. The ambivalence with which the nationalists viewed the mainstream churches – on the one hand, they were welcome purveyors of education, health care and other welfare benefits at a time when colonial administrations were often rather deficient in this regard; while, on the other, they were, at least potentially, agents of neo-colonialism – was carried into the post-colonial era, and provides one important reason why the relationship between African governments and the former mission churches has often been marked by equivocalness. With regard to

Muslim communities, the absence of an institutional church within Islam and the relative 'backwardness' of many Muslims led the majority of European-educated nationalist leaders either to ignore or to co-opt Muslims into the nationalist project as and when this was deemed necessary.

Part I of the book, comprising Chapters 1 and 2, thus covers the period from the late nineteenth century until about 1960. It shows that Christianity was largely associated with European colonial domination of large numbers of Africans. Many left to join the burgeoning African independent churches. Islam, for its part, was seen as a challenge both to mission Christianity and to colonial administrators. Nevertheless, Muslim communities by and large reached arrangements with European colonial administrators.

Part II of the book comprises Chapters 3 and 4. In Chapter 3, building on the analysis of the colonial period, I pursue the argument that it is quite understandable that leaders of 'mainstream' religious organizations in Africa – Christian and Muslim – have, since independence, usually performed an important role as interlocutors between their followers and the state. Partly because of the colonial tradition of mutual support between mainstream religious organizations – Christian and Muslim – and the state, and partly because of the normative desire of the former to seek stability and consensus, their position was often supportive of the government of the day, apparently irrespective of the latter's form (one-party, personalist, military) or type of rule (dictatorial, authoritarian). The situation changed quite remarkably in the early 1990s, however, when, following the eruption of democracy demands, the political climate underwent rapid change. What helped to maintain the supportive relationship between the organizations and the state was the interaction of three sets of concerns: first, the shared interests of religious and secular leaders in the maintenance of the status quo; second, the strong desire of the mainstream organizations to maintain their religious influence, which could be pursued most expeditiously in a climate of good rather than poor relations; third, a normative concern with political stability as a good thing in itself. As far as government was concerned, the role of mainstream Christian churches, both Catholic and Protestant, in providing public goods, especially education and welfare, was welcome; indeed, in some cases – for example, Zaire and Tanzania – it was a quite crucial supplement to their own, often increasingly feeble, efforts.

I also present in Chapter 3 a typology of relations between the state and mainstream religious organizations in Africa; this describes how three forms of relationship have been common in the post-independence period. The first is the apparent *severance of good relations between Church and State*, for example in the Marxist-Leninist countries of Ethiopia, Angola and Mozambique; the second is a situation of *religious pluralism*, as in South Africa, Ghana and Zambia; and, finally, there are instances of *extremely close relations between Church and State*, for example between the main Islamic reformist body and the government in Sudan. The point is that in each of these apparently different situations the claimed ideology of the regime in power was relatively unimportant in understanding the nature of the relationship between state and religious institutions. What emerges is that religious leaders were often as concerned with their own personal positions as with the corporate status and prosperity of their religious organizations.

Chapter 4 extends the analysis of the relationship between Church and State in order to examine the role of mainstream religious organizations in the current period of pro-democracy agitation in Africa. I argue that high-ranking religious figures usually seek as far as they can to defuse or reduce serious political challenges to the status quo. Yet, during the last few years, several leading Christian figures especially have been in the forefront of demands for democratization; as suggested above, mainstream religious leaders and regimes normally work together to seek to achieve or maintain a hegemonic ideology that stresses the desirability of stability rather than change, even when the latter is regarded by many as likely to be generally beneficial to many sections of society. An overriding concern with stability due to fear about the consequences of change provides a framework of norms and values which legitimizes the policies and behaviour of the state elite by the development of recognized forms of mutually supportive action and expectation involving secular power-holders and senior mainstream religious personnel. In order to maintain their influential positions as intermediaries between the state and sections of society, it is necessary – even crucial – for leaders of mainstream religious organizations to retain the loyalty of their followers and to prevent defections to rivals; it is equally important for them to keep religious 'dissidents' under their control. In recent times, hegemonic religious leaders of mainstream Muslim and Christian bodies have found themselves threatened by a remarkable increase in unofficial sects and churches – that is, popular religious groups.

In Part III, comprising Chapters 5–7, I direct the analysis to the political role of three types of popular religious bodies: community-oriented, fundamentalist, and syncretic groups. The emphasis here is on popular religions and their relationships with the mainstream organizations and the state. Popular religious organizations offer forms of theology which are often more suited to the understanding of, and are hence more appreciated by, ordinary people, than are the rather formal, somewhat inflexible theological messages of mainstream forms of Christianity and Islam. The importance of a popular religion in a society or community reflects the power of ordinary people to take charge of their own spiritual well-being. To speak of theology, Islam, Christianity, or 'the church' in the singular is to fail to appreciate that such concepts only have meaning in the context of class relations within which they are viewed. In short, religious unity within a faith is actually a chimera because of the different interpretations contained within the corpus of followers of one body of religious belief: some of the religious vehicles will be in the form of popular organizations that are usually beyond the control of the leaders of the hegemonic religions.

Three issues of importance have emerged so far in the relationship between religion and politics in contemporary Africa: democratization and religion's role in it; the relation between political and religious elites; and the role of popular religious groups in African politics. In the remainder of this introduction I want to look at each of these issues in turn, in order to make a number of analytical points which will be of use in later chapters.

Hegemony, State and Church in Africa

The issue of democracy and the prospects for its introduction and consolidation in Africa have emerged as important topics for political activists and scholars alike in recent times (Diamond 1993a and 1993b; Clapham 1993; Bratton and van der Walle 1991). It is often argued that in the process of democratization leaders of the orthodox Christian churches – especially the Roman Catholic and mainstream Protestant – have been important participants (Witte 1993; Diamond 1993a and 1993b; Joseph 1993; Gifford 1994). While according a degree of merit to this argument, I argue for a more nuanced view. Without doubt, *some* Christian leaders have been in the forefront of demands for democratization in a number of African countries in recent times. On the other hand, some have not. My contention is that leading religious figures are very often class actors in partnership with political elites to seek to achieve mutually advantageous goals; it is, as a result, rather aberrant for leading religious personnel to confront the state determinedly over a long period of time. In the book, I use a broadly Gramscian perspective to argue, *inter alia*, that recent, successful democratic initiatives in Africa involving religious figures have more often than not been little more than successful strategies of 'passive revolution'.[5] This is because leading members of religious hierarchies are often, but not always, intimately bound up with state representatives in a continuing project to maintain a hegemonic domination over society. The chief purpose of Christian leaders mediating between different political factions is to settle intra-elite disputes between those seeking state power, rather than between those involved in wider societal conflict involving upper and subordinate class forces (Bayart 1989a).

A Gramscian idea of hegemony is highly relevant to a conception of power in Africa (Laitin 1986; Chabal 1992; Schatzberg 1988). It involves the creation and institutionalization of a pattern of group activity in a state with the concomitant espousal of an idealized framework that strives to present itself as 'common sense'. Hegemony also helps to explain how such characteristics as culture, social formation and political institutions, involving individuals and corporate bodies, fit together in a concept of power (Chabal 1992: 217). The concept of hegemony enables us to locate better the state–civil society relationship, the elite–counter-elite dichotomy, and division between those with and those without adequate resources to prosper, within a useful analytical framework (Chabal 1992).

Central to an analysis of hegemony is the nature of *power*. It is insufficient to see power as merely the ability of one group or individual to achieve the acquiescence – or, at least, quiescence – of another because of the fear of the consequences of noncompliance. Power should rather be thought of as a two-faceted, sometimes contradictory force: in Cox's expression, 'power is a centaur, part man, part beast, a combination of force and consent' (Cox 1993: 286). This is the crux, the core of hegemony: the iron fist fills the velvet glove; the former is uncovered only when deemed necessary. There is an exemplary enforcement potential: force underlies the power structure; the strong can (and will) crush the weak when necessary, and the weak know this. Yet the use of force to gain compliance will be the last, or at least not the first, option. Indeed, force wielded by the dominant against the subordinate will not be necessary (or only very rarely) if that domination is seen as legitimate, even necessary. In other words, force will not be resorted to as long as the subordinate classes regard upper-class domination as right and proper, or at least tolerable. Subordinate classes will be more inclined to view their position with relative equanimity as long as the dominant class seeks to rule by at least a modicum of consent, rather than by unremittingly absolutist or dictatorial means. The dominant class must, therefore, be concerned with the *form* as much as the *content* of its rule. Might alone cannot routinely be effective; it must be tempered with a practical concern to keep social relations relatively trouble free; a concern to rule by law as far as possible must be evident. Above all, members of the ruling class must express their leadership by allusion to general, rather than specific, interests, such as 'national unity' or 'national self-determination'. The development of (more or less) popular and democratic institutions is the key to the long-term success of hegemonic strategy. This is because institutions help to coalesce diverse interests within a single body, giving rise to consensus and to a universalization of policy over time. Many ordinary people perceive that power relations are as they should be when the state achieves its objectives without dissent. That is, it is only 'right' that politicians and state officials rule authoritatively, that is their role. The goal of those involved in the hegemonic quest is to create what Williams calls a 'unified moral order', in which 'a certain way of life and thought is dominant, in which one concept of reality is diffused throughout society' (Williams 1960: 587).

In order to perpetuate hegemony successfully it is necessary for the dominant strata to maintain a more or less consensual moral order which has the status of common sense. Subordinate classes accept such a moral order, according to materialist analysis, out of a 'false consciousness' (Amin 1993). This allows the dominant political elite to rule through consent rather than relying too heavily upon coercion alone. Yet, this should not be taken too far in the African context: hegemony is rarely achieved on the basis of social and popular consent alone; coercion is always a highly useful option for the authorities to maintain social control. The 'false consciousness' argument is not a convincing explanation as to why subordinate-class Africans obey the authorities (when they do, which is by no means all of the time); obeisance is undoubtedly as often due in part to a well-founded fear of the consequences of not toeing the line. Because of the fear of the consequences as well as the social divisions extant in most African societies, it is usually difficult to see unified political actions undertaken by subordinate classes in pursuit of their class interests. It is by no means clear whether subordinate-class Africans perceive their interests to be best fulfilled by class action rather than by 'plugging into' the networks of reciprocity and by creating popular vehicles of mobilization, including religious ones. Before turning to the issue of popular religious vehicles, I want to discuss the nature of the relations between the African state and religious groups more generally.

Clientelism, the State and Religious Organizations

In order to locate the notion of hegemony in a form which is conducive to analysis, it is necessary to define at the outset what the African state *is*. The state in Africa is best understood as the sum of two theoretically separate, yet in practice connected, developments: first, it is a rapacious *structure* of interlinked interests (involving the creation and perpetuation of clientelistic relationships), where 'public institutions [are] colonized and emasculated' (Bates 1993: 419); and, second, it is at the same time the location of a hegemonic *process* whereby political figures engage in a pursuit of power. Forrest suggests correctly that 'state rulers are defined by and obtain their power and resources on the basis of their office-holding' (Forrest 1988: 439). Thus, the 'state' is not merely the sum of its official institutional parts; there is also a partial interpenetration of the state and society, where clientelist ties are the cement holding the system together, creating in the process a class structure which develops on the basis of a social differentiation rooted in the practicalities of wealth accumulation, rather than in relation to the productive process. As a result, a hegemonic striving unites individuals and groups within the national power structure, including mainstream religious leaders.

Religious leaders are by no means exempt from clientelistic concerns: the same forms of structure and process as operate in the state can be seen within many religious institutions. Leading figures join together in a theocratic 'class' which seeks to advance their personal and institutional position in relation to competitors. The crux of the matter for religious as for temporal leaders is that public office *can* bring private profit and influence. Certainly, some of the accrued wealth trickles down to those outside of the state parameters: it is assured by the conglomeration of clientelistic, familial and kin relationships. To many ordinary Africans the 'success' of a religion is reflected at least in part in the ability of its leaders to exhibit a high level of material wealth; how else is it clear that God smiles on the religion's leading figures?

It has often been noted how politics in Africa is characterized by the importance of patrimonial and clientelist relationships (see, for example, Joseph 1987; Bayart 1993a; Chabal 1992). 'The big man, small boy syndrome' often dominates political, social and economic relationships between individuals. Virtually everyone who has an official capacity has the essential wherewithal to benefit in some way from their position.

The intermingling of public and private concerns is by no means un-usual in Africa: the patrimonial notion of power and the position of the individual in relation to the community coalesce in an understanding that power, whether spiritual, political or economic, *can* bring profit (Chabal 1992: 258). Individuals develop mutually beneficial relation-ships with both subordinates and superiors. In political competition the cultivation of networks of reciprocity is a *sine qua non* for the aspirant politician and the incumbent power-holder. Those who fail to maintain their network of relationships are likely to fall prey to the shifts of politics, to find themselves ousted from their positions which gave them power in the first place. Because religious institutions have to survive in an environment of resource shortages, their structural characteristics and the types of interaction between individuals closely parallel those in the secular realm. There is extensive interaction between religious elites and the representatives of state power for mutual benefit (Forrest 1988: 429). Being a *de facto* member of the state framework gives senior religious leaders opportunity to amass personal wealth, in just the same way as other leaders of important societal groups, such as senior trade-union officials, leaders of professional bodies, top civil servants, and ethnic leaders, may do. There are, of course, no doubt quite a few senior religious figures who wholeheartedly devote themselves to the spiritual health and welfare of their followers without developing addi-tional sources of remuneration for personal well-being; nevertheless, many others do.

Networks of reciprocity involve religious organizations in Sub-Saharan Africa in three ways. First, as described in Chapter 4, religious leaders will normally, but not invariably, co-operate with state power for both pecuniary and spiritual advantage. Threats and rewards may be issued by the state's representatives to religious personnel. The aim either way is to ensure compliance with state objectives of societal control. Second, churches have been greatly influenced by what Gifford refers to as the 'Big Man model' of politics (Gifford 1993: 310). Senior and middle-ranking religious figures, while no doubt personally con-vinced of the spiritual efficacy of their religion, may in addition under-stand their job as a means to enhanced well-being. Family members and ethnic allies may be rewarded with jobs. Profits accrue to religious big men from their worldly business interests (Bayart 1989a, 1993a). In Togo, for example, some Catholic prelates are referred to as 'autoritaro-prébendier' (that is, both authoritarian and 'prebendalist')[6] (Toulabor 1991: 123). On the other hand, the position of less exalted priests and other religious personnel may be on the decline: some accounts suggest that a serious drop in applications to African Roman Catholic seminaries is related to the perception that the priesthood's social and economic position has seriously diminished in recent times (Luneau 1987). Third, as discussed in Chapter 4, some leaders of African religious organizations profit from their relationships with foreign non-governmental organizations (NGOs). Western NGOs, mindful of state corruption, which sees financial resources only too frequently disappear into private pockets, often prefer to deal with church organizations; they are deemed to use the money in more constructive ways, as well as being relatively independent of state control (Gifford 1993). Foreign donors, including those which have no formal links with religious organizations, such as USAID, pump money into church organizations, which are often judged to be more 'honest' and accountable than their state's governments in disbursing funds. Foreign funds rarely find their way to popular religious groups, although they are, by definition, concerned with ordinary people's interests. Generally lacking hierarchical leaderships, such groups usually fail to gain the ear either of government or of foreign actors, such as NGOs. They are, however, of immense importance in many parts of Africa.

Popular Religion and Politics in Africa

I understand a 'popular' religion to be one which serves as a community expression of a group desire to achieve a religious satisfaction which is not forthcoming from a mainstream religion. Both Marx and Weber stress how the 'contingent nature of the relationship between the content of an ideology and the social position of the group who are its "carriers" is of fundamental importance in understanding the social role of an ideology' (Giddens 1971: 211–12). What this suggests in relation to the hegemonic religions is that their leaders will be concerned with perpetuating and promulgating a version of religion which is also an ideology of domination, which aims to strengthen and bolster their own social and theological position. Popular religious organizations, on the other hand, will offer a more 'user-friendly' alternative to those who are less than impressed with what the mainstream organizations have on offer spiritually.

I examine three types of popular religious organization in the book. The first kind, which I call 'basic Christian communities', are reminiscent of Christian groups which emerged, *inter alia*, in parts of Latin America in the 1960s; they often have a clear political thrust to their activities (Haynes 1993a: ch. 4). I suggest that Africa's basic Christian communities did not generally develop along the same lines as those in Latin America – that is, as political vehicles of subordinate classes – except perhaps in South Africa. This was partly because in Africa the concept was more often than not imposed from above in order to overcome a serious shortage in priests on the ground; in other words, whereas in Latin America such communities were normally galvanized by radicalized priests, in Africa they were usually not. One result was that the African communities generally failed to develop as vehicles of popular power. The failure of African basic Christian communities to develop along the lines of their Latin American counterparts is also explained in part by the differing class structures of the two regions; that is, Latin America's class structure, located in reasonably high levels of industrialization, is more developed than in much of Africa, where appeals to class solidarity normally fall on deaf ears.

The second example of popular religious organization I examine is women's Islamic groups. They are to be found in many African countries where Islam is an important religion. They are especially notable in several countries, including Nigeria and Senegal, where they serve as conduits of women's liberation aimed at male repression. I shall argue in relation to women's Islamic groups that women use Islamic beliefs to defend themselves vis-à-vis men's attempted domination by skilfully employing Islamic precepts to their advantage.

The final example of popular religious organizations I examine are non-gender-oriented Islamic groups found, *inter alia*, in Kenya, Tanzania and Nigeria. They share a similar range of anti-state, socio-economic and political concerns, which sometimes also have an ethnic dimension. The aim of examining these examples of popular Islamic religious vehicles is to demonstrate how such groups may well develop political goals, the forms and orientations of which usually relate to the nature and characteristics of the effects of power dispersal within their societies.

In addition to examining the political concerns of certain types of popular religious organizations, the book sets out to explain the recent development of popular religious vehicles in relation to the upheavals occasioned by the modernization process in Africa since the early years of the twentieth century. An important benefit of popular religions, both as belief systems and as forms of community organization, is that they offer solidarity and group togetherness, which is particularly important at times of serious social upheaval and crisis. They help to fulfil people's spiritual, and sometimes material, needs better than other religious alternatives on offer. One of the main catalysts for the growth of popular religious organizations in Africa in the twentieth century has been the multiple effects associated with modernization. Modernization – a process involving, among other things, urbanization, centralization of government, and the growth of modern economies; in short, the multifaceted expression of almost unprecedented socio-economic and political change throughout the twentieth century in Africa as else-where in the 'Third World' – has been instrumental in stimulating the development not only of 'new', popular Christian churches but also of a range of Islamic and syncretistic religious vehicles. To Weiner, religion in 'Third World' contexts 'demonstrates the powerful attraction of transcendental sentiments as an ordering element in human relations and as a way of explaining collective misfortunes' (Weiner 1992: 317). Perhaps this is how modernization is most commonly perceived by many ordinary people in Africa: as the occasion of massive misfortune. Popular religion, seen in this way, is a means of attempting to come to terms with such transformation, to offer hope in the future of beneficial change, of improvements in people's lives, by the application of spiritual efforts. During the 1980s, a period which corresponded to a decade of particularly serious economic downturn for many African countries, there occurred, surely not coincidentally, what has been described as a 'mushrooming' of new churches in the region (Gifford 1994: 515). Africa's explosion of new religious vehicles paralleled a similar develop-ment in Latin America, which, similarly experiencing economic down-turn during a 'lost development decade', witnessed a widespread, popular turning to 'new' Protestant evangelical churches, many of which aggressively proselytized from their North American bases (Martin 1990; Haynes 1993a).

Many – probably most – African states have a fair number, and sometimes very many, popular religious faiths and sects, including various manifestations of Christian, Islamic and syncretic belief. I contend that the growth of popular religious organizations in Africa, especially in recent times, is due to the unsettling effects of moderni-zation on many ordinary people, as well as to the perception that the mainstream, official, orthodox religious organizations are rather remote from their concerns. Bayart suggests, in addition, that popular religions are the ordinary person's way of cocking a snook at authority (Bayart 1993a: 256–8). Mbembe argues that 'the current explosion of religious revivalism in Africa is another ruse by the common man to create a counter-ideology and alternative political space in response to the totali-tarian ambitions of African dictators' (Mbembe 1988: 96). I accept that various forms of popular religion may be a potent – and sometimes an overt – symbol or emblem of political opposition, yet maintain that this is not necessarily the case in all instances; that is, they are not always forms of anti-state political mobilization camouflaged in religious garb. It is necessary, I suggest, that disadvantaged people – commonly, but by no means invariably, the main followers of popular religions – should be regarded as following such religions for a variety of reasons. Political and material concerns have traditionally – especially but not only by Marxists – been conceptualized as somehow more 'real' than other kinds of needs. Yet, it is by no means obvious that poor people *only* define their demands along material and political lines. Spiritual and community benefits – delivered via religious vehicles – are, I shall argue, just as important for many people as material benefits alone.

In Chapters 6 and 7 I look at the political orientations of two types of popular religious organizations: syncretistic and fundamentalist groups. In Chapter 6 I look at what are commonly known as 'new religious movements' – those syncretistic religious organizations which emerged in many parts of Africa during colonialism and after it. I also examine the most recent manifestation of such movements in Africa: the 'fundamentalist' religious organizations – both Christian and Muslim – which have emerged in recent years and which governments and leaders of mainstream religious organizations alike often perceive to be directed by foreigners, such as Americans, Saudis or Iranians.

Syncretistic or 'new' religious movements are found throughout many parts of Africa. During the colonial era such movements flourished in the rural areas in a context of widespread dissatisfaction with aspects of colonial rule. On occasion, erstwhile foes – such as the Shona and the Ndebele in colonial Rhodesia (Zimbabwe) – combined to resist British colonialism. Religious identification was an important facet of such organization. Spirit mediums used 'medicines' to enhance warriors' martial efforts. They created a national network of shrines to provide an agency for the transmission and co-ordination of information and activities, a structure which was re-established during the independence war of the 1970s (Ranger 1985; Lan 1985). The use of medicine also helped galvanize the anti-colonial Maji-Maji rebellion of 1905–07 in German-controlled Tanganyika. The diviner and prophet Kinjikitili gave his followers medicine which was supposed to render them invulnerable to bullets. He anointed local leaders with the *maji* ('water') which helped to create solidarity among about twenty different ethnic groups and encouraged them to fight together in a common anti-European cause. In northern Uganda, the cult of Yakan amongst the Lugbara, which also centred on the use of magic medicine, galvanized the Lugbara in their short war against Europeans in 1919 (Allen 1991: 379–80). The list of such religio-political movements could be extended; the point, however, is hopefully already clear: many cults arose, led by prophets, stimulated by colonialism and the social changes to which it led. They employed local religious beliefs as a basis for anti-European protest and opposition.

After colonialism, similar cults continued to appear: clearly their existence could not be explained solely by the stresses and strains occasioned by colonial rule. The beliefs associated with the followers of syncretistic leaders such as Alice Lenshina and Joseph Kony in Zambia in the 1950s and 1960s, and the violence these beliefs engendered, should be located within a general background of upheaval which occurred as a result of the end of colonial rule (Allen 1991: 379). They can be explained as a response to extreme social trauma, a manifestation of collective despair at an unwelcome political outcome. As colonialism waxed and waned, the spread of both Christianity and Islam throughout Sub-Saharan Africa continued apace. Religious figures like Lenshina and Kony skilfully fashioned an ideology of resistance which used a blend of pre-Christian and Christian religious beliefs to create a potent mobilizational force. What these examples suggest is that in many rural areas of Africa threatened by crisis and the problem of profound social instability, provided there exists a sufficient degree of communal solidarity, prophet-led resistance, whether to colonial or post-colonial state or rebel attack, will succeed in organizing communities in self-defence. The lack of clear class differentiation in rural African societies has given the appeal of religious syncretist ideologies a wide currency. Oppressed and defeated peoples turned to the metaphysical in pursuit of their struggle against outside control. What seems clear is that such movements were not merely a reaction either to colonialism or to discrete post-colonial political developments. Rather, they were concerned with cultural, regional, ethnic, political and economic tensions which existed before colonialism (and which the latter helped to politicize), and which resurfaced in the post-colonial epoch when one group sought to achieve hegemony over others. Groups that resort to religious symbolism as political ideology are generally those that not only feel mistreated or abandoned by government, but that are also traditionally marginalized by both colonial and post-colonial political and economic structures and processes.

While the new religious movements mentioned so far have been mostly connected – albeit sometimes tenuously – to Christian ideas, it would be wrong to assume that none is Muslim. From the revisionist

Islam of Ahmadiyya to the near revolutionism of the Maitatsine movement based in Kano, northern Nigeria, the discussion in Chapter 6 indicates that a fairly wide range of Muslim new religious movements has formed in Africa over the last sixty years, with various spiritual, economic or political aims and objectives.

What is often of most importance in the context of state–society relations is how the state perceives a popular religion's aims. For example, as Fields (1985) notes, during the colonial period the Watchtower sect in Central Africa was regarded by the colonial authorities as a politically revolutionary movement masquerading as a religious group. So was Mau Mau in the 1950s in Kenya. Similarly, in the post-colonial era, orthodox Islam has done its best to dominate its Sufi rival because Sufism has often been regarded as a leading force of societal opposition among Muslims against the status quo. The state in Africa often has great difficulty in dominating popular religious sects, in order to ensure that they operate according to the official rules laid down in the context of the state's hegemonic politico-administrative framework (Forrest 1988: 428). During the last decade or so, states have been increasingly concerned with what they perceive as 'alien' religious influences penetrating their societies from beyond their borders and affecting the beliefs and goals of certain popular religious organizations. In Chapter 7, I turn the analysis to contemporary manifestations of what are commonly known as religious fundamentalist organizations – both Christian and Muslim – in order (1) to investigate their relationship with the state and with mainstream religious organizations, and (2) to ascertain the effect of the involvement of foreigners in their aims and objectives.

Fundamentalist religious organizations have emerged as challengers to their mainstream religious rivals in Africa over the last twenty years or so, part of an apparently global trend. Such is the concern with the haemorrhaging of their followers to their *arriviste* rivals that the mainstream Christian churches employ two strong lines of attack. On the one hand, the fundamentalist churches are accused of being little (if anything) more than American 'Trojan horses', while on the other the orthodox churches rush to incorporate evangelical elements (glossolalia, faith healing, copious biblical allusions) into their services (Mbembe 1988). The fact that millions of Africans – in common with many other regions in the Third World, including tens of thousands in Latin America, East Asia and the Pacific Rim – have converted to fundamentalist Christianity over the last twenty years or so, a period of enhanced modernization, suggests strongly that such people find something in it which is absent from the mainstream churches. At the same time, the dominance of some fundamentalist churches by wealthy foreign (especially North American) pastors helps to confirm the association between their religion and personal prosperity: they appear to offer a vision of Western consumerist success which serves as a powerful inducement to materially less successful people – an attraction for many converts in addition to the perceived spiritual benefits of the churches.

Several analysts have observed that many of the new churches in Africa are located at the fundamentalist end of the religious spectrum (Gifford 1994). By the end of the 1980s, in virtually all major African cities as well as in a number of rural areas, there were to be found many new churches which stressed their fundamentalist religious credentials – offering scripturalist forms of religious piety which affirmed the central relevance of the Bible for the day-to-day activities of their followers and which insisted upon the regulation of most aspects of social and individual behaviour.

Despite their leaders' claims to political neutrality, such churches are often strongly supportive of the status quo and of 'strong' government (Toulabor 1994). The political significance of the fundamentalist Christian churches is also manifested in a number of other ways. First, their followers apparently have no problem in endorsing their (American or Westernized) leaders' aversion to socialism. Whether this is due to their being controlled from abroad by conservative Americans or a result of indigenous beliefs is open to debate. Quite apart from the fact that to many Africans, whether followers of fundamentalist Christianity or not, socialism may well define itself as a negation of the very existence of God, further distrust for many follows first-hand experience with various types of 'African socialism', often associated with the bureaucratization, elitist power concentration, waste, and ideological inflexibility during much of the post-colonial period. Yet, any aversion to 'socialism' which may be present among followers of fundamentalist Christianity does not necessarily imply a lack of concern with community well-being *per se*. It appears that to some fundamentalist Christians at least, religion *should* be concerned with social and community issues, especially a communal sharing of fears, ills, jobs, hopes, and even material success (Marshall 1991, 1993). On the other hand, earthly misfortune is perceived as the result of a lack of faith: God will reward true believers. That is, it is held that those who believe sufficiently will reap material rewards in this life, rather than waiting for the next one to repay them for their earthly devotion to God. It appears that adherents of Christian fundamentalist churches in Africa often believe that people's spiritual redemption is in their own hands (or, rather, in God's and the individual's hands), and that expectations that government could or should satisfy all or even most of people's needs and deal with their material problems is misplaced. Consequently, it is unsurprising that fundamentalist Christians in Africa, unlike their counterparts in the United States, do not usually seek to join political parties to further their social and economic aspirations; instead, they appear to believe in the biblical idea that political leaders should rule and senior religious figures should stick to spiritual matters. What this implies is that followers do not ordinarily involve themselves in the cut and thrust of political competition; it does *not* mean that when a clearly political issue arises with significant implications for the fundamentalist Christian community they will remain silent. For example, as Chapter 7 explains, fundamentalist Christians in Nigeria have become a significant collective political voice in the context of the fear over perceived Islamization of the country.

Popular Muslim organizations generally offer ways of affirming the autonomy and the identity of a religious or ethno-religious community in many urban centres in Africa. Muslim community organizations, rather like Christian fundamentalist churches, serve to 'rescue' those who are 'drifting' in the urban milieu, including those who come to the urban centre for economic betterment but instead, finding themselves cut off from family and community, and alienated by social conditions, seek a religious-community vehicle to satisfy their longings for 'togetherness'. For such people, Muslim religious-community organizations offer an alternative 'family' which, like the Christian fundamentalist churches, serves as an expression of solidarity and cohesion (Charnay 1980: 241). Yet, African Muslim community groups below the Sahara are, for their part, very rarely 'fundamentalist'. I understand religious fundamentalism to involve scripturalist forms of religious piety which serve to testify the core appropriateness of a holy book for quotidian activities and which insist on the day-to-day regulation of most – if not all – practices of both individual and social behaviour.

There are two general forms of Islamic fundamentalist groups in Sub-Saharan Africa. On the one hand, there are the reforming groups, influenced by Iranian or Saudi Arabian conception of Islamic orthodoxy; these attract mostly the educated, intellectually convinced of the desirability of attaining an Islamicly 'pure' society. On the other hand, another kind of Islamic fundamentalism has also emerged, notably in Nigeria, in response to growing polarization between Christians and Muslims over the issue of which religion is to dominate in the country.

This is an Islamic fundamentalism less concerned with the introduction and promulgation of orthodox Islamic purity than with championing the 'rights' of Muslims in relation to those of Christians. It is a defensive Islamization which, calling on the closing of ranks of Muslims *qua* Muslims vis-à-vis Christians, serves to stress the 'apartness' of the two communities.

Conclusion

During both colonial and post-colonial periods in Africa, religion and politics have shown a significant, mutual concern for each other. Temporary confidence in the 1950s and 1960s that the growth and spread of urbanization, modern education, economic development, scientific rationality and social mobility would combine to diminish significantly the socio-political position of religion was not well founded. Instead, two broad trends were observable: first, mainstream religious organizations sought to retain or to build their influence by close partnership with governments, often in the face of growing challenges from popular rivals; second, popular religious organizations developed as vehicles of religious opposition or as foci of community self-interest. Threats emanating either from powerful outsider groups or from unwelcome symptoms of modernization sometimes galvanized popular religious reactions. Failure on the part of governments to push through programmes of social improvement exacerbated the trend towards the founding of local religious-community groups.

A notable feature of the development of religious praxis in Africa since the early 1960s was the emergence of popularly driven, community religiosity, often reform-oriented. A factor which such groups have in common is that religious professionals, while often respected, are not assumed to have the final word on religious praxis. The development of sets of community-oriented religious beliefs helps to develop mobilizing ideologies of opposition and self-expression. Each of the groups examined in this book has in common disaffection from and dissatisfaction with established, hierarchical, institutionalized religious bodies; a desire to find God through personal searching rather than through the mediation of institutions; and a focus on the ability of communities to make beneficial changes to members' lives through the application of group effort. This desire to 'go it alone', not to be beholden to 'superior' bodies, characterizes the relationship of nearly all popular religious groups to their mainstream rivals in Africa. The (at least temporary) demise of communism as a mobilizing idea leaves the ideological cupboard rather bare. Religion offers a rational alternative to those to whom modernization has failed or is in some sense unattractive. Its interaction with political issues over the medium term will be of importance, in carrying a message of societal resurgence and regeneration to both political leaders and economic elites.

Notes

1. 'Africa' in this book refers to Sub-Saharan Africa; other nomenclatures that will also be used for the sake of variety include 'Africa below the Sahara' and 'black Africa'. Any references in the text to North Africa will be made plain in the contexts in which they are used.

2. 'Syncretistic' religions are those which combine a variety of heterogeneous elements in their spiritual world-view.

3. Mainstream religious organizations are those which have established a regularized, systematic form of interaction with the state over time, and which are regarded by the latter as 'official', representative of large numbers of people. Examples include the Roman Catholic Church, the main Protestant churches, and the 'orthodox' versions of Islam championed by the ulama, i.e. the body of professional Muslim theologians.

4. Popular religious groups are those which are generally outside the control of the mainstream religious organizations. They offer to those disillusioned, or in some way dissatisfied, with the latter, alternative, community- or interest-group oriented religious vehicles which appear to serve their followers more satisfactorily.

5. The idea of 'passive revolution' denotes the way that any dominant sociopolitical group would have to change its manner of wielding power in some apparently fundamental way in order to preserve its hegemony at moments of great social instability.

6. A prebend is the share of revenues that a clergyman gains from officiating at some ceremony in the official course of his duties; in Toulabor's use of the term (which follows Joseph 1987), the prebend is an illicitly gained revenue, via perhaps a bribe or other form of corrupt wealth accumulation.

PART I

Religion and Politics in Colonial Africa

I

Religion, Colonialism and Hegemony

In order to understand the role of religion in political discourse in contemporary Africa – as, on the one hand, an ideology of attempted hegemonic control, and, on the other, as a vehicle for mobilizing community organization, often to help fend off that control – we need to refer back initially to the colonial era. In this chapter, we will examine the ways in which Christianity and Islam developed in relation to politics during the colonial period. Of particular concern will be their roles as important sources of popular resistance and mobilization of community concerns, which emerged in response to the social uncertainties that colonialism and modernization brought in their wake.

To highlight the importance of colonization for the development of the relationship between religion and politics in Africa, the analysis of this chapter is divided into four parts. We start with some general remarks about the role of religion in relation to colonial administrations. Second, we look at the growth and heterogeneity of Islam in Africa below the Sahara before European colonization. During the colonial era, a pattern of initial resistance to hegemonic rule by Christian Europeans developed over time into a more complex relationship, often characterized by the emergence of Muslim interlocutors presiding over Islamic counter-societies as an important facet in the system of indirect rule. Here can be seen the roots of modern popular Islam, which has had a major impact in the context of state–society relations in a number of African Muslim countries in the post-colonial era. Third, we move on to Christianity to examine the multifaceted nature of that faith in the colonial era, when the initial emphasis of the missionaries – on an active, morally concerned God – drew thousands of Africans into the mission churches only for them to find that their

23

chief concern, that spiritual forces could be called upon to improve their life chances in the here and now, was not always fully satisfied by the European versions of Christianity on offer. Finally, we examine the growth of African independent churches, which grew in part because of a felt spiritual need and in part because of the perception – linked to indignation at the racial intolerance within the mission churches – that Africans needed their own churches (Horton 1993: 155–6); as a result, many flocked out of the mission churches into their own independent Christian bodies, which were also manifestations of popular religion outside the hegemonic pull of the European-controlled churches, a role that these and other religious bodies continued to play in the post-colonial era. By the end of the chapter we will be in a position to appreciate the various political functions of religion during the colonial period.

State and Religion in Colonial Africa

The nature of the contemporary African state is in large part due to the legacy of the colonial era. Although the two main colonizing countries in Africa, France and Britain, were democracies, the institutions they created were little more than instruments of domination. Administrative networks were grafted on to pre-existing institutions; hegemony and security were very closely linked (Young 1988: 41). Colonial administrations attempted to employ religion tactically in their pursuit of political domination. Yet, religious interaction between ordinary Africans and the colonial authorities was by no means a straightforward relationship of dominance and dependence. Africans used religious belief as a means of adjusting the relationship between themselves and colonial authorities in their favour as far as possible. Whether through the founding of independent churches or via Africanized modes of Islam, leaders created relevant and popular religious vehicles for themselves and their followers. The point is that such religious communities functioned both during and after colonization as ways for ordinary people to come to terms with and to test the forces of change and modernization which the Europeans brought. They functioned as statements of social, political and economic interaction, as well as being important foci of community aims and strategy.

Mission churches, on the other hand, were an important facet of attempted colonial cultural domination, with both repressive and liberating functions: they were agents of both European superiority and political domination and the purveyors of modernization, especially Western education, which was quickly recognized by Africans as the key to advancement in colonial society. Pre-existing Muslim communities, on the other hand, attempted to deal with European-inspired modernization by seeking to come to terms with its effects without compromising Islamic ideals, once it became clear that it was not possible to defeat the Christian Europeans by force of arms.

We should regard religion's role in politics in contemporary Africa as arising from the multiple changes occasioned by European colonialism. Those few states which did not undergo formal foreign control (Liberia, for example, experienced Afro-American colonialism) nevertheless soaked up modernizing influences as though they had. Those countries where a majority of the population were neither Christian nor Muslim during the period of colonial rule (for example, Guinea-Bissau, Upper Volta [now Burkina Faso], Sierra Leone) were nevertheless ruled by Europeans; traditional religious activities had to function within their legal jurisdiction. Islam also had to coexist with European power and was ultimately under the latter's control.

The role of mission Christianity as an institutional force during the colonial period was not simply one of undifferentiated support of temporal political power. Whether the colony was settler-dominated or not is significant for an understanding of the relationship between Christian missionaries and colonial authorities. If large numbers of settlers were present (as in Kenya and South Africa), then a complex relationship developed between them, Christian missionaries and colonial authorities. Where substantive numbers of settlers were absent (as in most of West and west-central Africa and Uganda), Christian missionaries and colonial authorities tended to have mutually supportive relationships.

Yet, because the different Christian churches were in direct competition for converts, there was rivalry between them (Burns 1929: 261). Sometimes a truce would be declared in face of the common enemy – Islam. When Islam appeared a threat to Christian dominance, steps were taken by Western education to try to undermine its attraction. When Islam was already religiously and culturally dominant, however, even the temptation of education (and its attendant material rewards) was usually insufficient, in the face of cultural and community solidarity, to attract more than very small numbers of people to convert. Nevertheless, Muslim leaders were generally pragmatic enough, albeit often after serious opposition – the West African empire of El Hadj Oumar against the French, the Hausa-Fulani empire against the British, and Somalia being cases in point – to reach some kind of *modus vivendi* with colonial authorities (Boahen 1987: 49–54; Lapidus 1988; Sheikh-Abdi 1993).

One aspect of Islam, pan-Islamism, was of lingering concern for colonial rulers, who were worried that Germany and the Ottoman Empire were actively seeking Muslim leaders as allies in their strategic rivalry with Britain in the first few years of the twentieth century. Fears in the 1990s of a resurgent international Islam – directed from Tehran, some argue – can be seen, with the benefit of historical perspective, as a renewal of earlier fears of a resurgent, foreign-directed force whose aim is subversion of the status quo and its replacement by totalitarian domination (Krauthammer 1993). As we shall see in Chapter 6, although both Iranian and Saudi Arabian versions of Islam are important today as religious and financial influences among some African Muslim groups, there is virtually no chance of a pan-Islamic movement gaining supremacy in Africa. The reason for this is that African Muslims are fundamentally divided – by ethnicity, by country, by area of domicile (whether urban or rural dwellers), by whether they are reformists ('fundamentalists') or members of the conservative (and competing) Sufi brotherhoods, and so on.

Islam in Sub-Saharan Africa: From Pre-colonial to Colonial Times

This section seeks, first, to examine the spread of Islam during the pre-colonial period in order to place the faith's development in historical perspective in both colonial and post-colonial eras. Second, we look at the spread of Islam via the Sufi brotherhoods and its gradual super-seding of traditional religions in many areas. We then turn to two aspects of the interaction between Europeans and Muslims in the colonial period: (1) the forging of working relationships between Muslim leaders and colonial authorities in the context of indirect rule; and (2) the ways in which Islam spread in the early twentieth century during the process of modernization. As modernization gained pace in Africa in the colonial period, Muslims, like other Africans, sought to gain individual and community benefits.

Jihads ('holy wars') were examples of attempts in both the eighteenth and nineteenth centuries at religious reform which sought wider moral and social reconstruction of Muslim societies. In the late nineteenth century, the wider Muslim world experienced the slow demise of the Ottoman Empire and the (near) contemporaneous emergence of Saudi

Arabia as champion of Wahhabi reformist ambitions. The growth of the Sufi brotherhoods and their reformist rivals were two developments in African Islam that more or less coincided with the consolidation of European rule; others were the extension of Muslim networks throughout much of Africa and beyond, and the introduction of new modernizing ideas. During the first half of the twentieth century, Africa's Islamic communities often initially opposed European Christian rule, before they learnt to live with it and benefit when they could. Muslims joined Sufi brotherhoods to further their own commercial networks, and were often receptive to the reformist ideas of the Wahhabiya and of Pan-Islamic ideals in the context of urbanization and the development of ethnically oriented Muslim groups.

Statistics on the growth of numbers of both Muslims and Christians in Africa during the period of consolidation of colonization – in the decade around 1900 – should be regarded as impressionistic rather than precisely accurate. What seems reasonably clear, however, is that during the first half of the twentieth century in Africa below the Sahara, because of the imposition of European colonialism, the pace of growth of Christianity outstripped that of Islam; the numbers of Christians increased from around 10 million in 1900 to more than 250 million currently; numbers of Muslims in Africa grew from about 34 million to perhaps 300 million over the same period (Oliver 1991: 256–7).

Many of Africa's Muslims live in North Africa, but a substantial minority live below the Sahara. The continent is predominantly Muslim above the tenth parallel, which cuts through the northern regions of Sierra Leone, Côte d'Ivoire, Ghana, Togo, Benin, Nigeria, Cameroon, the Central African Republic, Ethiopia and Somalia. The same line roughly separates Muslim from non-Muslim in Sudan and Chad. Above the tenth parallel, the Gambia, Senegal, Mali and Niger are preponderantly Muslim.

Islamization in Sub-Saharan Africa went through three stages: first, converts accepted elements of Islamic culture and practice, especially distinctive clothes and some religious concepts; second, formal conversion to Islam was accomplished, with the ulama (religio-legal scholars) accepted as the sole representatives of God on earth; a third stage of conversion was marked by recognition of the principles of Islamic law, the acceptance of the five or six pillars of Islam (belief in one God, prayer, fasting, alms, pilgrimage, and – some would add – *jihad*), culminating in some areas with a comprehensive Islamization of local cultures. The process of 'full' Islamization was by no means uniform: some communities reached the first stage; others stage two; and a few, those nearest to the Arab heartland who received the longest and most focused exposure to Muslim religious culture, stage three. Often, especially in West Africa, indigenous ethnic and cultural factors interacted with Islam's universalist aspects to produce significant local variations which were distinctively African modes of Islamic belief.

Patterns of conversion to Islam tended to be quite different in West Africa than in East Africa. Parts of Africa closest to the Sahara Desert and thus North Africa were exposed to the effects of Islamization for up to a thousand years before European colonialism. The result was that entire communities became Muslim. In East Africa, on the other hand, Islamization was a much more patchy process. Islam was, of course, the faith of the region's slavers – Arabs from the Arabian peninsula – but they were much more concerned with collecting people for export than in spreading a religious message. In fact, the Arabs regarded themselves as superior precisely because they were Muslims and their victims were not. It was only in the late nineteenth century when slavery was finally replaced by more conventional trade that certain ethnic groups in East Africa – among them Gallas (Oromos) and Somalis – were able to adopt Islam, in part to facilitate trade with the more Islamized coast. Islam all but failed to reach southern Africa before the advent of European colonization; as a result the vast majority of people in those regions became Christian or remained devoted to traditional religious beliefs.

Such a great variety of African peoples and communities converted to Islam that it is very difficult to arrive at a simple, monocausal explanation for its appeal or to describe its socio-political impact on individual communities. What can be said is that Islam provided individuals and communities with a monotheistic religion, with attendant social and cultural norms, and with an attitude of cultural and religious superiority over non-believers. When Islam had sufficient time to become socially and culturally entrenched before the advent of European colonialism (as in northern Nigeria), then it contained within it the wherewithal of community solidarity which helped to ward off European-led modernization (Callaway and Creevey 1994). Islamic social solidarity was also important in Senegal, where the strength of the Sufi brotherhoods, especially the Muridiyya, facilitated a role as major agricultural producers of millet and groundnuts, with the latter crop grown largely for export. In this way modernization led to the entry of Senegalese groundnut producers into an international economic system controlled by Western interests.

By the time of the Muslim flight from Western Europe at the end of the fifteenth century, Islam had already established itself as the dominant socio-religious factor in North and much of West Africa. Islam spread from the Middle East via North to Sub-Saharan Africa in two ways: first, from the seventh century by a series of *jihads*; and, second, by trade in commodities and people. Slavery raged for a millennium. Where they existed, Islam followed pre-existing trade routes, such as the North African and Indian Ocean ways. The expansion of Islam from Egypt to Morocco in the seventh century, and from Morocco to West Africa in the tenth, was facilitated by the existence of such conduits. In West Africa the process of Islamization dates from the eleventh century, following the fall of the kingdom of Ghana to the Almoravids in 1076. The fall of Ghana to Muslims had two important effects on the advance of Islam in West Africa: first, it had considerable political and psychological significance because hitherto Ghana was one of the most important states in the area run by African non-Muslims; second, it led to the conversion of the elite, and to the subsequent dominance of local derivatives of universal Islamic culture. From this time on it was West Africans themselves – rather than Arabs – who spread Islam. This led to the Africanization of Islam in non-Arab West Africa, and to the Islamized kingdoms of Mali, Songhai and Hausa. A Moroccan invasion in 1591 destroyed the empire of Songhai, and the descendants of the invading army became the ruling elite in the Niger region. By the end of the eighteenth century, however, the once great Muslim kingdoms of the western Sahara had disintegrated into a plethora of small states (Lapidus 1988: 495).

As Islam spread from Mauretania to present-day Sudan between the sixteenth and nineteenth centuries, it was periodically 'purified' by *jihad*, until the coming of the Europeans put an end to such forceful means of religious reform (Boahen 1987: 14). A militant tradition grew up involving a determination to turn small colonies into Islamic states by defeating non-Muslim rulers, converting their people to Islam, and then ruling them according to Muslim law. The beginning of the Muslim thirteenth century in 1879 galvanized a further period of *jihad*. Islamic literature had prophesied the emergence of the 'awaited deliverer' (the *mahdi*), 'who would prepare the world for the end of time' (Stewart: 1986: 192). There emerged on cue the self-styled Mahdi in the Sudan, Muhammad Ahmad ben Abdallah, who led a determined revolt against the British. Although Muhammad Ahmad died in 1885, amid the political uncertainties following the partition of Africa Mahdism retained a populist appeal which endured until after World War I (Boahen 1987: 192–3). *Jihads* were finally brought to a close by the European conquest, although Islam continued to spread by way of the Sufi brotherhoods. As African societies rapidly urbanized during the colonial era, the Sufi brotherhoods established a reputation in many urban centres as the single most important facilitator of credentials necessary for newcomers – merchants and workers. In the post-colonial period, Sufism came to represent a form of 'uncaptured' Islam which was beyond the control of the reformist elites that dominated national Muslim organizations. For this reason, they were especially targeted as examples of 'corrupt' Islam.

Sufi brotherhoods as a popular challenge to the status quo

A significant proportion of Muslims in both East and West Africa belong to Sufi brotherhoods (*turuq*; sing. *tariqa*). Because of their importance both as purveyors of Islam and as vehicles of popular Islam, it is necessary to say a little more about them. While in theory brotherhoods are distinguished by not much more than variations in the form of prayer, in practice they often link ethnic groups, perhaps across state boundaries; as such they provide concrete examples of Pan-Islamic ties and represent popular vehicles of Islam which serve as counter-societies in the face of the hegemonizing tendencies of the Muslim reformists, such as the Wahhabites.

In the post-colonial period, Muslim reformists often attempted to control the brotherhoods' activities because of their promulgation of allegedly 'corrupt' forms of Islam. Generally – but not everywhere: Senegal is an exception – Muslim reformists gained control of national Muslim organizations to forward their own reformist aims and also to limit the power of the brotherhoods. In Senegal, leaders of the main Sufi brotherhoods play an important role in underpinning the state's hegemony. In furtherance of this aim they have found it expedient to link up with secular political elites. I will focus upon the growth and influence of the three most important brotherhoods: the Muridiyya, Tijaniyya and Qadiriyya during the pre-colonial and colonial periods.

The history and development of each was fashioned by their founders and by later leaders, including Ibrahim Niass, Abdul Aziz Sy, Sa'Idu Nuru Tall and Abdul Lahat M'Backe. The oldest of the Sufi orders in West Africa is the Qadiriyya, which gained widespread allegiance from the late eighteenth and early nineteenth centuries. Its stronghold is in Senegal, where it has more than half a million followers (Diallo 1988).

The Muridiyya brotherhood, with about 1,500,000 followers in Senegal, was founded in the late nineteenth century by Ahmadu Bamba (1850–1927), a holy man of Wolof and Tukulor descent, whose reputation was based on asceticism, piety and a lack of self-interest. Despite (or perhaps because of) Bamba's reputation, the French exiled him on several occasions, first to Gabon (1895), then to Mauritania (1902). He was allowed to return to Senegal in 1907. From this time the French authorities and Bamba reached a *modus vivendi* based on recognition of shared goals: Bamba accepted the futility of trying to rid the country of the French; whilst the latter, no doubt impressed by his apparent acceptance of the status quo, began to perceive the Muridiyya as a force for stability and economic growth (their collective farms were efficient groundnut producers), rather than rebellion. From this time, the brotherhood, at times assisted by the French colonial authorities, began to expand even more rapidly throughout Senegal.

By 1912, Bamba's brotherhood had grown to an estimated 70,000 members. Many had been displaced as a result of the political, social and economic developments that followed the advent of French colonialism. The brotherhoods in general were increasingly popular substitutes for a society and world that were being radically changed by European-inspired modernization. The brotherhoods played a role in relation to colonialism rather similar to that of African independent churches: both helped to establish African identities to facilitate community development, and on occasion economic growth, during a period of fundamental change. The brotherhoods' economic colonization of much of Senegal was inspired by Ahmadu Bamba's injunction, 'Work as if you would never die and pray as if you would die tomorrow' (Stewart 1986: 210). The brotherhoods offered those displaced by colonialism an Islamic-orientated society and authority structure which was quite distinct from that created by the colonial regime.

The Muridiyya's main rival, the Tijaniyya, entered Senegal from Mauretania in the early nineteenth century. The brotherhood exhibited an appeal which transcended ethnic and linguistic boundaries, and enabled it to expand rapidly throughout West Africa; it currently has some two million followers in Senegal. The Tijaniyya peacefully co-existed with colonial regimes, with the exception of one man, Ibrahim Niass, and his followers. Niass, the head of the 'Reformed' Tijaniyya, is of interest because of the transnational missionary activities of his group (Clarke 1982: 207). In 1937 Niass met Abdullahi Bayero, the emir of the northern Nigerian city-state of Kano, who apparently accepted Niass's claim to be the self-proclaimed 'Saviour of the Age'. Partly as a result, Niass sent his representatives all over West Africa to encourage people to join the Tijaniyya and to accept him as saviour. This brought Niass a large following in northern Nigeria (especially in and around Kano),

Burkina Faso, Côte d'Ivoire, the Gambia, Ghana, Guinea, Mali, Mauritania, and Togo. As with the rival Muridiyya, not all of Niass's followers were the alienated or politically powerless. Wealthy merchants, businessmen and professionals were also to be found in his brotherhood. This may be explained by the idea that Niass (following the message of the Quran) preached that commercial success was a gift of God: no opprobrium adhered to the wealthy, while membership of Niass's brotherhood would no doubt be good for the extension of commercial contacts.

Yet Niass was concerned to keep Western education at bay and to encourage Islamic learning and the acquisition of Arabic, the language of the Quran. In the sense of getting back to the 'fundamentals', he was a 'fundamentalist', although this should not be taken to imply that he was a political conservative. In effect, his anti-colonial message, manifested in the establishment of *zawaya* (communities), helped to popularize his interpretation of Islam (Cruise O'Brien 1988: 24). Some of Niass's followers saw him as an African whom God had singled out to lead the anti-European protest. The support which Niass enjoyed should be seen both as a reflection of Islamic and cultural self-assertiveness, and as an early manifestation of Pan-African politicization. Unlike Ahmadu Bamba, who is said to have imbued Islam in Senegal with many cultural characteristics of the Woloff, Niass was both internationally and Pan-Islam oriented.

On the East African coast the major brotherhoods at the end of the nineteenth century were the Qadiriyya and the Shadhiliyya. Black Africans in the hinterland had been denied access to the word of Islam by the Arabic and Swahili traders of the coast. Sufi brotherhoods allowed black Africans to 'build an Islam of their own', involving their own leaders and their own ethnic group (Cruise O'Brien 1988: 19). During the early years of the twentieth century, branches of the Qadiriyya, based in Zanzibar, Dar es Salaam and Bagamoyo, extended their influence inland to Rwanda, Mozambique, Nyasaland, Tanganyika, Kenya and Uganda, where Muslim communities were already established at commercial centres. The Shadhiliyya came to the East African coast from the Comoro Islands, and established itself sufficiently to branch out to Mozambique, Tanganyika and Uganda.

Islamization and the superseding of traditional religions

Despite the success of the Sufi brotherhoods in spreading Islam both before and during colonization, the faith did not everywhere dominate traditional religions. Part of the reason is that Islam's growth was slow, sometimes taking hundreds of years to travel from one population group to another by way of traders. *Jihad* speeded up the process in certain epochs; and during colonialism, Islam's growth continued in part because it was perceived by many Africans to possess anti-European, anti-Christian religious and cultural – and hence political – attributes. It is also important to note the relationship of Islam to the state's role in the context of social change. It is not obvious why Islam spread gradually and steadily in some areas of Africa, while it was prevented from growing elsewhere, even before European colonization (Owusu-Ansah 1987: 132).

It appears that Islamic influences were more readily accepted in West Africa than elsewhere because the new beliefs and religious practices were often adopted as supplements to pre-existing religious forms, rather than as substitutes (Levtzion 1971: 333). In the early stages of Islamization, proselytizers stressed the magical, ritual aspects of the faith rather than its political and legal characteristics; this meant that it was not usually perceived as a threat by incumbent rulers. This pragmatic adaptability of Islam was, however, counterbalanced by a bedrock of doctrinal and legal foundations. While magic and healing helped Islam to gain followers, its educational aspects helped to extend its teachings; trade, pilgrimage and membership of Sufi brotherhoods helped to build the idea of a Muslim universe.

Because the process of Islamization was often furthered by traders, the scope for proselytization was determined by the attitudes of the political institutions and leaders with whom they came into contact. An examination of Buganda and Asante, two pre-colonial African states on the margins of Islam's spread, shows how the welcome afforded to Muslims was intimately tied to the elites' perceptions as to how Islam would benefit them personally; in short, economic rather than spiritual concerns motivated rulers in their relations with Muslim traders, who for their part wished to deal with Muslims rather than pagans. Islam's differing rates of growth among the Asante and the Baganda – slow in the former, swift in the latter – is attributable to the different types of political system in operation. In Buganda, the Kabaka enjoyed virtually absolutist power, while that of the Asantehene was more constrained. The Kabaka (king) of Buganda was a ruler whose power was such as to render his word unchallengeable by lesser figures; the Asantehene's role, on the other hand, was that of a constitutional monarch who could be (and frequently was) ousted by political challenges. Asante contacts with Muslims began in the early eighteenth century, when it conquered northern states composed largely of Muslim traders. Islamic proselytization began in Buganda from the 1840s; by 1875, Islam had already experienced its 'Golden Age' of maximum influence (Ashe 1890). As Owusu-Ansah (1987: 138–9) notes, '[t]rade with Arabs and conversion to Islam served two important functions. It guaranteed the flow of commerce and enhanced the position of the Kabaka domestically and in the interlacustrine region. Hence the vigour with which Kabaka Mutesa pursued his Islamization programme.' By the 1890s, however, the spread of European missionaries' influence led to a reduction in the power of local Muslims in Buganda. British colonial authorities, in tandem with the Protestant missionaries, worked successfully to divide Uganda's Muslims between Baganda and non-Baganda, achieving the objective of removing the Muslim threat to a Christian hegemony – which nevertheless experienced its own difficulties at the time in the form of serious rivalry between Catholics and Protestants. In Asante, on the other hand, powerful trading interests managed to keep Muslim influence to a minimum by effectively vetoing the Asantehene's overtures concerning increased Muslim activity in the state. As a result, Muslims in Asante were a politically marginalized group both during colonialism and after independence.

I have suggested that the process of Islam's spread in both West and East Africa before colonialism was a complex one, with interacting political, economic and cultural factors resulting in an Islam characterized by a wide range of beliefs, religious practices, folklore and superstition. By the early years of the twentieth century the northern third of Africa was firmly integrated into the Islamic world by virtue of the spreading of the cultural norms of the faith itself and by the resulting economic networks which linked black Africa's Muslims with their counterparts in Egypt and the Middle East (Stewart 1986: 222). Reformist movements attempted to regularize Islamic practice, which resulted in increased spiritual and political authority for the ulama. European colonizers found an array of forms of Muslim community with which they had to deal. After initial hostility, European colonial administrations often found it quite easy to establish working relationships with leaders of Muslim communities, based on the principle of mutual benefit. The emergence and political significance of such relationships form the focus of the next section.

Colonial authorities and Muslim communities

During the period of European colonialism, African conversion to Islam often became a symbol of anti-Europeanism, an alternative modernizing influence in opposition to the hegemony of the European Christian missionaries and their system of putative enculturation. In other words, Islam provided its followers with an alternative modernizing world-view, not defined by the colonial order and its norms (Stewart 1986).

By the time of World War II, Muslims probably constituted about half of Africa's population (Oliver 1991: 256). Islam was the basis of local communal and social organization, but not of state power or national identity. Nevertheless, because of the European policy of cultivating interlocutors between administration and society, Muslim leaders were able to carve out for themselves niches within the structure of power, to advance both their own interests and those of the constituencies from whence they derived. Sufi brotherhoods prospered under colonial rule in many areas, including Senegal, Mauretania, northern Nigeria, Tanganyika, Sudan and Somaliland (Cruise O'Brien 1988: 25–6).

During the colonial period, French and British administrations often preferred to deal with those Muslims they recognized as following a relatively 'civilized' religio-cultural code. Pagans, on the other hand, often appeared to exhibit to the Europeans all the worst aspects of a lack of appropriate religion in their lives. Yet pagans and Muslims alike often opposed European rule, not least because it tended to be accompanied by an aggressive Christian evangelization (Trimingham 1980: 103). New eruptions of *jihad*, as noted above, were encouraged by the beginning of a new Islamic century across the Maghreb and the Sudanic belt. During the 1890s and the first years of the twentieth century, Muslim resistance flourished in Sudan, Somaliland, Libya and Morocco, before a *modus vivendi* was established between Muslims and European colonial authorities. Both Libya and Morocco were in the first flushes of an Islamized militancy at the time following the recent founding of polities espousing Muslim values. In Morocco, it was a feeling that the sultan had been compromised too far by successive European demands that led to Islamic resistance. In Somaliland, it was the deprivations of Muhammad Abdallah Hasan, called by the British the 'Mad Mullah', who unleashed a reign of terror against local people who refused to join his Salihiyya brotherhood, which focused Islamic militancy. The British sent in four expeditions between 1900 and 1904 to attempt to quell the *jihad*, but Hasan retained his influence in the north of Somaliland until as late as 1920 (Stewart 1986: 195–6).

The initial effect of *jihad* was both to stiffen the resolve of Muslims to fight European encroachment, and to identify Islam more generally with a militant anti-colonial stance. Aggressive European intrusion against various African peoples sometimes led to their mass conversion to Islam as a potent signal of continued resistance. In West Africa, for example, the Mandinka people converted *en masse* following French campaigns against them in the last two decades of the nineteenth century, while in German East Africa the bloody repression of the Maji-Maji revolt between 1905 and 1907 resulted in a turning to Islam by the persecuted Ngindo people (Stewart 1986: 198).

If localized Islamic militancy was often not sufficient to disturb the sang-froid of colonial authorities, the threat of a militant Pan-Islamism certainly was. Not only were there links between Mahdists in the Sudan and in northern Nigeria in the first years of the twentieth century, but there were also Pan-Islamic influences associated with the Ottoman Turks. Sultan Abdulhamid, Caliph of Islam for over thirty years (1876–1908), attracted many African Muslims, who saw him as the leader of the only Islamic power which could confront the Europeans with any hope of ultimate success. At the outbreak of World War I, the Ottomans issued a call to *jihad* against the Europeans which circulated widely in North Africa and parts of Kenya and Mozambique, although without conspicuous numbers of African Muslims heeding the call. The end of the war stimulated the fall of the Ottoman Empire, and Egypt, with its national programme which sought to emulate Turkey's example, became in turn a model of Islamic reform for some African Muslims.

The crushing of the Ottomans, coupled with the apparently inexorable spread of European power, confirmed to many African Muslims that the Europeans could not be defeated by force. *Jihad* was increasingly regarded as somewhat anachronistic. Muslims who wished to distance themselves from European suzerainty physically withdrew themselves from their ambit. Whereas a few examples of militantly separatist Muslim communities developed – such as Chinasala, which emerged in Malawi at the end of the nineteenth century in reaction to the hegemonic policies of the Presbyterian Church and to taxation (Shepperson 1954: 245) – a tactic more common than militant separatism was the institution of a policy of 'separate development', whereby Muslims refused to join Christian educational systems but in other respects maintained reasonably good relations with Europeans. The result was that by World War I most Muslims had not only resigned themselves to European colonial rule but many had also responded positively to the new economic opportunities it offered. Sufi brotherhoods were a moderating influence and, as Stewart (1986: 202) suggests, this confirmed the wisdom of colonial policies which aimed at the incorporation and appeasement of Muslim authority within the structures of indirect rule.

While the concepts and forms of Islam purveyed by the Sufi marabouts (holy men) and shaykhs (preachers) were regarded as the epitome of a corrupt form of Islam by the ulama, the adhesion of the latter to a 'purer' or reformed version of the religion did not prevent them reaching an accommodation with European authorities. Such people, with their knowledge of Arabic, their contacts with the outside Muslim world, and their understanding of Islam as spiritual world-view and as political ideology, were initially difficult for colonial authorities to work with. In many respects they were similar to Christian Africans: educated to university level in Europe or North America, both ulama and educated Christians developed international and internationalist world-views which coloured their relationships with colonial authorities. Later, after World War II, a new generation of Islamic reformists challenged conservative ulama. In the process of attacking these religious leaders, they also threatened the strata which had reached an accommodation with European imperialism. Representatives of the colonial administration unhesitatingly threw their weight behind the conservatives, and attacked the reformists.

Colonial policy towards African Muslims was affected both by earlier experiences of dealing with Muslims elsewhere (in India especially) as well as by the nature of African Muslims' response to European intrusion. French colonial authorities, who were on the whole somewhat more sensitive to the political reaction of Muslims than were the British, discovered, as a result of their long colonial sojourn in Algeria, that it was easier to reach accord with marabouts, who had a limited, somewhat localized view of Islam, than with ulama, who had often studied outside the region in Egypt and elsewhere. The British attitude to Muslims, on the other hand, especially in Sudan and northern Nigeria, was moulded by Indian experiences. Of particular salience was the policy of individual administrators. Both major colonizing powers utilized the policy of indirect rule, which could easily accommodate compliant Muslim leaders. By the 1920s, many colonial administrators had forged a *modus operandi* with Muslim leaders; the latter promised to deliver their people's support for (or at least quiescence in) European policies, while the former established Muslim notables within the structure of indirect rule. Islamic law was codified and administered by Europeans, sometimes leading to the establishment of both Islamic and European courts.

One of the best examples of a mutually beneficial relationship between Europeans and local Muslim rulers was to be found in northern Nigeria, where Lord Lugard's system of indirect rule (actually first developed in Uganda, following Britain's Indian colonial experiences) owed much of its success to the fact that it tampered hardly at all with pre-existing socio-political structures and cultural norms. The local Fulani elite, albeit that they were slave owners, became intermediaries with the colonial administration as a reward for putting down the Mahdist revolt of Satiru in 1906 (Bayart 1993a: 126). While northern Nigeria emerged as a testing ground for the efficacy of the policy of indirect rule, the Fulani political leaders were able to enlarge their sphere of influence by extending their supremacy over previously autonomous non-Muslims, especially those in what were to become Plateau and Borno states.

Even though Muslim elites found it useful to deal with Europeans on a political basis, they were less willing for the modernizing effects of European education to be promulgated in areas they controlled. After independence, Muslims living in areas where European education had been discouraged found themselves unable to compete with mission-school-educated Christians for control of national political institutions; this led to the political marginalization of the Muslim voice, often already fragmented by ethno-religious rivalries, even in countries like Ghana, Kenya or Côte d'Ivoire, where they represented up to a quarter of the population.

Although European education did not find favour among more conservative Muslim communities, once it became established that European administrations could count upon a cadre of loyal, moderate Muslims with standing in their communities, they began to found colleges to undertake studies in Arabic to equip putative Muslim bureaucrats (Stewart 1986: 204). Such educational establishments were created in northern and southern Nigeria, Sierra Leone, Kenya and in parts of French West Africa. Nevertheless, most Muslim boys and nearly all Muslim girls remained outside of this Westernized educational system. For their part, the providers of European education – the Christian missionary societies – criticized colonial policies towards Islam as being too favourably disposed to it. Christian missionaries were concerned about utilizing Muslims in the indirect rule system, about the *de facto* acceptance of Islamic law where administrators considered it appropriate, and, in general, about the continued expansion of Islam throughout much of Sub-Saharan Africa. Colonial administrators, if they were torn between encouraging Christian evangelizing and the smooth running of their domain, chose the latter. It is significant that, although Christian missionaries were opposed to the administrative recognition of Islamic norms and structures, they were unable to deflect colonial rulers from the policy. Evidently political accord, and especially the consolidation of European rule with the minimum of social and political friction, was of greater importance to colonial administrations than the triumph of Christian proselytization over Islam. One result was that in a number of areas, such as parts of south-east Nyasaland (where there were conversions to Islam in the 1880s) and northern Nigeria, Christian proselytizing was curbed at the behest of Muslim heads of communities.

The practical effect of indirect rule was not only to encourage acquiescent Islamic leaders but also, as Stewart (1986: 203) notes, 'to confirm and reinforce the importance of Islamic institutions'. Not all Muslim leaders were by any means initially acquiescent, yet many later became agents of colonial rule, while many ordinary Muslims were willing to serve in colonial military and police forces. This suggests that collaboration between Muslims and colonial administrations became increasingly common. The latter took pains to enlist respected Muslims – such as Sufi shaykhs – who had standing within their own communities and who would be useful as tools of the administration to moderate and mediate with their constituencies.

The social and political corollary of the concord between Muslim notables and colonial administrations was that the former found themselves in positions of personal influence, and by extension gained a more significant role for Islam, only when they were prepared to work with colonial administrators. The forging of mutually advantageous working relationships between Muslim leaders and political authorities was to continue into the post-colonial era. For many Muslim leaders, collaboration with both colonial and post-colonial governments was the best way of achieving both individual and community benefits. Thus, during the colonial period, as modernization gained pace, Muslims, like other Africans, sought to gain such benefits. In the next section we look at the ramifications of modernization on the spread of Islam in Africa below the Sahara.

Modernization and Muslims in colonial Africa

From around the time of World War I, urbanization drew increasing numbers of Africans, Muslims and non-Muslims alike, into the towns and cities of Sub-Saharan Africa. Whereas in West Africa, as previously noted, whole communities converted to Islam, in coastal East Africa, on the other hand, Islamization remained a mostly localized phenomenon, until after the war. Until then, Islam had largely remained the religion of foreigners: Arabs, 'Persians', Indians and Swahili merchants, culturally oriented away from Africa usually towards the Arab world. After World War I, the spread of Islam was facilitated by the existence of Swahili as lingua franca, by the social need to establish a common identity amongst heterogeneous peoples, by a desire for new bases of social and political organization, by the need to establish a trading network of trustworthy individuals, and by the need for a mechanism of defence against the practice of Europeans favouring African Christians for jobs.

Urbanization, and by extension other aspects of modernization, resulted in the founding of separate organizations for discrete Muslim groups in the coastal population centres of East Africa. The formation of Muslim associations during the colonial period reflected a three-way ethnic and economic division, which was to remain of political significance after independence. It involved a division between Muslims of Arab descent, historically recent arrivals from the Indian subcontinent, and indigenous black African Muslims. Intra-Muslim political competition reflected historic ethnic and economic antagonisms – in part, the result of lighter-skinned Arab and Indian Muslims being granted political favours over indigenous black Africans by European colonizers. The favouring of certain groups over others can be illustrated by alluding to the composition of the colonial legislative council in Kenya. From 1920, it included one seat for a nominated Arab member. In the following year the Coast Arab Association was formed to seek elective representation on a wider basis. This was obtained in 1923, but elections increased factional rivalries to the extent that two separate organizations for Kenyans of Arab descent were founded in 1927 and 1928 – the Afro-Asian Association and the Arab Association (Stewart 1986: 217). In the post-colonial era, numerous Muslim associations were formed to serve the separate ethnic communities; these include the Kenya Muslim Welfare Society, which sponsors schools and clinics. This suggests that during the period of swift modernization the 'glue' of Islam was insufficient on its own to overcome ethnic and cultural differences between different groups of Muslims – that is, to unite them against Christian Europeans.

There was a similar situation in Tanganyika, with the swift growth in the numbers of Muslims in the decade after World War I. At that time, the proportion of Muslims rose from about 3 to around 25 per cent of the population, as the result of a series of social upheavals, including Germany's withdrawal, the British entry, an influenza epidemic, and an accompanying famine (Tripp 1992: 224). In effect, there was a swift demographic shift from belief in the old gods who had failed to keep European colonization at bay and other traumas, to Islam which offered both spiritual benefits – an alternative, more powerful God – and material improvements. As in Kenya, separate ethnically divided Muslim associations were founded during colonialism: the Arab Association (*c.* 1900), the Indian National Association (*c.* 1914), the African Association (1934), and, for Zanzibaris, the Shirazi Association (1939). Each professed Islamic ideals of solidarity while promoting members' particularist economic interests. What this suggests is that urbanization increased the differentiation between distinct Muslim groups separated by ethnicity. Each group established its own organization to press for its advancement. The result was that a number of different Muslim groups were formed with a range of religious, welfare, educational and economic activities and goals. This fragmentation of Muslim interests across a variety of associational groups led to a diffusion and thus diminution of any putative Muslim voice in East Africa, which was of great value to post-colonial regimes whose leitmotif was national unity. A symptom of the breakdown of the efficacy of the national unity ideal, as well as of the growth of foreign Islamic influences, emerged much later – in the 1980s – in both Kenya and Tanzania. In both countries Muslim reformist groups were founded to further specific groups' interests after decades of constraint imposed by single party rule. As we shall see in Chapter 5, the stultifying effects of one-party rule were highly efficacious for the growth and development of Muslim counter-societies in many African urban contexts, forming foci of social solidarity which surfaced in sometimes overtly political forms in the 1980s as tentative democratization moves began.

A further factor in the multiple processes of change affecting African Muslim communities between the world wars was the emergence of reformist strands of Islam. In the 1930s and 1940s, reformist groups – especially the most important of them, the Wahhabiya – were influenced by the activities of the Egyptian Muslim Brotherhood, which sought to radicalize the country's quiescent Islamic establishment. The Wahhabiya's main stronghold in the 1940s and 1950s was at Bamako (Mali), at the junction of trade routes between Senegal, Guinea, Côte d'Ivoire, Burkina Faso, and the Niger region; its central position, which aided communication with distant regions, helped to disseminate its message of Islamic reform and unity. The ideas of Wahhabiya were also spread by higher-education students who studied in Egypt and came into contact with the radical Islamic ideas of the Muslim Brotherhood and other neo-Muslim movements. Pilgrimages to Mecca and Medina were also efficacious in this regard in helping to develop the reformist movements' popularity. As the political climate edged towards increasing articulation of nationalist concerns around the time of the end of World War II, Wahhabiya leaders found it expedient to ally with secular nationalists. The growth of Wahhabiya in Côte d'Ivoire, for example, was closely associated with the rise of the Rassemblement Démocratique Africain (RDA). As we shall see in Chapter 2, leaders of the RDA and the Wahhabiya made common ideological purpose despite their religious differences.

In the next section of the current chapter the discussion moves to an account of Christianity and politics in the colonial period. The main difference between African Muslims and African Christians was, of course, that while the former saw themselves as fundamentally distinct from the Europeans who came to their lands, the Africans who adopted Christianity did so, at least in part, *because* that religion was associated with European-ness and 'progress'. We trace the political role of the purveyors of Christianity in Africa during the colonial period – the Catholic and Protestant mission churches – in order to put the post-colonial relationship of mainstream Christian churches in political perspective. Following that, the emergence of independent African Christian churches – in effect, vehicles of popular Christianity – is discussed. It will be argued that they emerged in the early years of the twentieth century in response to the deficiencies which many Africans perceived in mission Christianity.

Christianity in Sub-Saharan Africa: The Coming of the Europeans

Mission churches and colonial power

If the situation involving Muslims and colonial administrations resulted from the very inequality between the power attributes of each group, that involving the Christian mission churches and the same authorities was based on a quite different relationship. The Christian mission churches were perceived by many Africans to be in the vanguard of the advance of European hegemony. Yet, initially, African Christians' response to colonial rule and the advance of the mission churches was generally favourable. While Europeans were usually perceived as *de facto* representatives of foreign cultural and political hegemony (Mbiti 1969; Birch Freeman 1968), to some Africans this was not unwelcome in it-self. Many educated Africans, at least initially, regarded the Christian missionaries as welcome harbingers of coming civilization and modernization (Boahen 1987). Yet there were differences in the relationships between missionaries and colonial authorities which probably escaped many Africans. Although these were differences of degree rather than anything more fundamental, and the mission churches had relationships involving varying degrees of cordiality with the colonial administrations, there was a range of kinds of association between the Catholic and Protestant churches and the various colonial authorities. In French and Portuguese colonies, for example, the Catholic Church had a much closer relationship with colonial authorities than it did in British areas. Protestant churches in the British colonies, on the other hand, tended to be split among a number of competing sects, which served to diminish the corporate influence of the Protestants with the colonial administrations. This issue is of significance not only for historical analysis but also for the current era, because if it can be established that individual churches as corporate entities had a particular view of their relationship with secular authorities during the colonial period, then the post-colonial arrangements with African regimes would appear in clearer perspective. In the context of Christianity's relationship with colonial rule, I want to look first at the association between the Catholic Church and colonial authorities, before proceeding to examine how the latter and the Protestants interrelated politically. Finally, we shall turn to the emergence of independent African churches. These, I shall argue, developed as popular Christian vehicles reflecting both the racism of the mission churches, which severely inhibited the ability of African clergy to move up the churches' leadership hierarchy, and the desire of Africans to indigenize Christianity to make it of greater relevance to their own lives and pre-exisiting spiritual world-views.

The Catholic Church and the colonial authorities

Oliver claims that the Catholic Church in Africa during the period of colonial rule was relatively independent of ties to European secular power (because Catholicism was not associated with any particular European colonizing state, unlike the Anglican Church with its close links to the English political establishment), and that in the post-colonial era it emerged as a sturdy corporate opponent of governmental authoritarianism and capricious behaviour in many parts of Africa (Oliver 1991: 257). He argues that

> [t]he success of the Catholic church [in allegedly gaining three-quarters of Africa's Christian converts by the mid-1970s] was important, in that it left the majority of African Christians affiliated to a strong international structure

which was comparatively untainted by colonial associations. In this way, Christianity (*sic*) overcame the crisis of African independence, and indeed found itself in the new situation to be almost the only institution which was capable of facing up to the increasingly authoritarian states of the new era. (Oliver 1991: 257)

The claim is that the Catholic Church in Africa was (and remains) a staunch defender of citizens' human and civil rights against African authoritarian governments in both colonial and post-colonial periods. Yet Rueschemeyer et al. (1992: 281) are correct when they note that the Catholic Church has often been characterized as an 'uncompromising opponent of liberalism and democracy'. In the 1920s and 1930s, for example, the Catholic Church dealt with the rise of fascism in Germany, Spain and Italy by giving it at least tacit support. After World War II the church enjoyed a close relationship with avowedly conservative Christian Democrat parties in Western Europe, as the latter sought to defeat socialism (and those generally advocating socially progressive measures) electorally. It was not until the Second Vatican Council (1962–65) that the Pope and other senior Catholic figures rather belatedly expressed concern over human rights and democracy issues (Hastings 1979: 173). The context for this expression of concern was the transition from colonial to post-colonial rule in both Africa and Asia, and the rise of liberation theology in Latin America. Significantly, senior Catholic officials in both Latin America and Africa were usually implacably opposed to the socially progressive articulations emanating from the Second Vatican Council, and did nothing concrete to further them (Vaillancourt 1980).

Oliver's claim that Catholicism had a 'strong international structure which was comparatively untainted by colonial associations' neglects the way in which the colonial administrators of European Catholic countries (France, Portugal, Belgium) had relationships of varying cordiality with the church. In France's African colonies there was certainly a *degree* of distrust between the Catholic Church and the colonial authorities. The mutually suspicious relationship stemmed from the time of the French Revolution, when the Jacobins' anti-clericalism was of fundamental importance in creating a new relationship between Church and State. Yet, it is necessary to remember that both Catholics and secular authorities were French; their suspicion of each other was limited by recognition of certain shared aims – continuation of French rule, antagonism to Islam and Protestantism, and antipathy to other colonizing powers.

In the Belgian Congo there was a closer relationship between the colonial authorities and the Catholic Church. The *entente* between the

Catholic missions and colonial authorities only began to diminish after World War II as leaders of the church, receptive to unambiguous signs that European colonial rule was declining (independence of India, liberation wars in Southeast Asia, and so on), sought to Africanize the church hierarchy and to disengage it from such close links with the state. The goal was to ensure the continued pre-eminence of the church in the post-colonial era (Markovitz 1973: 144–64).

In Portugal's main African colonies (Angola, Mozambique, Guinea-Bissau) the friendly relationship between the domestic fascist government and the Catholic Church was reflected in the 'Missionary Concordat' of 1940, as well as in a statute of 1941 which collectively endorsed especial privileges for the Catholic Church; the effect of these was to ensure the continuation of a close relationship between Church and State, which only came to an end in 1974 when Portugal's African colonies achieved independence following long-running wars of liberation. One of the main reasons for both Frelimo's and the MPLA's unceasing hostility to the Catholic Church was precisely because it was seen as an extension of colonial rule. To many Africans in French, Portuguese and Belgian colonies, the Catholic Church, by virtue of its ubiquitous solidarity with secular authorities, was just as much an element of European rule as they were. In short, it is by no means clear that the Catholic Church in Africa during the colonial period was more than a willing partner in the creation and consolidation of European hegemony. After colonialism, I will argue in Chapter 4, the church continued with its pragmatic policies because its corporate concerns were paramount.

Protestant churches and colonial rule

Although it is difficult to generalize, there was usually a somewhat different story in colonies where Protestant churches dominated. The position of the Protestant missions in relation to the colonial authorities was dependent on a number of factors: whether the colony had a substantive proportion of European settlers; whether there was serious rivalry between Christian sects; whether Islam appeared to pose a serious threat; and whether the dominant Christian denomination was favourably disposed to eventual African independence from colonialism. As we have already noted, where the Catholic Church was dominant its officials tended to forge a *modus vivendi* with political authorities which reflected both flexibility and concern with corporate strength. This was the case when settlers were present, as in Mozambique and

Angola, as much as when they were not in substantive numbers, as in Guinea-Bissau, Equatorial Africa, the Congo and throughout much of Francophone West Africa.

Protestant missions tended to predominate over Catholic bodies in British and German colonies. Until Germany was stripped of its African colonies (Togo, Cameroon, Tanganyika, South-West Africa) after World War I, there was often mutual distrust between German mission societies and political authorities; the same situation pertained in British colonies (Strayer 1976: 9). Missionaries frequently found themselves in antagonistic situations involving white rulers, employers and traders. According to Etherington (1983: 130), there was 'a direct contradiction between the white settler and the [Protestant] missionary in most parts of the continent'. In Uganda there was a testy relationship between the local Anglican Missionary Society and the colonial authorities, with the former enjoying few special privileges over rival missions (Hansen 1986). Christian missionary work in Kenya only began 'with colonial rule, not before ... missions interacted with colonial governments from the outset' (Spencer 1989: 116). Nevertheless, by the 1920s and 1930s there was a three-way relationship, at times conflictual, between missionaries, settlers and colonial authorities over three issues: treatment of indigenes, land and education (Strayer 1976: 9). There was a different situation in Nyasaland (post-colonial Malawi), where the Presbyterian mission had a strong popular position with which the colonial authorities were obliged to coexist. What these examples suggest is that in the colonial era the relationships between European authorities and the various Protestant churches were the product of a number of factors, including the corporate clout of the individual missions and the perception of those missions held by the authorities themselves.

Generally, however, the relationship between church missions in Africa and the colonial administrations was undoubtedly reflective of a joint hegemony, tempered at times by certain disagreements over policy issues. The dissatisfaction felt by many African Christians, both concerning the quality of spiritual help they obtained and the fact that the mission churches were controlled by Europeans, was reflected in the growth of African independent churches. Most authors who have looked at the issue stress Africans' positive response to Christian teaching, with its focus on the idea of a supreme being (Horton 1993; Boahen 1987). Some of the most flourishing examples of extant Christian churches in Africa today are those where a decisive Africanization has taken place, that is, where beliefs are often rather different from those associated with mission Christianity (Horton 1993: 155). African independent churches were founded in great numbers between about 1914 and 1925, with a second wave of growth from the 1930s to the 1950s, followed by a third wave from the 1970s onwards. Each of these periods was associated with multiple changes in Africa, reflective, first, of modernization and then of the impact of economic decline and social instability. In the final section of the current chapter we are concerned with the formation and growth of African independent churches during the colonial period, that is, in the context of European control of the mission churches and of a more diffuse modernization.

African independent churches, modernization and colonial rule

By the early 1940s it was estimated that there were about 800 independent churches in South Africa alone (Sundkler 1961). By the 1960s there were about 3,000; while elsewhere in the region there were about '500 separate church bodies of independents in West Africa and 500 in Central Africa, [and] about 300 in East Africa' (Parrinder 1976: 149). By the 1980s, Barrett (1982: 782, 791) estimates that there were 7,000 (overwhelmingly Christian-oriented) independent churches in Africa, with an estimated 32 million adherents. In comparison there are about 1,000 churches in Africa which claim close links to their former mission 'parents'.

The growth of independent Christian churches should be seen, first, as an attempt by Africans to indigenize Christianity, involving forms of social mobilization and political resistance to European hegemony. Second, their development should be regarded as a function of the mission churches' failure to deal with Africans' major concerns: sickness, health, fortune, misfortune. The inability to deal with what Africans perceived as the biggest threats to their well-being was also directly responsible for an outbreak of Christian revivalism in East Africa after World War I, and to the popularity of sects like the Watchtower (Jehovah's Witnesses) in Central Africa, which overtly challenged the mission churches' conception of what Christianity was about (Fields 1985). Third, the racism of the mission churches was another reason for the growth of independent churches. Of the competing mission churches, the Roman Catholic Church took higher education and the training of local clergy most seriously. Among Anglicans, however, there was a distinction between the mission, financed by donations from Britain, and the so-called 'Native Anglican Church', locally supported. Even though the living standards of expatriate Anglican missionaries were frugal, African Anglican clergymen and their families were even poorer materially. This caused widespread ill-feeling among African clergy. Other Protestant denominations were slower to ordain local men; this gave the appearance of trying to keep control of church affairs as a European prerogative. One result was that many African clergy broke from the parent churches to found their own religious organizations where they would be in positions of responsibility and power.

In relation to the independent African churches, one issue that has been particularly controversial is whether such churches were predominantly 'cultural' or 'political' in orientation and *raison d'être* (Buijtenhuis 1985). The literature often focuses on such issues without addressing sufficiently the fundamental question: is it really possible to separate out aspects of social reality as neatly as some social scientists appear to wish to do? The question of whether a religious vehicle is actually political or cultural in orientation is surely a somewhat artificial dichotomy, reminiscent of the felt necessity of dividing the social sciences into subdivisions – economic, politics, sociology, and so on. The question does not arise in accounts of Islam because it is generally accepted that for Muslims, politics and religion are inseparable. Buijtenhuis's (1985) painstaking concern to determine whether new religious movements in Africa are in general either counter-societies aiming to escape a hostile environment or actual political movements aiming to achieve political power misses the point in some respects, assuming as it does that the only purpose of politics is to achieve power at the centre. Of course, the successful creation and consolidation of a counter-society (as, for example, Kitawala in Zaire) is intensely political if it achieves its aim to capture state power for itself. As admirable as Fields's (1985) study of Watchtower in Central Africa is, she failed to raise the question of *which* social groups were attracted to Watchtower and which were not. She is so anxious to separate her analysis from a 'vulgar' Marxist approach – that social conditions 'cause' religious ideology – that she ultimately manages only to separate social consciousness (ideology) from social experience (class), without answering the important question of where the two meet. In other words, to what extent are non-mainstream manifestations of Christianity in colonial Africa characteristic of popular concerns at the time to escape from European hegemonic domination?

Fields is anxious, it would appear, not to repeat Sundkler's error in creating ideal categories of religious groups which in reality cannot be so easily separated. Sundkler's 1961 classic study of Christian churches in South Africa distinguishes between two ideal types of indigenous Christian churches, the Ethiopian and the Zionist. Ethiopian sects, he argues, are either direct or indirect offshoots of European mission churches, whose forms of organization and doctrines of biblical interpretation they followed fairly closely. They tended to be Africanized churches which left the missions chiefly on racial rather than theological grounds; their essential character was encapsulated by the notion that Africans could lead and organize churches as well as Europeans (Parrinder 1976: 158). In other words, most of the Ethiopian churches stressed what may be described as a proto-nationalist outlook, although this should not be taken to imply that they were forerunners of secular nationalist movements, which as we shall see in Chapter 2, arose for quite different reasons following the end of World War II (Shepperson 1954).

'Ethiopianism' began in South Africa in the early 1880s and spread to both British Central Africa (Nyasaland, Northern Rhodesia) and south of the Zambesi. The chief early influence was Joseph Booth, a black American missionary, who founded his first churches in 1892, encouraged by the religious fervour in the United States at the time, which led to the formation of numerous Africanized churches with pentecostalist leanings. Ethiopia was regarded as synonymous with Africa as a whole; biblical references to Ethiopia were cited in support of claims for the antiquity of an African Christian church. The political consequences of the defeat by the Ethiopian Emperor Menelik of the Italians in 1896 at Adowa furthered the idea of Ethiopia as a metaphor for Africa. Some of the churches had links with so-called 'Negro sects' in the United States, ties strengthened in some cases by the Jamaican-born black American leader, Marcus Garvey. Garvey travelled widely in the 1920s and 1930s, spreading the idea of independent black churches as a means to liberation. He was regarded as an important prophet by Rastafarians, militant Jamaican descendants of West African slaves, who regarded the Ethiopian emperor Ras Tafari (Haile Selassie, who ruled 1932–74) as God. From the founding of the sect in the 1930s, Rastafarians sought a meaningful creed distinct from the teachings of white colonial Christians (Hall 1985: 269–96). The Ethiopian African churches paralleled the development of Rastafarianism in Jamaica, with one major distinction: the essential aim of the African independent black churches was to be both African and Christian – Christian in the essentials of doctrine and practice with only minor modifications to accommodate the first aim, that of being self-governing and independent of white control.

Zionist sects, on the other hand, according to Sundkler, are more overtly syncretist, that is, with a fusion or blending of traditional and Western Christian religious ideas. Interestingly, something similar arose in Peru, Colombia, Equador and elsewhere in Latin America during the drive to implant Catholicism as the dominant religion. Zionist sects taught divine healing, triple immersion, and the imminent second coming of Christ (Parrinder 1976: 159). Their leaders emphasized healing by faith; speaking with tongues in ecstasy; rites of purification; and taboos on blood, pork and alcohol in accordance with Old Testament teachings.

A number of the Zionist churches were modelled on American pentecostalist churches, such as the Assemblies of God, the Church of God in Christ, the Church of God, and the United Pentecostal Church (Hoekema 1966). Specifically Africanized derivatives developed in Nigeria and elsewhere in West Africa, including the Harrist and Aladura (literally, 'praying') churches, founded between 1918 and 1930.

In general, the rise of African 'Ethiopian' and 'Zionist' independent churches involved a combination of social, religious and political factors. It is not analytically helpful to separate out ideal types because it is clear that Ethiopian and Zionist forms of independency have as much in common with each other as either does with the mission churches. In other words, both are examples of Africanized Christianity which adapted to particularistic cultural and ethnic contexts. Social and political elements were of significance because of the multiplex effects of modernization, including urbanization, the creation of centralizing polities, their incorporation into the capitalist world economy, and the breakdown of traditional communities. In short, the independent churches aimed to (re-)create a sense of community in quickly emerging urban environments and in the changing context of rural life. Colonial authorities tended to regard them as a sinister manifestation of revolution. Many authors have stressed how independent churches led by, for example, Simon Kimbangu, John Chilembwe, Reuben Spartas Mukasa and Odadaiah Basajjakitalo, among many others, were persecuted by colonial administrations because of their political activities (Desanti 1971; Shepperson 1954; Milton Yinger 1970; Wilson 1985; Goldthorpe 1984; Parrinder 1976).

In sum, African independent churches arose between the world wars as a reaction to situations characterized by severe instability and change, following the European conquest. The culturally specific religion of the conqueror, though often strongly promoted by missionary activity, was embedded in the whole social system of the dominant group and thus unacceptable to some subordinate groups. Unifying religious vehicles of popular mobilization helped in dealing with the effects of cultural and political subjugation during colonization. Despite the ending of colonization, such anti-hegemonic religious vehicles did not die out. In the post-colonial era, the Jehovah's Witnesses, with their world-view moulded by the coming millennium, maintain a substantial number of lay missionaries in Africa. Because of their unwillingness to recognize earthly rulers, they have been widely persecuted by state authorities (Wilson 1985: 309). As we shall see in Chapter 5, the existence of popular Christian vehicles in Africa in the post-colonial period is explained by the fact that they are expressions of community solidarity and aspirations which continue to serve important social and religious functions.

African independent churches are manifestations of popular religious movements with a number of interrelated religious, social and political goals. In the early part of the twentieth century they were the result of attempts by ordinary people to organize themselves spiritually and communally in religious vehicles which were of particularistic relevance. While there does seem to be something of a correlation between the harshness of European rule and the numbers of independent churches – it may not be coincidental that the main area of growth was South Africa – other factors are of relevance in explaining their growth, such as divisions between the mission churches, which in turn encouraged further schisms within Christianity. It is, however, too much of a simplification to view independent Christian churches in Africa solely within the context of the nationalist struggle against European rule, if only because such churches continued to be founded in the post-colonial era.

Conclusion

The main purpose of this chapter was to examine the effects of the impact of European colonization on African Muslims and on various types of Christianity in Sub-Saharan Africa. Colonization facilitated the expansion of Islam, an unexpected outcome given the aim of hegemonic consolidation of European power, as well as of Christianity, which was much more likely given the generally cordial ties between mission churches and colonial authorities. Protestant missions vied with Catholic for influence and converts, while, after an initial period of quite explosive growth, the limitations of culturally specific, Europeanized versions of Christianity led many Africans into independent churches. Over time, both Christianity and Islam became Africanized – that is, adapted to the specific needs of the African communities which adopted them; various vehicles of popular religion developed in opposition to the hegemonic versions of both Islam and Christianity. One of the chief differences between the two faiths for many Africans was that Islam was not associated with European hegemony, while Christianity was. Because of Islam's socio-cultural entrenchment in some areas – especially around the southern fringes of the Sahara Desert and beyond – Christianity's aim of Cape-to-Cairo proselytization was never achieved. In fact, colonial authorities failed to 'push' Christianity fully, as they found it expedient to inculcate Muslim leaders into the structures of indirect rule. The result was that by the end of the colonial period Islam and Christianity alike were composed of discrete vehicles of both popular and hegemonic organization. The ulama-led reformist strands comprised the latter in Islam; the Sufi brotherhoods were their popular counterparts. As far as Christianity was concerned, the mission churches were manifestations of European hegemony, while their African independent counterparts provided alternative popular Christian vehicles.

Finally, this chapter has sought to show how the impact of Christianity and Islam was moulded by European colonialism and the multiple changes accompanying it, which I have labelled 'modernization'. One result was the emergence of educated African nationalist leaders whose views on religious institutions were coloured by the closeness of the mainstream churches to temporal rule. Religious institutions were often seen as at least potential rivals by nationalist leaders for people's hearts and minds. As a result, as we shall see in the next chapter, the attitude of African nationalists to both Christianity and Islam was rather ambivalent. One outcome was that in the post-colonial era African governments continued to regard religious institutions as *political* actors whose support for government has been regarded as an important stabilizing attribute within the context of often volatile state–society relations.

2

Nationalists, Religion and the
End of Colonial Rule

This chapter aims, first, to examine the attitude of nationalist politicians to the mainstream religious institutions – the Catholic and Protestant mission churches, as well as Islam – in order to show how religious institutions were often putative obstacles to nationalist leaders' aims of achieving power. Second, I want to show how the mainstream Christian bodies were initially opposed to, then sceptical of, and finally won round to the idea of African independence. As for Islam, the wide variety of religious vehicles and the varying circumstances of Muslims' relationships with nationalist politicians ensured there was no clear-cut 'Muslim' response to moves towards African independence. In the course of the chapter it will be demonstrated how the relationship of the mainstream religious bodies to governments after independence arose in part from the circumstances which led to the end of colonialism; chief among these was the suspicion of many, but by no means all, nationalist leaders that the mission churches were the tools of neo-colonialism. Partly due to this suspicion, and partly due to the immensely useful role in education and welfare that the mainstream churches carried out, an ambivalence in government–church relations remained a discernible feature of the post-colonial era.

Modernization and the Growth of African Nationalism

The effects of rapid social change

During the first fifty years of the twentieth century Africa underwent a period of unprecedented modernization, almost revolutionary in its medium- and long-term effects. Urbanization was an important effect of this process, leading to mass migrations and slow industrialization. Towns expanded and new urban centres grew following the formal establishment of colonial rule. Abidjan, Takoradi, Port Harcourt, Lusaka, Nairobi and many other towns and cities were founded as ports and harbours, administrative and mining centres, and as transportation – especially railway – points. Urban centres expanded swiftly. The population of Accra, for example, increased from about 18,000 in 1901 to nearly 136,000 fifty years later; Nairobi's population more than doubled in little more than a decade in the 1930s from around 12,000 people to more than 25,000; while Casablanca's population rose a hundredfold from just over 2,000 to a quarter of a million people between 1910 and 1936 (Boahen 1987: 103–4).

Urbanization and the development of transportation infrastructures were accompanied by rapid population growth. Due in part to improvements in health care and to the progressive conquest by medical science of illnesses like bubonic plague, yellow fever and yaws, Africa's population grew by about 40 per cent between 1900 and 1960. Migrants flooded into the urban centres, while traditional communities were everywhere disrupted and consequently changed as a result of their gradual insertion into the modern world economy and the effects of an increasingly centralized political environment. The result of population growth, urbanization, increased educational and employment opportunities, the introduction of cash crops, and the cessation of slavery was that a new social order developed. The colonial system emphasized achievement rather than birth alone. While it would be going too far to claim that a purely meritocratic system developed – racist ideas put paid to that – it was certainly the case that for many Africans upward social mobility was for the first time something that could be earned rather than bestowed by circumstances of birth. There also emerged an increasing urban–rural divide. By the 1930s, rural dwellers were separated from those who lived in the towns and cities by differences in employment, access to health care, better housing standards, and so on; later, after World War II, further subdivisions of class, ethnicity and occupation also became clear. Taken together these developments had the effect of stimulating many Africans, especially the educated elite, to question the appropriateness of European colonial rule.

From the 1880s, as a result of the effects of European colonization, African society had begun to polarize into two main groups. On the one hand, there was a small but growing educated and professional elite; on the other, there was an 'overwhelmingly large traditional and illiterate group' (Boahen 1987: 35). The educated elite was subdivided between

Christians and Muslims, with the latter concentrated in the coastal regions of West and East Africa. The majority of educated Christians initially welcomed colonialism; their Muslim counterparts were often more ambivalent. Boahen (1987: 36) claims that it was the educated African Christians, in tandem with the European missionaries, who in the 1880s put pressure on both the local administrations and the metropolitan governments to annex adjoining areas before other European powers could move in. The West Indian Pan-Africanist, Edward Blyden, went so far at the time to claim that West Africa had 'been partitioned, in the order ... of providence, by the European powers ... [T]his partition has been permitted for the ultimate good of the people and for the benefit of humanity' (Blyden, quoted in Boahen 1987: 36). Largely due to their teaching at the hands of Christian missionaries, educated Christian Africans had been led to believe that Africa could only be 'civilized' through the combined activities of Christianity, education, capitalism and industrialization – in short, by a process of fundamental modernization directed by European Christians. Fifty years later, however, in 1936, I.T.A. Wallace-Johnson of Sierra Leone bitterly attacked the role of the mission churches for the way they had used Christianity as the justification for a brutal ideology of domination, using force to subdue and convert pagans to Europeanized Christianity:

> I believe the European has a god in whom he believes and whom he is representing in his churches all over Africa. He believes in the god whose name is spelt Deceit. He believes in the god whose law is 'Ye strong, you must weaken the weak'. Ye 'civilized' Europeans, you must 'civilize' the 'barbarous' Africans with machine guns. Ye 'Christian' Europeans, you must 'Christianize' the 'pagan' Africans with bombs, poison gases, etc. (Wallace-Johnson 1936)

The difference between Blyden's optimistic expectations of Christian development and Wallace-Johnson's disgust at the way the process appeared to him to have turned out may be explained by the fact that Christianization was used as a justification for sometimes brutal tactics. In other words, the attempted imposition of ideological domination was to seek to create, consolidate and then maintain political quiescence by masking subordination and exploitation in order to preclude popular revolt by any means deemed necessary (Schatzberg 1988: 27). To this end, Christianity was a double-edged sword of civilizing and oppressive propensity.

The Second World War is rightly regarded as a watershed in the emergence of African self-rule. Before the war few plans had been articulated by Europeans for African independence. British and French colonial administrators may have acknowledged that, at some time in the (perhaps distant) future, Africans would have been taught by them to rule themselves successfully; other colonial powers – Belgium, Portugal, Spain – appeared to reckon that the sun would never set on their African imperial sagas. For African nationalists it was the very duality of colonial rule which became the focal point of their attentions. For example, on the one hand, the French imposed the corvée on their African subjects; on the other, they proclaimed that the colonies and their inhabitants were integral parts of a Republic whose motto was 'Liberté, Egalité, Fraternité' (Crowder 1984: 5). Initially, the African nationalist demand was only for greater participation in the political institutions imposed by colonialism. Later, partly due to the success of anti-colonial movements elsewhere (especially the independence movements in the Indian subcontinent), partly because of postwar European economic weakness and political uncertainty, and partly as a result of increasingly effective nationalist challenges which attracted growing popular support, African champions of independence found themselves with increasing influence. Tentative questioning of the moral right of Europeans to rule Africans swiftly gave way to demands for independence sooner rather than later.

African nationalists and mission Christianity

In the face of the multifaceted changes, both domestic and international, outlined above it is hardly surprising that the ideas of some educated African Christians underwent a sea change. Wallace-Johnson was by no means an extremist. By the 1930s, Europeans were clearly no longer uniformly regarded as the benign purveyors of civilization; instead they came to be increasingly seen as the problem of Africa's future development, rather than its solution. Scattered, often religiously motivated, anti-colonial actions (such as the Maji-Maji rebellion and the founding of African independent churches) occurred around the time of World War I; they were to intensify from the mid-1930s. One of the chief catalysts was the Italian occupation of Ethiopia in 1935; before then only a relatively small number of African nationalists had demanded a complete overthrow of the colonial system. Mussolini's invasion and subsequent annexation of previously independent Ethiopia served to push both African and Caribbean public opinion against colonialism. Wallace-Johnson's anti-colonial diatribe was almost certainly at least in part an expression of righteous indignation in response to Italy's actions in Ethiopia (Furedi 1994: 25–7).

Partly as a result of particular events, such as Italy's action in Ethiopia, and partly in response to more general developments, the hitherto scattered anti-colonial groups became fully fledged nationalist movements able to absorb and direct the energies of both moderates, who desired only the modification of society, and militants, who wished to see the overthrow of the colonial system. Independent churches were sometimes vehicles of nationalist aspirations. In Nigeria, for example, the Zikists, followers of the radical nationalist Nnamdi Azikiwe, were regarded as extremists by the colonial authorities, even though many were relatively well-educated, urbanized young men who considered that their legitimate aspirations were thwarted by the structure of Nigerian society. British officials, according to Furedi (1994: 244), regarded Zikists as psychologically disturbed individuals without popular support, representative of the 'ubiquitous troublemakers' of the imperial world-view. In reality, the Zikist movement found its support among mostly urbanized workers, chiefly low-level white-collar grades, who found their upward mobility restricted; and among demobilized soldiers and small business people, especially from Eastern Nigeria, Azikiwe's home region (Furedi 1994: 245). The Zikist movement not only controlled a number of associational groups, such as trade unions and ex-servicemen's organizations, but also had close ties with an independent church, the National Church of Nigeria and Cameroons (NCNC) (Furlong 1991), which put forward a kind of religio-nationalism involving the divinity of a black God and social and political equality between blacks and whites.

Christian mission churches, in contrast, were regarded by some nationalists with great suspicion, even though in many cases they had been educated at schools founded by missionaries, especially in relatively developed areas like coastal West Africa. Nearly all African nationalist leaders were Christians; yet many, especially in British colonies, where there was much less of an attempt to create 'Europeanized Africans' than in French colonies, regarded the mission churches as vehicles of European hegemony. This was despite the fact that by World War II many Christian missionaries in West Africa were in fact black Africans. Local clergy were introduced from the mid-nineteenth century, because of the high death rate among European missionaries there. By 1949, in the Gold Coast, for example, of the Anglican Church's thirty-seven priests, thirty-two were Africans and only five Europeans (Pobee 1977: 391). The Methodist Church also developed an organizational structure which involved local Africans. Most Gold Coast nationalist politicians were products of mission education, and retained close links with

Christian churches (despite the acceptance by some of the efficacy of Islamic talismans [Cruise O'Brien 1988: 27]). Yet, to the Gold Coast's first mass nationalist leader, Kwame Nkrumah, the mission churches themselves were integral parts of the structure of colonial control, an instrument of social oppression by the colonialists rather than a force for beneficial change alone (Nkrumah 1967: 23). For their part, the main mission churches in the Gold Coast (the Anglican and Methodist) entirely reciprocated Nkrumah's suspicions, and were very concerned by his Convention People's Party's (CPP) 'communist' programme. In 1951, when the CPP gained a measure of power in a dyarchy with the British, and in a move redolent of the passing of material power from Europeans to Africans, education was taken out of the hands of the churches and transferred to the control of a government which was partly controlled by Africans.

The alarmed reaction of the churches to what they perceived as the start of an attempt to subdue religious institutions to governmental fiat was compounded in 1958 by a Preventive Detention Act which Nkrumah's government used to incarcerate many opponents without trial; and again in 1961, when his regime ordered the mission churches to open branches of the CPP in each community's church building. According to Pobee (1977: 395), however, the mission churches adopted a 'quiet approach [in relation to the CPP government] because they felt … the Church should be concerned to conserve what she had [in order] to ward off open hostilities' from Nkrumah's regime.

In Northern Rhodesia, in contrast to the Gold Coast, the colonialist–nationalist relationship was moulded by the particular circumstances of its being a settler colony. As with Azikiwe's NCNC, senior nationalist politicians, including the long-serving independence leader Kenneth Kaunda, turned to independent African churches, including the African Methodist Episcopal Church (AMEC). The AMEC had some 50,000 members in the 1950s, and was renowned for its nationalist militancy (Cook 1978: 285). The growth of the AMEC, and of other independent churches in the colony, was in part a reaction to the impact of a substantial white settler community and its links with mainstream Christian churches: 'By the 1920s most mission churches could be clearly seen to be part of the white establishment' (Cook 1978: 286). The result was that aspiring nationalists turned to African alternatives for spiritual as well as organizational purposes. Kenneth Kaunda was both a local preacher and a choir leader at the Lusaka branch of the AMEC in the 1950s, which gave him an opportunity to hone his political skills. Yet, following independence in 1964, the AMEC refused to join with a number of other Protestant churches to form the United Church of Zambia, which later became virtually the state church. The significance of the AMEC and its role as a focal point for many nationalist politicians was that, once independence was won, its political purpose came to an end as nationalist leaders sought to establish a church which could be counted upon to work closely with government.

This section has described how educated Africans – especially when, for the most part, they became nationalists during the 1930s and 1940s – often changed their position regarding the benefits of European colonialization and the virtues of mission Christianity. In the next section I want to examine how the period leading up to independence and the first few years of the post-colonial period were crucial for the later relationships of mainstream religious institutions and the state. During these formative years the mission churches were caught in a difficult situation, while many of them became increasingly Africanized: on the one hand, in order to keep the favoured position they had enjoyed under colonialism, it was necessary not to appear to post-colonial governments as a threat to the aspirations of national unity; on the other, it was essential for the local churches' relationships with their parent churches in Europe that they would use what influence they had to persuade their new governments to rule in as humane and Christian a way as possible. I will look first at the general position of the mainstream religious organizations and African nationalists, before proceeding to an examination of the Catholic and Protestant churches and, finally, of Islam.

African Nationalist Leaders and Religious Institutions

There is in theory little real difference between the colonial and post-colonial African state. Both sets of leaders sought to rule by legal precepts, recognized the need to take into account their people's concerns, and ostensibly sought to address themselves disinterestedly to solving developmental problems. Whatever the theory, however, post-colonial African governments in reality often became Janus-faced. As Morris-Jones (1992: 220) notes: '[T]he post-imperial state is at once a reflection of and a reaction against the preceding imperial state.' African nationalist leaders sought both to bring down what had gone before and to rebuild. European-led regimes were both anathema and a model worthy in some respects of preservation or imitation. The creation of constitutional frameworks for independent African states involving all the trappings of political independence – a prime minister and/or president, a legislature, competing political parties, an independent judiciary, state security services, and so on – helped to obscure crucial questions about the nature of the successor states. Constitutions were invariably selected from the Western examples: the French, British and American were popular, yet their adoption was in some respects beside the point. What is of greatest relevance is not that European colonial administrations changed Africa so radically that newly installed nationalist leaders had a tabula rasa on which to inscribe their plans for progressive change, but rather the opposite: the colonial period was a hiatus; the 'traditional' may have been changed, but it was not transformed. After brief periods of colonial rule (only fifty years or so in some cases), the post-colonial state was grafted on to an essentially pre-colonial socio-political order where diktats from the centre were translated into policy at lower levels. At independence, popular representation was introduced, and formally expressed through Western-style political institutions; in reality, however, power was often wielded through a network of personal relationships beginning in the capital city and spreading to regional, district and local levels (Chabal 1992: 69).

While African nationalist leaders were almost invariably the products of the Christian mission education system, this did not necessarily prevent them from making selective appeals to their own ethnic groups. Even though the church associated with Nnamdi Azikiwe, the NCNC, was ostensibly a national alternative to the mission churches, it actually gained the major part of its followers from among Azikiwe's fellow Ibo (Furlong 1991). In Zaire, the Kimbanguist Church – which became one of the triumvirate of legal Christian churches – found its major support among the Bakongo. Generally, the religious allegiance of ethnic groups tended to conform to a pattern based on corporate identity; this was especially true of Muslim groups. The significance of this for nationalist politicians was that an appeal to co-religionists and members of their ethnic group was likely to be successful, not only because of the attractiveness of their policies but also as a result of communal solidarity. Once a political constituency was forged as a result of a combined religious and ethnic appeal then it became easy to reject other politicians' programmes on the grounds that they were from the 'wrong' religious and ethnic backgrounds (Morgenthau and Behrman 1984: 650–51). Given that, with the exception of South Africa, every African colony was predominantly rural, it was essential for nationalists to forge an appeal which found favour among the bulk of the people who lived in rural areas. Groups which might emerge as competitors, such as trade unions and professional organizations, counted their support primarily from urban populations; rural power-holders, such as chiefs, were politically important within a specific area only and could be recruited as local representatives of the party. Nationalist politicians managed to eliminate the threat to their goal of political dominance through a combination of domination and co-optation, often creating the impression that their popularity was colony-wide. The combination of carrot and stick was used during the drive to independence in order to crush or buy off political rivals, just as it was after independence. With regard to the mainstream religious organizations, however, there was by no means a clear-cut position.

The role of mainstream religious organizations in the context of the drive to independence was both complex and multifaceted, the result of a number of discrete but related factors. Whether they were early (principled) or late (opportunist), supporters of African independence depended on a number of issues, including, in the case of the mainstream churches, the attitude of the European parent church and whether individual leaders of the local churches themselves welcomed independence or not. No clear, unambiguous conclusions can be drawn on this issue in relation to the Protestant mission churches, which were often divided among themselves. The lack of formal central Islamic religious authorities, though not an absence of hierarchy, coupled with the fact that colonial authorities were adept at striking a deal with influential Muslim leaders, meant that the issue of political independence was often viewed with a degree of agnosticism by ordinary Muslims, although not by the ulama and reformist groups anxious to establish their influence in the post-colonial period. Ordinary Muslims, in addition, understood that national political power was in the hands of Christians. Because of this they tended to adopt a wait-and-see attitude based on a reluctance to be too concerned over which particular group of Christians – whether local or foreign – was to rule. This is not to suggest that African Muslims necessarily lacked a normative vision of the future, but rather to acknowledge that in the Muslim world-view only an Islamic state could be a truly appropriate vehicle for aspirations and values.

The different relationships between religious institutions and African nationalist authorities may be summed up as follows:

(1) The Roman Catholic Church, controlled by the Vatican, was initially highly suspicious of African nationalism, as it was often equated with communism; as time went on, however, the church sought to make

the best of a situation which was beyond its control, by seeking to forge close ties with nationalist leaders and, later, independent governments.

(2) Protestant mission churches were rather agnostic about African independence, but often had a theologically derived view which was more liberal than the Catholic. The Protestant churches attempted to fit in with new political arrangements by a process of swift Africanization of religious hierarchies.

(3) Muslims who were not residing in states where co-religionists were clearly in the majority – as in, for example, Senegal – were prepared to 'wait and see', being suspicious of all governments, whether colonial or post-colonial, which they perceived as being run for the most part by Christians. On the other hand, Muslim communities were often regarded with suspicion by colonial and post-colonial rulers alike, especially as the desire for national unity in the post-colonial period effectively forbade the manifestations of community separateness sometimes associated with Muslim communities.

Religious allegiance sometimes became an emblem of political factionalism and competition in and around the independence era. The Catholic Church, because of its wide geographical spread and its hierarchy's close ties to colonial authorities, was particularly involved in independence struggles. In Uganda, rivalry between Protestants and Catholics was the main political issue in the 1950s and into the 1960s. The conflict focused on the role of the Baganda and their king in the political structure of the country. Kabaka Mutesa was exiled in 1953; two years later he returned in triumph as constitutional monarch of the Baganda. The political establishment of Buganda – the Kabaka and his senior chiefs – had long been Christian, following the diminution of the influence of Islam in the 1870s. Yet a civil war between Catholics and Protestants in the 1880s had served to illustrate how sectionally polarized Buganda's Christians were. The outcome of the civil war did nothing to reduce incipient rivalry and, as it subsequently turned out, political conflict. Although the Kabaka was a Protestant, some of his more important chiefs were Catholic. His temporary exile in the 1950s – judged necessary by the British colonial authorities, who were concerned that the Kabaka was becoming a powerful symbol of Baganda nationalism – in fact achieved what the British most feared: an upsurge of Baganda nationalism with Protestant overtones. Catholics felt discriminated against and consequently used the opportunity occasioned by the Kabaka's exile to organize themselves into a predominantly Catholic organization, the Democratic Party (DP), founded by a leading Catholic politician, Matayo Mugwanya, in 1955. The aim was to challenge the Protestant-traditionalist alliance favoured by the Kabaka (Hastings 1979: 88–9). The Democratic Party was to lead the colony's first internally self-governing administration in 1961–62, with the mainly non-Baganda Protestant Uganda Peoples' Congress (UPC) and the Baganda-led Protestant party, Kabaka Yekka (King Alone), taking over later in the decade until Milton Obote seized power for the UPC alone, before he in turn was overthrown by Idi Amin in 1971 (Twaddle 1988: 81).

The Catholic Church and African independence

The political acumen of Catholic politicians was illustrated in Congo-Brazzaville, where the priest-politician Foulbert Youlou led the country to independence in 1960. Three years later, however, he was deposed in a populist *coup d'état* led by trade-union activists. In neighbouring Congo (Zaire), where the Catholic Church was the largest, the withdrawal of the Belgian colonial administration was the signal for an all-out battle for political power. Representatives of the Catholic Church – identified by some Africans as a bastion of authoritarianism and racism – were notable victims in the outbreaks of violence. Dozens of Christian missionaries were killed as Zaire entered a period of civil war upon achieving independence. Attacks on Catholic missionaries in Zaire during the civil strife and anarchy of 1960–65 testified to the 'overbearing manner in which missionaries had often behaved: "You are as wicked as a priest" (Tu es aussi méchant qu'un père) was commonly heard at the time' (Hastings 1979: 136).

The role of Catholic professionals and politicians in both Congo-Brazzaville and Zaire in and around the time of independence raises the issue of the church's involvement in, and attitude to, African independence more generally. The Catholic Church is of importance in Africa not only because of its presence in nearly all African countries and its nearly 100 million followers throughout the region but also because of its unique position as a church which is also a state. Its position in relation to African independence should be seen in dual perspective: from both the religious and the strategic point of view.

At no time had relations been better between African imperial governments and the Catholic Church than during the final years of colonialism. There existed a widespread harmony of outlook and degree of close practical co-operation, particularly in the educational and welfare areas. In British Africa relations warmed between the Catholic

Church and the colonial authority, after cool beginnings; in French Africa little of the old suspicious anti-clericalism remained within government circles. Once independence was clearly on the way, even though the Catholic Church was slower than the main Protestant churches to Africanize the ranks of its leading personnel, 'it soon had an adequate number of native born archbishops and bishops to indicate its full participation in the new political era' (Hastings 1979: 148). The trend towards Africanization was also the result, especially in Europe, of a strong – and growing – intellectual anti-colonialism during the late 1950s and 1960s. The result was that progressive Catholic thinking and nationalist aims dovetailed neatly to produce a coherent policy for Church–State relations after independence. Catholic professionals on the ground were more ambivalent: white missionaries were mostly, according to Hastings (1979: 97), 'apolitical'; although what this appears to mean is that they considered that religion and politics 'did not mix'. Most, however, accepted the legitimacy of both a benevolent colonialism and nationalist aspirations; that particular circle was squared by a hope that independence would not come before Africans were 'ready' for it. Many missionaries appeared to be disturbed by the rise of political parties; many were inclined to see a loosely defined 'communism' everywhere. Yet, once it became clear that the rush to independence was unstoppable, once Sudan (1956) and Ghana (1957) achieved their independence, many Catholic missionaries pragmatically considered that the next best thing to continued colonial rule was the 'right' kind of mildly socially aware political parties led by sound Christians (Hastings 1979: 98). In short, the preference was by and large for a certain kind of liberal, tolerant, ideally ecumenical, ethnic-blind, political party. As the 1950s advanced a number of such political parties and movements appeared, including those led by Houphouet-Boigny in Côte d'Ivoire and Léopold Senghor in Senegal, which expressed solid Western virtues of democracy, ethnic harmony and anti-communism.

The ease of transition from colonial to post-colonial rule was aided in many French-speaking colonies by the way the education systems had been run by the Catholic Church to produce nationalists who were usually by no means political radicals. While in English-speaking African colonies there were a few elite Protestant schools such as Alliance High School in Kenya, King's College Budo in Uganda, and Mfantsipim in Ghana which produced a number of nationalist politicians, in their French-speaking counterparts most senior nationalist figures were products of the Catholic mission schools, socialized by its corporate ethos of a certain conservative kind. Most members of the nationalist elite in

Dahomey (Benin), Congo-Brazzaville, Togo, Cameroon, Côte d'Ivoire and, to a lesser extent, Senegal, were products of the Catholic educational system. Some of the nationalists had even closer links to the Catholic Church – as noted earlier, Foulbert Youlou was a priest before leading his country to independence. In addition, Léopold Senghor was seminary-educated, although he never worked as a priest; Kayabanda of Rwanda was a former Catholic Action activist; while Houphouet-Boigny later demonstrated his commitment to the Catholic Church by spending over US$100 million (of his own money, it was claimed) on the construction of the world's second largest basilica at his home village, Yamoussoukro. Significantly, and reflecting a conservative consensus among many of the French-speaking nationalists, these leaders formed themselves into the conservative Brazzaville group in 1960, motivated by the twin aims of measured social change and anti-communism (Hastings 1979: 403–4).

Given the close ties between many nationalist leaders and the Catholic Church, it is unsurprising that senior Catholics managed to retain close links with nationalists once they became the new political elite (Morgenthau and Behrman 1984: 650–651). In effect, their ideological, religious and class affinities were of greater practical import than the somewhat idealized conflict for power between 'whites' and 'blacks' which the nationalists portrayed as their main struggle. In order to illustrate the development of the relationship between the Catholic Church and temporal rulers, it is necessary in addition to examine how the Catholic Church hierarchy regarded its African domains from a strategic viewpoint.

The relationship of the Catholic Church to African nationalist leaders is placed in perspective when we recall the former's generally close ties with governments in many parts of Western Europe and Latin America. This is not to deny that the Catholic Church in France, Mexico and Portugal at the end of the nineteenth century was confronted by decidedly anti-clerical governments. Yet, significantly, the church did all it could to rehabilitate itself – and with some success – in the eyes of secular opponents. Its pragmatism was stimulated by a ferocious anti-Communism, especially after the 1917 Bolshevik Revolution, which led to a toleration of Fascism as definitely the lesser of two totalitarian evils – Communism denied the existence of God. The defeat of Fascism in World War II was followed by the ascendancy of conservative Catholic political parties in Europe, most notably in Italy, Germany and France. The predominantly Catholic Christian Democrat parties espoused two main aims: the consolidation of a particular form of conservative liberal democracy and the maintenance of a strong commitment to capitalist development. This Catholic ideology – mixing social conservatism with strong support for capitalism – spread after World War II, supported by organizations like Catholic Action.

In Africa, the Church's ideology was closely related to its 'civilizing' mission: before Africans could take charge of their own development they had to become more like Europeans. The bishop of the Congo from 1910 until the 1950s, de Hemptinne, a friend of Belgian royalty and member of a wealthy banking family, typified the attitude of the church to its African 'flock'. De Hemptinne saw as the role of church and colonial authorities the development of a form of Christianized civilization which was both authoritarian and disciplinarian. He believed that American missions were unacceptably liberal, and even that there was an 'identity' between them and Moscow in aiming to communize Africa. He considered that African education up to secondary level should be under the church's jurisdiction and should consist in part of cultivating a fear of authority in order to achieve popular acquiescence (Markowitz 1973: 44–5). De Hemptinne is not only important because of the length of time he spent in charge of Catholic policy in the Congo; the substance of his ideas constituted Catholic orthodoxy until after World War II (Hastings 1979: 64). The ideology of an authoritarian anti-communist Catholicism also informed the behaviour of the French bishop of Douala (Cameroon) in 1945. In the course of the colonial authorities' brutal suppression of a railway workers' strike in 1945, he allowed troops to shoot fleeing strikers in Douala Cathedral. No doubt he regarded the strikers as dangerous political militants who brought their own deaths upon themselves (Mfoulou 1978: 217–18).

After World War II, the independence of the Indian subcontinent and the near contemporaneous eruptions of anti-colonial wars in North Africa and Southeast Asia raised the issue of whether imperial states had the moral right – and, increasingly, whether they possessed the political will – to seek to retain colonies against the wishes of the local inhabitants. The Catholic Church, along with other Christian denominations, also began to shift its attitude towards independence. In France, theological opinion was split on the desirability of seeking to retain colonies. Younger Catholics and liberal church figures tended to be in favour of African political self-determination. Mgr Chappoulie, Bishop of Angers, spoke for many when he declared: 'The Christian and human calling [of France] forbids us to oppose in a brutal manner and without reception the legitimate aspirations of our overseas populations who were yesterday subdued without division to our authority' (Grenet

1989: 210). Pragmatism was the order of the day: senior Catholic figures in France began to recognize that support for decolonization was a sign of their concern for justice, a 'noble example of disinterestedness which [France] shows to the world in regard to the young African nations' (Déclaration de l'Assemblée des cardinaux et archévêques de France, quoted in French in Grenet 1989: 210).

It is important to link the development of Catholic colonial policy with developments in the church itself, rather than to regard it solely as reactive to external events. The First Vatican Council (Vatican I, 1869–70) was organized at the time of Italy's unification when the church considered itself under threat from the forces of nationalism. Its main task was to proclaim papal infallibility and to urge that physical force could not be used within the Vatican City by any organization (including the Italian state); it suggested that religious and secular power were henceforward separated in Italy (Bax 1987: 4). Vatican I also marked the emergence of the Roman Catholic Church as a transnational and international body which had no overt interest in any state; organizationally it confirmed the development of the church into a centralized, supranational body with a strongly hierarchical structure. The church had a transubstantiated form as a kind of state almost without physical substance, but significantly with an unparalleled international network of interests and influence which gave it considerable status at a time of African empire-building.

During Pope Pius XII's pontificacy (1938–58), the church consolidated its position in several areas of Africa where it had been of importance for some time. By 1960 the Catholic Church was the major Christian church in Africa. Between 25 and 50 per cent of people living in Angola, Cape Verde, Equatorial Guinea, São Tomé, Congo-Brazzaville, Uganda, Rwanda, Burundi, Kenya, Tanzania, Malawi, Zambia, Togo, Cameroon, Central African Republic, Mozambique, Lesotho, Madagascar, the Seychelles and Zaire were baptized Catholics. Substantial minorities (between 10 and 25 per cent) were Catholics in Côte d'Ivoire, Ghana, Benin, Nigeria, Guinea-Bissau, Chad, Zimbabwe, Swaziland, Namibia and South Africa. By the 1980s Africa's approximately 100 million baptized Catholics were around one-sixth of the continent's total population (Grenet 1989: Table 2, 216–17). To facilitate its administration, the Vatican divided up Africa among the different Catholic orders in the 1880s in an ecclesiastical version of the contemporaneous political division of Africa at the Congress of Berlin. The church also tentatively began its Africanization programme at this time; both the Spiritains and White Fathers independently opened a number of seminaries in Tanganyika and eastern Congo. Africanization had its limits, however: in 1939 there was just one African Catholic bishop, Joseph Kiwanuka. In 1949, there were fewer than 750 African Catholic priests in mainland Sub-Saharan Africa (out of a total of about 12,000 [Hastings 1979]); ten years later there were more than twice as many, as well as twenty-seven bishops (Grenet 1989: 216). By the 1960s, despite the increase in the number of African priests, most Catholic clergy in Africa were still Europeans. Independence speeded up the Africanization process: by the beginning of the 1970s there was a black Episcopal majority in, *inter alia*, Zaire, Tanzania, Uganda, Cameroon and Nigeria (Hastings 1979: 237). Rome's continued control of church activities was, however, ensured by the Papal nuncios (ambassadors), who continued to be mostly Europeans until well into the 1970s. The Vatican built up its network of nunciatures across Africa, staffed by diplomats, in order to ease contact with African political leaders and to help the Catholic African hierarchy with their political problems. The latter remained highly dependent on Rome for financial support.

The Catholic Church's ability to deal with the uncertainties accompanying the emergence of independent African statehood was aided by its institutional strength and ability to prevent serious schisms within the faith itself. Whereas both Islam and Protestantism frequently divide into competing sects, the Catholic hierarchy has always been very concerned to perpetuate a doctrinal unity encompassing all Catholics. In particular, much effort has been expended to prevent a separation between the intellectual stratum at the head of the church and the ordinary believers. As a result, Catholicism has been notably willing to allow into the faith many beliefs and practices from non-core areas such as Latin America and Africa in order to prevent divisions. The organizational capacity of the clergy also helped to keep the unity of the faith. Nevertheless, soon after African independence in the early 1960s three developments seriously affected the church's unity, which in turn led it to regard maintenance of good relations with temporal rulers with even greater concern than hitherto. The first was the serious decline in the number of practising priests, which later facilitated the drift of Catholics in Africa, as in Latin America (Berryman 1994), to rival Christian churches and sects, especially Protestant fundamentalist. The second was the traumatic intellectual division in the church between conservatives and radicals over the issue of social development as a prerequisite for strengthening the faith. This debate followed the Second Vatican Council, which ended in 1965; this was paralleled and fuelled by the growth of an African theology within the ranks of thinking

African Catholics. The third development was a reflection of economic and political developments within African states since independence: the growth of an all-encompassing clientelism involved the Catholic Church in the same way as it did nearly every social organization. The overall result of these developments was that the church sought to maintain its standing with African leaders as a means of maintaining its institutional role during a period of change for the church itself.

Internal conflict was focused upon the outcome of the Second Vatican Council (Vatican II), which reported in 1965. Vatican II was the main doctrinal event of the twentieth century for the church. Its main concern was the issue of religious flexibility within the corpus of Catholic doctrine. The results of the deliberations of Vatican II included the idea that the church should seek to restrict the uniformity of its spiritual guidance policy in order to allow for cultural distinctiveness outside of Europe where most of the church's followers were to be found; second, and more generally, Vatican II also underlined the church's support for religious liberty, its opposition to racism and colonialism, and its commitment to social and economic development, peace and cultural pluralism (Conus 1975: 50–53).

Despite Vatican II's unequivocal support for socially progressive themes and policies, Catholic hierarchies around the world were split between those who saw the church as basically a group of like-minded churches confederated under the loose tutelage of Rome, and those who saw the Roman Catholic Church as an essentially unipolar organization which might allow a few local peccadilloes, but not alternative perceptions of the religion itself, the form of which would be settled by the figure of the Pope himself. The post-Vatican II conflict within the church paralleled political events on the ground in Africa: conservative Catholic figures increasingly sided with secular leaders in order to ensure the latter's support. Socially progressive theologians, on the other hand, sought to create a new Catholic model of interactive, flexible religious concerns which would be of greater relevance to ordinary Catholics (Hastings 1979: 234–5).

Vatican II both stimulated and reflected two developments in Catholicism in Africa and Latin America. In the latter region the main revisionist trend took the form of liberation theology, with its revolutionary message for the necessity of radical change in this world in order to create God's kingdom on earth (Haynes 1993a: 95–109). In Sub-Saharan Africa, within different cultural, ethnic, religious and social contexts, liberation theology had much less impact, except in South Africa as we shall see in Chapter 5. Instead, there developed attempts to indigenize Catholicism, to develop a specifically African theology which strove to make the church more relevant to the lives of the mass of Catholics in Africa. Prominent African champions of the latter included Archbishop Emmanuel Milingo (Zambia), and Bishops Gantin (Benin), Zoungrana (Burkina Faso), Jago (Côte d'Ivoire), Malula (Zaire), Thiandom (Senegal), and Souza (Rector of the Catholic University of West Africa at Abidjan). Other influential figures included Englebert Mveng (secretary-general of the Association of African Ecumenical Theologians), Efoe-Julien Pénekou (Professor of Theology at the Catholic University of West Africa), and Professor Jean-Marc Ela of Cameroon (Errasova 1989: 221).

These champions of African theology sought to establish a direct link between Catholicism, with its emphasis on one supreme being and its rituals, with traditional African religious values and beliefs. This development was regarded with ambivalence within the hierarchy of the Catholic Church: some viewed the overt Africanization of Catholicism as a significant stage in the process of creating a new religion, and therefore as completely unacceptable; others regarded such a cultural revolution as necessary to retain existing African Catholics within the church, as well as to attract new followers at a time of growing competition from the burgeoning Protestant evangelical or 'fundamentalist' churches.

This section has provided an account of the Catholic Church's close ties with colonial authorities in areas where the church was demographically significant. Its later post-colonial ability to coexist with authoritarian rulers and their one-party states should be regarded as a triumph of the church's pragmatism in retaining, and in many cases building upon, its position during a period of major upheaval and change. A second point to emerge is that close social links between senior nationalist and church figures reflected wider concerns of shared interest involving a desire for political stability and the perpetuation of moderate socio-economic policies. As we shall see in Chapter 4, ideological and material concerns often coalesced in the post-colonial period to ensure good relations between secular and church leaders. In the next section we turn the analytical spotlight on the mainstream Protestant churches.

The Protestant churches and African independence

The relationship between Protestant mission church leaders and African nationalists may be dealt with more summarily than that between the latter and the Catholic Church. This is because the mainstream

Protestant churches were not a unified force in the way that the Catholic Church was during the colonial period and, as a consequence, individually possessed much less spiritual and religious clout. In addition, whereas the Catholic Church possessed its own state which aided its unity vis-à-vis both colonial authorities and African nationalists, the main Protestant mission churches – the Anglican, Methodist, Presbyterian and Lutheran – were in competition with each other as well as with their common Catholic rival and with Islam. Protestant churches individually achieved close relations with some colonial administrations, as for example in Kenya, yet the sectarian divisions between them meant that they never individually possessed the same corporate significance as the Catholic Church. Generally, the division between liberal and conservative outlooks within the Protestant churches paralleled those of the Catholic Church. On the whole, conservative Protestants believed that Christians should not involve themselves with political concerns, while their more liberal colleagues stressed that such involvement was desirable to achieve greater social justice. Nevertheless, '[n]either of the two Protestant theological traditions ... encouraged the churches to play a prophetic role in society, to act as the public conscience of the state' (Lonsdale 1978: 268). Until the 1950s, many leaders of the Protestant mission churches in Africa accepted the correctness and appropriateness of European imperialist rule provided it was seen to be to the medium- or long-term advantage of local Africans. As independence loomed, however, they tended to accept the end of European rule as inevitable, doing all they could to ensure the continuation of their churches' influence in the coming new order.

Islam and African independence

Muslims are divided by sectarian and ethnic divisions, to say nothing of different theological interpretations. As noted in Chapter 1, individual Muslim leaders were often important in the structures of indirect rule, but they rarely achieved close political relations with the colonial powers. This was because their relationship was built on a mutually convenient pragmatism, subject to change over time. Yet, in the drive towards decolonization, the role of Islam was relatively insignificant compared to that of the mainstream Christian churches.

Like the Catholic Church in Africa, Islam too is a very important faith in a number of countries. At least 80 per cent of the populations of Senegal, Somalia, Mauritania, the Gambia and Niger were Muslim by the 1960s. Inhabitants of Guinea, Mali, Chad, Nigeria and Sudan were at least 50 per cent Muslim, while Côte d'Ivoire, Ghana, Tanzania, Sierra Leone, Cameroon, Ethiopia and Burkina Faso each had sub-stantial Muslim minorities of between 10 and 40 per cent. It might be expected, given these substantial populations of Muslims in a large number of African states, that Islam's universalism would have been welcomed by nationalist leaders as a unifying ideology; able to transcend ethnic exclusiveness and individualism. As it turned out, however, Islam was usually unavailable as a social and political cement at national level, even when it enjoyed apparently overwhelming demographic salience. As already noted, Muslims in Sub-Saharan Africa are divided into competing Sufi brotherhoods, by ethnicity and by country. Nation-alist leaders – nearly always Christian – for their part associated Islam with backwardness and conservatism. The ulama, on the other hand, tended to be satisfied with the status quo, distrusted the new tendencies towards nationalism, and were lukewarm or opposed to the new post-colonial order (Trimingham 1980: 114).

Nationalist leaders were sometimes suspicious of the motives of minority Muslim populations; nowhere was this more noticeable than in Ghana. Between 1948 and 1980 the percentage of Ghana's popula-tion which classified itself as Muslim rose from 4 to over 20 per cent. Northern Ghana is substantially Islamic; elsewhere in the country Muslims are concentrated in three main population centres – Accra, Sekondi-Takoradi and Kumasi. The Muslim presence in Kumasi – divided between Hausa from Nigeria and immigrants from Mali and Burkina Faso – is the longest established outside the northern regions; it grew as a result of trade between the Ashanti state and Muslim areas to the north which predated European intrusion. In Accra, the Muslim community is also divided on the basis of ethnicity, as it is in Sekondi-Takoradi: Hausa and Zabrama from Burkina Faso are the most signifi-cant Muslim immigrants (Pobee 1992: 107). A colonial umbrella body, the Gold Coast Muslim Association (GCMA), was founded in 1932 as a national voice for the colony's diverse Muslims during the phase of modernization associated with colonization. Later, in the early 1950s, Muslims that were also supporters of Nkrumah's Convention People's Party (CPP) sought to infiltrate the GCMA in order to turn it into a pro-CPP body. Failing in its attempt, CPP Muslims formed a rival association, the Gold Coast Muslim Council (GCMC). In 1954, the anti-CPP GCMA evolved into a fully fledged political party, the Muslim Association Party (MAP). The MAP was 'based on sectarian and parochial interests, which was a serious challenge to the efforts of Nkrumah to build a nation out of congeries of tribes' (Pobee 1992: 114).

Nkrumah's response was to create a pro-CPP rival to the MAP, the Muslim Youth Council (MYC). Nkrumah 'adopted kid-glove methods in his dealings with' the MAP, according to Pobee (1992: 114), although he deported or detained in prison the organization's activists when he believed it necessary. It is clear that Nkrumah, whose reputation was built upon an espousal of the Pan-Africanist cause and 'ethnic blindness', was willing to be ruthless in extinguishing any communal challenges to his rule in the run-up to independence and in its immediate aftermath, when national unity was essential. The crushing of dissent to CPP rule from Ghana's Muslim opposition was made easier by the fact that no single important ethnic group was predominantly Muslim.

In Cameroon, as in Ghana, a one-party state was created soon after independence. Unlike in Ghana, however, Muslims from the north of the country were politically dominant. The proportion of Muslims to Christians in the country is approximately 2:1 – that is, some 40 per cent compared to around 20 per cent; the remainder are followers of traditional religions. Muslims in Cameroon are virtually all Sunnis; despite this religious solidarity, ethnically the north of the country is far from homogeneous. The Fulani (Peul) Muslim minority, along with Hausa traders and Kirdi converts, coexists, sometimes uneasily, with the majority of Kirdi, who are pagans (Bayart 1993a: 45). Christians – divided equally between Roman Catholics and Protestants (Evangelical and Presbyterian) – dominate in the south. Christianity is concentrated among the Beti, the Bulu and the Bamileké.

While religious divisions were socially important, the power struggle within the nationalist movement was played out according to ethnic allegiance. The (Muslim) president of Cameroon from 1958, Ahmadu Ahidjo (replaced by the Catholic Paul Biya in 1982), had an uneasy relationship with the country's Roman Catholic Church over the role of the state vis-à-vis religious bodies. Or, to put it another way, southerners (who were Christians) were suspicious of a state which appeared to them to be dominated by Muslim interests. 'Southern Roman Catholics were particularly strong among the ethnic groups most hostile to [Muslim] northerners' (Kofele-Kale 1987: 143). The example of Cameroon shows how difficult it is to pinpoint specifically 'political' and specifically 'religious' issues of contention between state and society. In Cameroon an issue may, in effect, be regarded as religious in one light, cultural in another, or straightforwardly political in a third.

A clearer pattern of Muslim–Christian interaction was discernible in the nationalist movement in Côte d'Ivoire. As in Ghana, Muslims are scattered among several ethnic groups and small communities, although the bulk of the country's Muslims – 25 per cent of the population – are to be found in the north-west of the country. Nationally, the reformist sect the Wahhabiya is of political importance. Wahhabiya leaders were in the forefront of the nationalist movement in the 1950s; their twin aims were to rid the country of the French colonial presence and to ensure their own leading role once the country gained its independence (Lapidus 1988: 850).

Wahhabiya leaders associated themselves with the main nationalist political movement, the Rassemblement Démocratique Africain (RDA), in order to achieve their objectives. Most leading nationalist politicians were Roman Catholics who nevertheless employed readings from the Quran to appeal to local Muslims for political support. Cultivation of the Muslim communities helped to increase the RDA's political salience and to gain strong national support in a way that the CPP in Ghana was never able to do. At independence in 1960, Wahhabiya leaders were given jobs in state institutions. They also benefited directly from Houphouet's policy of reasonable state prices for agricultural commodities – such as cocoa and coffee – for, like the Mourides in Senegal, they were often medium- to large-scale farmers. This policy helped to ensure the loyalty of most Muslims in the country, as the Muslim notables were adept at championing Houphouet's government, even though it was led by Catholics.

The type of mutually supportive relationship that existed between Muslim leaders and Côte d'Ivoire's government was also apparent in Senegal. As already explained in Chapter 1, in areas where Islam was already the dominant social force it was crucial for colonial administrators at least to neutralize powerful Muslim leaders, and preferably to co-opt them into the framework of administration. Following early friction between French colonialists and the Muslim Mourides in Senegal, the latter became staunch allies of the former. Rather than seeing Muslim resistance as an early example of proto-nationalism, it is analytically more satisfactory to regard their communities as examples of counter-societies. As Coulon notes,

> Such communities are forms of opposition characterized by leaving the existing social order and entering 'societies that openly defend other values and claim to set up, at least within their midst, a new order'. The aim ... is not to conquer the colonial power but to get away from it by creating ... a parallel power structure. (Coulon 1985: 358)

Such counter-societies were founded during the colonial era as a result of anomie and social crisis rather than as a clearly nationalist response to colonial rule. Maraboutic counter-societies in Senegal were later reintegrated into the colonial economic framework by the French, anxious to develop the country agriculturally in order to dissipate opposition to their rule. Initially charismatic in form, the power of maraboutic leaders over their followers was gradually routinized into a mutually beneficial patronage relationship. Muslim leaders forged a role as intermediary between government and community which has endured from the colonial period in Senegal to the present day. Over time the initially messianic nature of the maraboutic communities evolved into an overtly hegemonic structure which 'exercises control over a civil society that the political society cannot or does not want to control directly' (Coulon 1985: 364). As in Côte d'Ivoire and elsewhere in Sub-Saharan Africa where Muslim leaders have a high social and political standing, successive regimes in Senegal were content to co-opt marabouts into the economic and political élite for each group's mutual benefit.

Conclusion

This chapter, in its examination of the relationship between African nationalists and the end of colonial rule in the context of Catholic, Protestant and Muslim responses, has shown that the mission churches shared the fears of colonial administrations concerning African nationalist leaders' aspirations to independence. What would be the position of the church in the new order? While the Christian churches may well have had a theologically derived moral viewpoint on colonialism, involving as it did foreign political domination of Africans, it was generally agreed in the 1950s that the time was 'not yet right' to grant Africans self-rule. Once it became clear – by the late 1950s, exemplified by the accession to independence in quick succession of Sudan (1956), Ghana (1957) and Guinea (1958), before the independence floodgates opened in 1960 – that the demand for African independence was an unstoppable force, then the Christian mission churches sought to adapt as quickly as possible to the changing political climate: that is, they sought to accommodate themselves to new political realities and to strive, as far as possible, for positions of influence with the new leaders. Much was made of the close social, educational and cultural links between African nationalists and the churches, especially the Catholic Church. Local leaders of the church generally considered that their nationalist protégés were honourable men who would seek to rule in a way reminiscent of their former colonial predecessors, and that the churches would find it fairly easy to coexist with them. Suspicion of the Christian churches was greater in those states run by more radical regimes, as in Ghana; whereas in many of the French-speaking former colonies, senior Christian figures enjoyed close relations with nationalist leaders.

The Catholic Church in Africa is, of course, part of a global, transnational organization which could and still can bring considerable influence to bear upon African governments. The Protestant mission churches, on the other hand, found themselves in a more ambiguous, less secure, position. The attitude of their leaders to independence, like that of their Catholic counterparts, was pragmatically to seek to coexist with post-independence regimes with as few problems as possible.

Nationalist leaders (usually products of Western education and of their own efforts at self-advancement), for their part, spouted ideologies gleaned from their familiarity with Europe and European philosophies and ideologies. They sought to wrest power from the hands of a conservative, foreign stratum and to consolidate it in their own hands and those of their 'modernizing' supporters. Being aficionados of modern nationalist precepts, it was quite in order for them to decry the power of Islam as symbolizing an 'unmodernized' past which had to be transcended; nationalism had built Europe's states, where spiritual and secular power were officially quite separate. Muslims had to be incorporated into the nation even though they were suspicious of Christian leaders' objectives. The colonial rationale for meddling as little as possible in extant religious power hierarchies – that it was easy and cheap to rule through pre-existing elites (or to create them if necessary) – was not duplicated by the new nationalist brooms which displaced them. Their task was to create a modernized state built on nationalist ideals; religion was potentially a dangerous competitor for hearts and minds. In the post-colonial period, as we shall see in the next chapter, mainstream religious leaders often found themselves in ambivalent positions in relation to the new political elites which formed the post-colonial governments. Whereas nationalist politicians demanded unequivocal loyalty from all groups, including religious bodies, in the context of a drive for national unity, religious leaders for their part were often more or less compelled to seek accommodation with government in order to ensure their own positions and not to be seen to be undermining attempts to build national unity among often highly heterogeneous populations.

PART II

The State and Religious Institutions
after Colonialism

3

African States and
Mainstream Religious Organizations
in Comparative Perspective

In this chapter I argue that leaders of mainstream religious organizations in post-colonial Africa have often been strongly supportive of the government of the day even when regimes seemed to be ruling neither wisely nor well. I suggest that three factors have been important in these supportive relationships: (1) shared class concerns on the part of both sets of leaders, religious and temporal; (2) a strong desire by religious leaders to maintain influence as far as possible with political elites; (3) a normative concern on the part of both sets of elites that political stability was a good thing in itself.

State and Society

The state in Africa is often regarded as a powerful force in relation to society. Yet, as Hyden (1983) among others has argued, society's ability to organize itself beyond the state's jurisdiction suggests that the state's importance has sometimes been overestimated. Sanneh, for example, claims that the state in Africa is 'omnipotent', gaining for itself 'a wide channel of power, being not merely content to restrain and arbitrate but seeking to prescribe faith of a fundamental kind and conformity of an absolute form' (Sanneh 1991: 212). This, however, is to overstate the state's capacity to secure obedience from all of its people all of the time. Given that the post-colonial state was the inheritor of the colonial entity's political, economic and social framework of rule, then it is not surprising that it would attempt to govern in the same authoritarian, hegemonic fashion. Yet, the attempt to rule in this way was more of an indication of the state's *inability* to achieve its objectives by the creation

79

of societal consensus through a forging of national unity and direction. Above all, state leaders seek a comprehensive penetration of society whereby control over other political actors and social units is sought (Forrest 1988). Success has been patchy: the African state is far from being either omnipotent or able to enforce absolute conformity. It is the state's inability to penetrate society fully that actually demonstrates its weakness or 'softness'. In fact, the state–society relationship is nearly everywhere in Africa moulded by a network of clientelist interests which extends widely through the region's societies. This network of association resembles nothing so much as a spider's web. This suggests that there is no clear boundary between state and society; each interacts, feeds off and helps to sustain the other. Thus, state and society 'interpenetrate each other in more or less complex ways and at different levels (symbolic, normative, or structural), evolving over time into patterns' (Lemerchand 1992: 178). Political leaders are connected with allies throughout the state, sharing goals and orientations, although this should not imply an absence of conflict between different groups seeking state power. As economic crisis, triggered by the oil price rises of the 1970s, deepened throughout the 1980s in most African countries, so access to the state for resources became more and more difficult as it became increasingly desirable. Often as a direct consequence of economic reform and restructuring programmes imposed by the International Monetary Fund (IMF) and the World Bank, state jobs became harder to come by; access to state resources via patronage mechanisms remained a more likely possibility for many individuals. In the context of increasing shortages of fungible resources, the state became increasingly a patrimonial state (Lewis 1992: 47). The need to penetrate the state was transmuted into the ability to tap resources at a distance, a system characteristic of 'the rhizome state' (Bayart 1993a: 218). The idea of the 'rhizome state' is straightforward: the more difficult the penetration of the state itself, the thicker and more extensive the patrimonial links between individuals become. One of the (unintended) effects of IMF programmes has been to produce extensive new opportunities for clientelistic interaction, which has given increased opportunity for the disbursement of financial favours (Brittain and Watkins 1994).

My argument is that most representative and associational groups – including religious ones – are organically linked with the state to perpetuate the role and position of a certain hegemonic stratum. Organizations within civil society serve to internalize the relations of domination, creating the consensus indispensable for the reproduction of this domination; leaders of mainstream religious organizations play their part in the maintenance of the status quo. On the one hand, the leaders of these organizations epitomize, as figurehead and leader, the normative beliefs of their religion in terms of a reorganization of society which may well transcend the merely spiritual level. It is for this reason that they may join – yet rarely inaugurate – societal attacks on governments which appear to have been trampling for too long and too heavily on the collective rights of society. On the other hand, however, religious leaders are products of the society within which they live: they are affected in the same way by basic shortages of goods; their salaries may well be low in relation to their status; they will of necessity cultivate 'contacts' who can help them with their material problems. There is also the issue of the nature of the relations *within* religious institutions, between 'big men' (archbishops, bishops, members of the ulama, leading marabouts, and so on) and those who serve local populations at the grassroots (priests, mallams, and other ministers of religion). Such men are nearly always poor, usually badly served by their religious organizations, and, as a consequence, often resentful of their leaders' superior material positions (Bayart 1989a, 1993b).

Attempts to redefine the three-way relationship between mainstream religious organizations, the state and society should take into account the plethora of independent churches and the manifestations of popular Islam which are common throughout Africa. There are many extant studies of popular religions – that is, those uncontrolled by the state or the mainstream religious organizations – and their impact upon secular politics in the region (see Ranger 1986 for an exhaustive survey; and Lan 1985 and Ranger 1985 for case studies of Zimbabwe during the liberation war). In the colonial period they were generally understood as manifestations of proto-nationalism; after independence they were often seen as one result of popular dissatisfaction with the outcome of independence – that little seemed to improve for many ordinary people despite the ending of European political domination. In sum, as we shall see later, popular religious vehicles are manifestations of community mobilization against both state heavy-handedness and unresponsiveness to demands for change, as well as a protest against mainstream religions which seem to be somewhat remote from many ordinary people's concerns. In other words, they are potent symptoms and symbols of African governments' common inability to satisfy their constituents, a means for ordinary people to organize themselves to gain spiritual and material benefits which neither the state nor the mainstream religious organizations appear to be able to deliver (Mbembe 1988; Ranger 1985;

Lan 1985). The contemporary growth of popular religious organizations in Africa thus not only reflects a widespread disaffection with mainstream religious organizations; it has also meant that the spiritual and material lives of increasing numbers of ordinary people have been enhanced. As Chabal notes,

> the deployment of new or re-invented local 'indigenous' religions which the state, unsurprisingly, perceives as a direct political challenge are best regarded along with 'ethnic politics' and 'corruption' as one of the political idioms by means of which state and civil society joust with each other. (Chabal 1992: 97)

Before we can examine the role of popular religion in the relationship between state and society, we need to look more closely at the association between the state and the mainstream religious organizations in Sub-Saharan Africa in order to place the various vehicles of popular religion in perspective. It is to this task that we now turn.

Tension and accord

The expectation of material resources from the state helps to forge close ties between leading religious figures and senior government officials. An additional and sometimes more compelling reason for routine – but not always total – compliance on the part of the former to the latter is that the state has force at its disposal to underpin its authority. Lacking, as they do, the state's ability to back up its demands by the use of force, religious figures must know at the back of their minds that if they are perceived by the government of the day to be challenging it in a serious fashion, then they run the risk of incurring its wrath. To make the point bluntly: religion's power is no match for the state's so long as the latter can rely upon the loyalty of its security forces. Because, ultimately, religion only has 'mere' morality and right on its side, the state or other political actors, with superior force at their disposal, are quite capable of silencing religious 'troublemakers'.

Recent examples of such brutal treatment include: the murders of five American nuns and a Ghanaian priest in separate incidents in Liberia in 1992, allegedly at the hands of soldiers of Charles Taylor's National Patriotic Front of Liberia (*West Africa* 1993b: 1987); General Idi Amin Dada's killing of Archbishop Janani Luwum in 1977 because of his opposition to Amin's rule (Pirouet 1980); the 'accidental' death of a Kenyan bishop, Alexander Muge, in a car crash in August 1990 (many Kenyans believe he was executed by the regime because of his vociferous opposition to the Arap Moi government's growing totalitarianism)

(Africa Watch 1991); the late President Samuel Doe's execution of a number of 'pastor-politicians' following his *coup d'état* in 1980 because of their alleged corrupt and self-serving rule. The 16 February 1992 massacre in Kinshasa, when at least thirty people were killed by soldiers during a peaceful march for 'la paix et l'éspoir' (peace and hope) organized by the Catholic Church, confirmed how the state is prepared to use force even against religiously motivated actors in order to crush challenges to its domination (Collins 1992).

In Burundi, the whole-hearted support of the Catholic hierarchy for the democratic government of Melchior Ndadaye, elected in June 1993, was no bar to the Tutsi military's murder of Ndadaye and three prominent colleagues three months later. These killings stimulated a Hutu backlash against the Tutsi minority which led to many further deaths. Most recently, in neighbouring Rwanda in June 1994, the Catholic Archbishop of Kigali and twelve other priests were murdered by soldiers of the Tutsi-dominated Rwandan Patriotic Front (Huband 1994).

The examples above are merely some of the better-known instances in recent years of political authorities killing religious professionals and activists. Religious critics of the status quo who seek to alter the prevailing relationship between Church and State may also suffer in terms of their career prospects. For example, Bishops Emmanuel Milingo (Zambia) and Patrick Kalilombe (Lilongwe, Malawi) were forced to leave their countries following governmental consultation with the Vatican – 'troublesome priests' may receive short shrift, it appears, if they seem to be threatening the status quo. It is clear that religious professionals' fear of punitive treatment at the hands of political authorities is a factor which may impel them towards relatively muted responses to instances of state heavy-handedness. This helps to explain the silence of religious leaders on many occasions in the face of clear wrongs perpetuated by secular power-holders. That is, over and above shared class interests, there also exists a well-grounded fear of retribution should they be seen as a focus of popular discontent and opposition.

Gramsci and Weber share an observation on the role played by mainstream religion in politics. They both suggest that different strata in society pursue their own conceptions of religion. The religious elites, for their part, seek to monopolize the administration and content of religious values, while religious intellectuals who are not in positions of power may challenge them on theological grounds. Weber notes that, generally, 'the individual's quest for salvation ... has been considered highly suspect ... and ... controlled hierocratically ... Every body of *political* officials, on the other hand, has been suspicious of all sorts of individual [and, it should be added, community] pursuits of salvation' outside of the state's control (Weber 1969: 37; emphasis in original). This points to the likelihood of the establishment of a working relationship between state and religious organizations to pursue their individual and collective hegemonies by the domination of society. Before looking at this issue more closely, it is necessary to establish the nature of the duality in religious thought which separates religious leaders, concerned primarily with the perpetuation of their own positions, and intellectuals of their faith, who will often seek to criticize the nature of the relationship between their leaders and the state.

Intellectuals and the forging of state–religion hegemony

African intellectuals often have conceptions of their religion which involve primarily issues of equality, fairness, human rights, and so on. As a result, they are often in the forefront of criticisms of religious leaders in Africa, whom they charge with failing to confront governments over issues of human and civil rights and the lack of democracy. Frequently they bemoan the apparent inability or lack of will of their church leaders to confront bad government (Gitari 1988; Okullu 1978). Such critics often argue that the Christian churches have not discovered 'an answer to the question of how best to relate to political, social and economic structures' (Gitari 1988: 12). A 1976 colloquium organized by the ecumenical World Council of Churches (WCC) sought to come up with some answers. Four positions were outlined by the WCC: (1) Churches may 'adapt themselves actively' to prevailing secular power – that is, identify themselves with state goals; (2) churches may 'adapt themselves passively' to secular power – that is, withdraw into the purely religious sphere and not comment on state programmes and policies; (3) churches may 'engage in critical and constructive collaboration' – that is, evaluate political programmes from a theological perspective and react accordingly; (4) churches may 'resist or oppose' state policies – that is, campaign against state policies because they are fundamentally unjust (Gitari 1988: 12).

As will be discussed in the next chapter, there has undoubtedly been a common coalescing of human rights, democracy and developmental concerns in Africa, especially in the 1990s, with which religious leaders have involved themselves. Yet it is not clear that the most senior religious leaders have always been in the vanguard of recent demands for social and political change. I shall argue that national religious leaders have often viewed the mushrooming of opposition initiatives with misgivings or at least ambivalence, a position which is traceable back to the colonial period.

In colonial Africa the mission churches by and large helped to sustain the European administrations because of shared cultural and 'civilizing' goals. Demerath (1991: 37) argues that mainstream religious organizations generally possess a significant political *potential*; yet those 'with the greatest organizational resources to place at the disposal of a political perspective rarely fulfill their political potential'. This is because if the mainstream organizations wish to retain their independence, it is advisable for them to keep their political utterings to a minimum, both for fear of losing the material benefits which go with their favoured position and because of the potential consequences if the state uses its power to silence them. Obviously, loss of official approval is not to be welcomed. Yet, it would be incorrect to claim that African religious leaders *never* criticize their governments. Leaders may well add their personal voices and their organizations' corporate clout to societal attacks directed against government once a sufficient groundswell of criticism has built up. The point is that criticism of the government must be both vociferous and broad-based before senior religious leaders add their weight to it. If, on the other hand, religious leaders fail to join in attacks against a clearly unpopular government once they have reached a certain stage of intensity it would no doubt suggest to ordinary people that they and the regime were as one; the result might well be popular criticism of the religious leaders themselves for keeping silent while others attack the government. It seems that recent pro-democracy initiatives matured from scattered innovations in civil society coupled with international pressure (Bratton 1994). In both Kenya and Ghana, for example, a combination of international and domestic pressure did much to undermine one-party states and to compel the regimes to allow multi-party elections in 1992 (Haynes 1993b; Gifford 1994).

Pressure by religious leaders on government appears to have been particularly significant in Kenya. Fifteen Catholic bishops and six leading officials from the National Council of Churches told President Moi to his face in 1992 that the people had lost confidence in his regime, and that changes to the one-party system should be made immediately (Gifford 1992b). Given that the leading Christian churches in Kenya were renowned for their fulsome support of the very same one-party system, it seems that two processes combined to produce the volte-face: pressure from ordinary Kenyans interacted with international disquiet concerning the Moi regime expressed by human rights and church organizations to produce a groundswell of criticism to which the Kenyan bishops added their voices (Gifford 1994). Kenya's Christian leaders were faced with a stark choice: take a leading role in the ranks of the reformers or be tarred with the same brush as unrepresentative leaders who dig in their heels and refuse to leave the political centre stage. Yet, this is not to suggest that *all* senior religious leaders joined the attacks against the Moi regime. For example, the leader of the independent African Gospel Redeemed Church (AGRC) claimed in 1992 that, 'in Heaven it is like Kenya has been for many years. There is only one party – and God never makes a mistake' (quoted in Ranger and Vaughan 1993: 261). The leader of the independent Maria Legio church, Moi's minister of employment, also supported the status quo. What this suggests is that independent churches like the AGRC or the Maria Legio, which theologically are towards the 'fundamentalist', conservative end of the religious spectrum, regard government as divinely sanctioned – that they rule because God allows them to. The mainstream Christian churches in Kenya, on the other hand, were part of an international constituency which increasingly regarded the Moi regime as illegitimate. Mainstream Christian leaders may *prefer* not to involve themselves in political issues but, at times, it becomes very difficult indeed to remain silent. Further, the fact that the Maria Legio church leader, as a minister in the government, benefited materially from the status quo made it natural for him to support the pre-existing one-party state system.

In the next section, I want to illustrate further my contention that mainstream religious leaders will often be content to back a regime – at least implicitly – as long as popular pressure for change is muted. I will refer to a number of extant typologies of state–religious institutions in order to examine the relationship between state and mainstream religious organizations in a variety of ideological and religious contexts. I will refer to three of Africa's erstwhile Marxist states – Mozambique, Angola and Ethiopia; to Africa's only theocracy, Islamic Sudan; and, finally, to apartheid South Africa, where the largest Christian church, the Dutch Reformed Church, was a supporter of the notion of 'separate development' – a defender of apartheid as an aspect, it was believed, of God's will. I will argue, *inter alia,* that the official ideology of a regime is relatively unimportant when seeking to ascertain the nature of its relationship with certain mainstream religious organizations. What will emerge is that religious leaders have been more concerned with their personal positions and with the standing of their religious institutions than with seeking to confront regimes over policies which were often disastrous for much of society.

Typologies of State–Religion Relations in Africa

Weber's classic typology of state–religion relations identifies three types
of relationship between secular and ecclesiastical power: *hierocratic*, where
secular power is dominant but cloaked in a religious legitimacy; *theocratic*,
where ecclesiastical authority is pre-eminent over secular power; and
caesaro-papist, where secular power holds sway over religion itself (Weber
1978: 1159–60). More recent attempts to develop typologies of state–
religious organization interaction have taken into account the growing
separation between Church and State as a function of modernization.
Parsons (1960) suggests that the church may form part of the 'establishment' at one extreme and may be totally separate from the state at the
other. Mazrui (1974) argues that a common middle position on such a
scale – what he called the 'ecumenical state' – is where a government
is not religiously monopolistic but is, intent, rather, on upholding
religious pluralism. The ecumenical state is obviously different from
one with an established church, although it may of course have either
a pro-Christian or pro-Islam bias.

  More recently, Medhurst (1981) extended the range of types of state–
religious organization interaction from Weber's three to four. Medhurst
proposed the following four categories: 'The Integrated Religio-Political
System' (IRS); 'The Confessional Polity (or State)'; 'The Religiously
Neutral Polity (or State)'; and 'The Anti-Religious Polity (or State)'.
The IRS is a type of theocracy, virtually extinct globally, with only
Saudi Arabia offered as an example by Medhurst. It pertains to premodern political systems where religious and spiritual power converge
in one figure, as in pre-1945 Japan or ancient Mesopotamia. It is very
rare in the contemporary period because one of the most consistent
effects of modernization has been to separate religious and secular
power. The 'Confessional Polity' (CP), on the other hand, emerges
when the 'traditional "religio-political system" begins to crumble and
gives way to a new situation of religious or ideological pluralism'
(Medhurst 1981: 120). In other words, this is a situation characterized
by a (more or less) formal separation of state and (dominant) religious
organization, although in practice close links are retained between the
two. Medhurst gives examples from both Muslim and Christian
contexts. The latter include Ireland and Colombia; and the former,
post-revolutionary Iran. The 'Religiously Neutral Polity' category
denotes constitutionally secular states such as India, the USA, and the
Netherlands, where no religion is given official precedence over others,
rather like Mazrui's ecumenical state. Finally, the notion of the 'Anti-

Religious Polity' pertains to Marxist states where religion is, according to Medhurst, 'throttled'.

I want to look next at an example of each of the three extant types of relations involving religious organizations and the state in Africa. Examples of apparent severance between Church and State are provided by the Marxist states of Ethiopia, Angola, Mozambique and Guinea-Bissau; examples of religious pluralism, with a bias towards one church, is provided by apartheid South Africa, with further illustrative examples from Ghana and Zambia. Finally, an example of a regime which is in close partnership with a religious organization is provided by Sudan, where the regime of General al-Bashir has ruled in partnership with the radical National Islamic Front since 1988.

Christian Churches and Marxist States

It might be thought that the idea of religious organization and state in more or less symbiotic relationship would only pertain when the former is fully accepted as a welcome stabilizing factor by the latter. Yet, when apparently serious threats to the mainstream Christian churches' survival followed the accession to power of Marxist governments in Ethiopia, Angola, Mozambique and Guinea-Bissau in the mid-1970s, they appeared remarkably to choose a line of only minimal or quite limited resistance: a serious diminution of spiritual activities, which however turned out to be only temporary, was a price that church leaders were apparently willing to pay to Africa's revolutionary Marxist regimes for their continued existence.

The apparent threat to the survival of Christian churches in the African Marxist regimes came after socialism in Africa entered a new, revolutionary, phase in the mid-1970s. From that time, 'African socialism' à la Tanzania was challenged conceptually by the creation of 'scientific' socialist regimes in Angola, Mozambique, Guinea-Bissau and Ethiopia. Three characteristics of the 'scientific socialist' trend are relevant to the current discussion. First, in contradistinction to the ideologies of several of the initial post-independence African regimes, a possible third way (that is, communitarian 'African socialism' or ujamaa socialism) between capitalism and scientific socialism was rejected by the leaders of Africa's Marxist regimes. They adopted the techniques and aims of class analysis in order to identify internal class enemies supposedly working to hold back national development. Second, there were attempts to create Leninist-style vanguard parties, alliances of modern-sector workers and farmers, in order to transform society along revolutionary lines. Third, in Angola, Mozambique and Ethiopia, attempts to create socialist societies coincided with the outbreak of civil wars, caused in part by differences of ideological interpretation within the contending political movements. In Guinea-Bissau, on the other hand, the absence of civil war did not significantly advance the development goals of the post-colonial government, as the country remained one of the poorest in Africa. In addition, the demographic insignificance of the Catholic Church – despite the fact that the country had been a Portuguese colony – meant that it was never an important player in the post-revolutionary period. Christianity was (and is) the religion of only about 5 per cent of the population of one million – that is, 50,000 people, mostly Balanta. Muslims, about 40 per cent of the population, were 'le fer de lance de la lutte antiportugaise' (the iron spearhead of the anti-Portuguese struggle), and retained a leading role in post-colonial politics (Grenet 1989). Because of the limited religious and social significance of the Christian churches in Guinea-Bissau, I will not be concerned with them in the following analysis.

The creation of 'scientific socialist' regimes in Ethiopia, Angola and Mozambique followed revolutions made exclusively by soldiers rather than by class action led by workers or peasants. One advantage for the revolutionaries of overturning the old political structures was to be able to replace them with new ones where the old elite would be denied their former positions of dominance. A new elite would emerge, defined by membership of the single Marxist party and their revolutionary fervour, able to gain new economic opportunities commensurate with newly achieved political dominance. Additionally, by proclaiming themselves Marxist-Leninists, cadres gained the chance to enter into new alliances with the then-extant 'scientific socialist countries' of Eastern Europe, and, as a result, emphatically to distance themselves from their former colonial masters. In other words, they would be able to use for their own ends opportunities offered by the Cold War between East and West. As far as religion was concerned, the Marxist rulers of Angola and Mozambique, in common with their Soviet allies, regarded the Christian churches as the epitome of conservatism and false consciousness; in the colonial context, they were also regarded as the epitome of Western imperialism and colonialism. Due to these factors, they were perceived as the Trojan horses of the former colonial powers and had to be cut down to size. In Ethiopia, on the other hand, the situation was different. Because the country was never properly colonized, the Christian churches were indigenous to the country, enjoying nearly 2,000 years of existence and with strong popular allegiance reflective of their cultural affinity with many ordinary people. Yet, for Ethiopia's Marxist rulers the churches had to be tackled, for they were obvious foci of dissent for anti-revolutionaries. How they went about this forms the substance of the next section.

Ethiopia

Ethiopia's population of more than 50 million people is divided fairly equally between Christians and Muslims. About 40–45 per cent are Sunni Muslim; many of them live in now-independent Eritrea. About 45 per cent of the population belong to the Ethiopian Orthodox Church, an indigenous African church, which was founded nearly two thousand years ago, and which has historical links with the Egyptian Coptic Church. Less than 5 per cent of Ethiopians are Protestants or Catholics, while about 12 per cent are followers of traditional African religions (Clapham 1989: 73).

Although Ethiopia was not really a colonial country its ruler, Ras Tafari, Haile Selassie, judged by radicals a stooge of the United States, ruled his country dictatorially. After the 1974 revolution, the Derg (Provisional Military Administrative Council) lacked a coherent policy relating either to individual religious freedoms or to Christianity and Islam more generally. During the fervour of revolution in the late 1970s, the government stripped the Ethiopian Orthodox Church of most of its landholdings. The Derg leaders were, however, astute enough to realize that religious traditions formed an important, even integral, facet of Ethiopian life and that it was somewhat counterproductive to attempt to crush religion completely. By the early 1980s, as problems with the revolution became apparent, the government courted the two most senior religious figures in the country, the Orthodox patriarch and the chief Muslim mullah of Addis Ababa, seating them both close to the Marxist rulers at important state events.

The Orthodox Church's reaction to Ethiopia's revolution had initially been marked by apparent passivity and resignation. Its great disadvantage, in common with former mission churches in Africa, was that in the revolutionaries' eyes it was heavily inculcated with symbols of the past, especially the feudal system based on oppression and exploitation of ordinary people. During Haile Selassie's rule the Orthodox Church was the established church, supported by the state, with its organization and administration governed by law (Barrett 1982: 284–5). The Catholic Church with some half a million members, and the Protestant churches with perhaps four or five times as many, on the other hand, had not hitherto been politically influential in the country, and had no close links with the *ancien régime*. Leaders of the Catholic Church were, however, cautious in denouncing the revolutionary regime. There was no serious confrontation between the Catholic hierarchy and the state, while the church's welfare activities continued as before.

Angola

While the attitude of the Ethiopian Orthodox Church was marked by resignation and that of the Catholic hierarchy by caution, the authorities in Angola mounted an intense state campaign against the dominant Catholic Church. About 70 per cent of Angola's 10 million people are Roman Catholic, concentrated in the west where the Portuguese colonialists had lived, while another 20 per cent belong to various Protestant churches, including the Methodist, the Baptist and the Plymouth Brethren. Membership of African independent churches is very low – about 1.5 per cent of the population (150,000 people); there are even fewer Muslims residing in the country.

Southern Ovimbundu people were often strongly supportive of Jonas Savimbi's Unita (National Union for the Total Independence of Angola) rebels, as well as being staunchly Christian (Marcum 1987). The Ovimbundu's chief ethnic rivals, the Kimbundu, along with mixed-race mesticos, dominate the upper levels of the Popular Movement for the Liberation of Angola (MPLA) government, even though in the late 1970s the MPLA Political Bureau had also included four Mbundu, three Bakongo and two Cabindans. This amounted to representation of all the country's main ethnic groups except for the Ovimbundu (Rothchild and Foley 1988: 247). Conservative American evangelical Christians, in cahoots with both the American CIA and the South African government, cast Unita's resistance to the MPLA government as a religious war against Marxist atheism, and supplied the rebels with monetary aid and arms. Yet, the putative religious orientation of the civil war oversimplified what was actually a complex, multifaceted conflict, involving a mixture of ethnic, regional, economic and religious issues; it also underlined how the role of religious organizations in Angola was heavily influenced by the civil war itself.

The Roman Catholic Church is the predominant church in Angola, yet, like the Orthodox Church in Russia after the October 1917 Revolution, it found itself in the unwelcome position after 1974 of having to come to terms with a revolution, a political upheaval which resulted in the laicization of the state. The Angolan Catholic hierarchy had always been extremely loyal to Lisbon; as late as April 1974, the Angolan Church was still condemning armed insurrection and expressing support for the colonial regime. Two months later, after the MPLA's victory, it was forced by events to backpedal and to denounce the 'atrocities' and negation of human rights systematically practised by the colonial regime. The 1976 Constitution stated with regard to religion that Angola was a secular state with religious liberty and freedom of conscience. What this meant in practice was made plain the following year, when the president of MPLA, the late Agostinho Neto, the son of a Methodist minister, stated: 'No party member can be a church member, and no church member can be a member of the party.' In other words, Angolans were perfectly at liberty to follow the religion of their choice, yet if they did they would be expunged from the party with the loss of attendant privileges. This uncompromising position on religion had a serious impact on the MPLA's ability to recruit new members, until Neto's guidelines were relaxed after his death in 1979 (Webber 1992: 129).

During the period of Neto's leadership, all religious holidays, including Christmas, were abolished (Mews 1989: 10). The root of the MPLA's hatred of the Catholic Church was that the party perceived it as the very epitome of neo-colonialism. Its position as a foreign church was made clearer by the fact that most priests in Angola were not Angolans – of the 527 priests in Angola in 1985, only 117 in the fourteen dioceses were Angolan-born (Clévenot 1987: 232). The MPLA government, true to its Marxist-Leninist understanding of the nature of religion as 'false consciousness', believed religion to be a factor of alienation which would naturally evaporate as the new socialist society was built. The Catholic bishops made it plain, in a pastoral letter of 22 November 1976, that they did not object to Angola becoming a socialist society provided the guarantees of the Constitution pertaining to religious liberty were upheld. The Methodist bishop, for his part, claimed to regard the new order as a potentially fertile environment for the promulgation of a socially conscious Christianity. While it would be easy to regard this statement as one fashioned for the delectation of MPLA leaders and cadres, and best viewed in the context of religious leaders' jockeying for position, the Catholic hierarchy in fact expressed somewhat similar views. Provided there was no effort made to crush religion per se, the episcopate would attempt to find a way to work with the regime. The bishops did, however, object to what they called the 'active promotion of atheistic propaganda in the schools and at public meetings' (Pro Mundi Vita 1982: 13). Yet, despite their appeals, courses in

Marxist theory were introduced in the schools, and all religious education was discontinued. This, the Catholic bishops argued, infringed the rights of parents by interfering in the education of their children. The full extent of the state's attempt to clip the Catholic Church's wings were revealed when the MPLA government nationalized Church schools – the bulk of the religious establishments in the country – while its hospitals, seminaries, printing presses and radio station were confiscated by the state. The result was that the ability of the state to build a strong welfare sector was heavily circumscribed, for most of the competent professionals were also religious figures; in their absence the sector largely failed to function. The inability of the state to fill the developmental role of the church encouraged President dos Santos to meet with the twelve Catholic bishops for the first time in 1981; both sides agreed to respect the position of the other and to work together for the development of the nation. Archbishop Muaca noted on that occasion that '[t]oo many points of interest unite us' for it to be different (Pro Mundi Vita 1982: 14). The gradual transfer back to the church during the 1980s of its welfare functions underlined how both Church and State could function in mutually supportive ways which transcended ideological differences (Webber 1992).

Mozambique

In terms of the relationship between Church and State the situation in Angola and Mozambique was similar; both countries experienced civil war and both adopted Marxist-Leninist ideology, with its strong views on the negative social effects of religion. In addition, American-linked, Protestant evangelical churches were suspected of assisting the anti-government guerrillas of the Mozambique National Resistance (Renamo), just as their counterparts were in Angola (Gifford 1989). Mozambique is, however, considerably less christianized than Angola: the population of more than 16 million is only about 40 per cent Christian; of those, about 30 per cent are Catholics. Around 6 cent of Mozambicans are Protestant, and about 13 per cent are Muslim, reflecting Mozambique's position in relation to the Arabian peninsula and a history of Muslim penetration. Half of Mozambicans follow traditional African religions.

The local organization and structure of the Catholic Church in Mozambique was largely a copy of that which pertained in Portugal, although unlike the church in Angola its personnel saw increasing Africanization after the 1974 revolution. As in Angola, religious organizations were allowed to function, although they were certainly not encouraged. The late president, Samora Machel, like Agostinho Neto in Angola, frequently denounced the four centuries of alienation produced by the Portuguese Catholic Church (Clévenot 1987: 231). Muslims were also denounced for their alleged alliance with the Portuguese colonialists. Restrictions on religion in Mozambique went further than in Angola: for example, Christian missions were closed down for several years after 1974. The Presbyterian Church was allowed to reopen its missions several years later, in advance of the Catholic Church, because it was perceived by the Frelimo leadership to have identified itself with the liberation struggle (Pro Mundi Vita 1982: 14).

In March 1981, the archbishop of Maputo, Dom Alexandro Maria dos Santos, was able to report that the previously cool relationship between Church and State was improving. He noted that,

> in recent months, the relations between the [Catholic] Church and the state have greatly improved. Indeed, Church and state start from different ideologies. We know and respect this fact, but we also know and acknowledge that Church and state pursue one and the same goal: an independent and strong nation ... Basically, we can carry on our pastoral activity without interference from the state, and our cooperation is requested whenever major problems of the country are discussed. (Pro Mundi Vita 1982: 15)

As in Angola, the government of Mozambique confiscated many church buildings and assets after 1974. In 1988 they were returned, as part of a process of religious rehabilitation and a lessening of hostility by the state, symbolized by a visit from the Pope that same year. The process of reconciliation began in the early 1980s, as in Angola, and for the same reasons: the Frelimo government could not do without the church's involvement in health, literacy and development projects, while the Christian bodies had to co-operate with the state if they wished to run their missions and to proselytize freely.

To conclude this section, it should perhaps be emphasized how army-led revolutions similarly empowered radical political actors in Ethiopia, Angola and Mozambique in the mid-1970s to seek to change religious and social values and political norms. In Ethiopia, the Marxist rulers sought as far as possible to reach a *modus vivendi* with national Christian and Muslim figures alike. Obviously, it is one thing to proclaim a revolution from the top down, yet it is quite another to infuse a set of radical political changes throughout society – that is, to gain widespread acceptance for the validity, comprehensiveness and practicality of such ideas. The unexpected characteristic of Ethiopia's revolution was retention of the personal support of both Christian and Muslim leaders. In Angola and Mozambique, on the other hand, both Christian and Muslim institutions were regarded primarily as manifestations of colonial rule, imposed institutions whose relevance to people's lives would quickly wither away in the new socialist order. Within a few years, however, the MPLA and Frelimo regimes made overtures of reconciliation to the Catholic Church. What this account of the relationship between mainstream Christian churches and African Marxist-Leninist states has shown is that neither significant religious institutions nor the state have the ability to thrive without the sanction of each other. The state can make life difficult for religious institutions, although the latter, because of their social and cultural importance, can also be crucial for the state in the context of gaining and maintaining popular acceptance.

Religious Pluralism and the State

South Africa

In the second category of state–religious organization relations – those states which profess to encourage religious pluralism – I want to look first at the role of the Dutch Reformed Church in South Africa. In this example, the apartheid state looked to the church as its major religious ally. Because the struggle to end apartheid was for many a religious struggle, it was of great importance for the state to continue its historically close links with the church because of its social and religious significance for many Afrikaners.

South Africa's population of about 38 million comprises about 4.5 million whites of European origin, nearly 3 million 'Coloureds' of mixed race, about 1 million 'Asians' (mostly of Indian subcontinent and East Asian origin), and about 30 million black Africans. About two-thirds of black South Africans, and four-fifths of whites, are Christians. The traditional English-speaking denominations are predominantly black, and have consistently opposed apartheid. There are over 2 million Roman Catholics, slightly fewer Anglicans, and less than 1 million Lutherans. Some 12 million black Christians belong to African independent churches. It is claimed that South Africa has the greatest proliferation of independent churches in the world, more than 3,250 in 1980 (Oosthuizen 1985: 71).

Muslims comprise around 1.5 per cent of the population, some 400,000–500,000 people. They are roughly equally divided among

Asians of Indian subcontinent extraction (20 per cent of the total, pre-dominantly Sunni) and Cape Coloureds (Afrikaans-speaking ethnic Malays). Until recently, few black South Africans were followers of Islam (Moore 1989: 238). The Call of Islam was formed in Cape Town in 1984 to inform non-Muslims about the beliefs of Islam; it achieved some success in recruiting black South Africans by projecting Islam as an anti-colonial, anti-white religion, and in seeking to relate the way that the *tauhid* (way) of Allah was violated in South Africa during the apartheid era. It aimed to bring Muslims back on to the path of right-eousness by making them more conscious of their religious duties to build a 'just' society. What this implied, in effect, was that Muslims in South Africa were involved in political struggle against an 'unjust' secu-lar state, rather than opposing spiritual leaders for religious laxity, which is much more common generally in Africa.

The largest Christian church, to which about 2.5 million Afrikaans-speakers of Dutch ethnic origin belong, is the Dutch Reformed Church (Nederduitse Gereformeerde Kerk: NGK). The NGK is the denomina-tion of most members of the former apartheid government. There are two ultra-conservative whites-only breakaway churches from the NGK: the Nederduitsch Kerk, established in 1858; and the Gereformeerde Kerk (the 'Doppers'), established in 1859, to which former state president de Klerk belongs. Until 1986 the NGK sought to produce theological justifications for apartheid. Non-white members of the NGK had to belong to one of three sister churches established by mission: the Nederduitse Geregormeerde Sendingkerk (NG Mission Church) for 'Coloureds'; the (Asian) Reformed Church in Africa for 'Indians'; and the Nederduitse Gereformeerde Kerk in Afrika (NG Church in Africa) for blacks. After 1990, the four churches attempted to overcome the racial divisions between them, without success. A February 1993 sum-mit meeting between them failed to agree on conditions for unity. On this occasion, the NGK leaders refused to recognize the errors of the past, failing to declare apartheid to have been a heresy, or to repudiate the members of the Broederbond – former prime ministers, D.F. Malan, Hans Strijdom and Hendrik Verwoerd – responsible for introducing the racial system in 1948. President de Klerk described these three as 'men of great personal integrity, sincere in their belief that separate development could bring justice to black South Africans' (Sparks 1993).

The NGK has a historic role in South Africa which is analogous to that of the Orthodox Church in Ethiopia, or that of the Roman Catholic Church in Angola and Mozambique. It is regarded by many as the church of the colonizers, a conservative force acting to reinforce the political dominance of a white, Afrikaner elite. The role of the other main Christian denominations – Roman Catholic, Anglican and Evangelical Lutheran – was, on the other hand, to lead public critiques of apartheid. What this points to is that the struggle against racial discrimination in South Africa was regarded by many to be as much theological as it was political. Even though the great majority of South Africans are Christians, their commitment to their faith is heavily conditioned, as elsewhere in Africa, by class interests and religious interpretations (Fine 1992). The NGK was, in effect, an element in the structure of apartheid which maintained its relationship with government right until the end of white minority rule.

Ghana and Zambia

Unlike the NGK in South Africa, several leading churches in both Ghana and Zambia were in conflict with their governments in the early 1980s. The churches protested when their own positions appeared threatened. The activities of the Marxist governments of Angola, Mozambique and Ethiopia were regarded nervously by Christian churches in these two countries; they feared that their own governments would act in some fundamental way to curb them. In Zambia, the proclaimed adoption in 1981 by the then president, Kenneth Kaunda, of 'scientific' socialism as the official state ideology was the catalyst for the creation of a coalition *in extremis* between the labour movement and the mainstream Christian churches; the former thought the creation of a socialist state would result in the complete erosion of their bargaining powers, real wage levels and their ability to protest, while the latter feared marginalization, perhaps even abolition. The alliance between religion and labour was to have profound political effects over the next decade. In 1991 the 'born again' Christian and former chairman of the Congress of Trade Unions, Frederick Chiluba, was elected president of Zambia, ousting Kenneth Kaunda who had been in power since independence in 1964. As in Poland in the 1980s, the struggle between Church and State in Zambia later developed into one for participatory democracy (Sklar 1986: 24). The significance of this was that during a period of perceived threat the mainstream churches in pluralist Zambia joined forces with another organization which felt itself under attack; owing in part to their combined efforts the Kaunda regime was later toppled, and as a result both churches and trade unions re-established their previously good relations with government.

The populist, military regime of Jerry Rawlings in Ghana also had a tense relationship with the mainstream Christian churches in the early 1980s, although, as in Zambia, the position was later rectified. The regime's apparent espousal of socialism as its guiding ideology after it grabbed power in a military *coup d'état* at the end of 1981 was followed by the banning of the *Catholic Standard* newspaper in 1986. The Protestant and Roman Catholic Church hierarchies joined forces to attempt to prevent what they saw as a concerted attack by the state upon their positions. They linked up with the political opponents of the Rawlings regime – the so-called 'professional' groups, including lawyers, doctors and journalists – to push the government gradually towards democratic elections, which took place in late 1992 (Haynes 1993b). The confrontation between Ghana's government and the country's Christian hierarchy took place at a time when the former appeared to be threatening the very existence of the latter. The point is that an apparently concerted attack upon Christian religious institutions in both Zambia and Ghana led to a strong, sustained response from their leaders, who felt that their own personal positions and that of their churches were under threat from the state. This is not to suggest that Ghana's and Zambia's Christian leaders confronted government solely out of self-interest, but to note that once those particularist concerns were evoked then sustained opposition to unwelcome state policies became much more likely. For the last example of state–religious organization interaction in the current chapter we turn to Sudan, where a strongly Islamic government has been in power since the 1980s. The case of Sudan is illustrative of the third position established in our typology: where the state and 'church' join forces to pursue common goals of societal control.

'Theocratic' Government in Africa: The Case of Sudan[1]

At the time of African independence in the 1960s, Islamic ideas were rarely regarded as progressive by most nationalist leaders. Most of the latter were Christian, educated in mission schools and perhaps foreign universities. They were fired by the fervour of anti-colonial success, looking to modernist, temporal ideologies – especially socialism – to express and convey national unity even in predominantly Muslim countries like Guinea, Senegal and Niger. Many first-generation independence leaders appeared to believe that Africa was on course for a general process of modernization, and – if the European model was anything to go by, which many thought it was – of secularization as part of that process. Islam, like Christianity and traditional African religions, may have been important from a cultural, social and historical perspective, but not politically.

With the benefit of hindsight, it is clear that generally optimistic expectations of Africa's trouble-free development fell rather wide of the mark. Economic progress has often been highly problematic, and class inequalities have by and large increased. Africa *was* partially transformed, but in a not altogether welcome way: social, economic and political disarticulation of the bodies politic was widespread. Sometimes, as in Liberia, Sierra Leone and Zaire in recent times, the state appeared almost to fall apart. Islam, like other religions in Africa, lost none of its social relevance; on the contrary. Yet Islam's impact in Africa has been decidedly variegated over the last two decades or so: in northern Nigeria, for example, the faith is judged variously to be conservative, seditious, subversive, or even revolutionary, depending on the observer's viewpoint; in Mali, Niger, and to an extent in Senegal, on the other hand, it is often regarded as the cultural cement keeping society together; whereas in Kenya, Uganda, Cameroon and Tanzania, Islam is regarded with great suspicion by political leaders who see within its social concerns the seeds of communal strife; in Eritrea it is something else again – the *leitmotif* of ethnic culture and pride of a people freed at last from Amharic dominance.

It is, however, only when there are substantial Arab populations, claims to Arab identity, or long-term Arab hegemony – as in Mauritania, northern Sudan, Somalia, northern Chad and the coast of East Africa (which experienced Arab political and/or commercial hegemony over several centuries) – that national identity in Africa expresses itself in self-consciously Islamic terms. It is only in those regions where Islamization engendered a process of Arabization that Islam and Arab are relatively synonymous. In effect, these regions in the West and East of Africa were the 'periphery' of Arab centres of political and commercial power. In Mauritania, Mali, Niger, Chad, Sudan and Eritrea, which straddle the geographical Muslim/non-Muslim divide (that is, the area around 15 degrees north of the Equator), the nature of politics is largely dependent upon the proportion of Muslims to Christians, or Arabs to non-Arabs. That is to say, where ethnicity melds with religion, it tends to focus political issues and allegiances. In Mauritania, an Islamic state was declared in 1980 through the alliance of the native Hausa regime with the Muslim Brotherhood; Sharia law was introduced and slavery officially abolished (Mews 1989a: 178). Almost the entire population of Mauritania are Sunni Muslims, which is the only cultural point of similarity between the light-skinned northern nomadic Arab-Berbers and their black African pastoral co-religionists in the south. Politically, southerners are highly apprehensive about domination by the north. In order to prosecute its hegemony, the northern-dominated government emphasized the Islamic rather than Arabic features of the national culture (Gerteiny 1971).

Sudan is unique among African countries south of the Sahara, because it is only there that Islam has achieved the status of state ideology. Its institutionalization manifests itself in a society where human rights and political freedoms appear generally to have been quite seriously downgraded and where certain ethnic groups – including the Dinka, Nuer and Nuba – have been victimized in the name of the ruling Islamic-military dictatorship and state homogeneity.

The process towards Islamization in Sudan began in the early 1980s. The then state president, Ja'far al-Numeri, began to adopt Islamic dress in public: the *jellabiya* (robe) and *anima* (turban) were worn for many public appearances, in preference to the military uniform that Numeri had hitherto appeared to favour. He also issued new currency which showed him resplendent in his new Islamic persona. Sharia law was imposed in 1983 (although never made to stick in the largely Christian/ animist south of the country). Such acts, as Bernal (1994: 48) notes, served to assert 'Sudan's Muslim and Arab identity while associating Islam with power and nationalism'. Foreign and domestic pressures coalesced to convince Numeri of the appropriateness of his policy of Islamization: Sudan's chief aid provider of the time, Saudi Arabia, as well as the most important domestic Islamic actor, the Muslim Brotherhood, joined forces to demand a more trenchant imposition of Islamic norms. Political discourse in the country became increasingly phrased in Islamic terminology; Numeri's political opposition also adopted the language of Islam to press their case. Since the early 1980s, successive regimes have attempted to emphasize their power by stressing Sudan's proclaimed Muslim-Arabic identity. Following the rupture of Sudan's relations with Saudi Arabia during the Gulf War of 1991, Iran emerged as an important new patron of the now Islamic regime.

The current military-Islamic regime of Omar Hassan al-Bashir, which achieved power following a military *coup d'état* in June 1989, sought to combine Islamic social control with the organizational skills of the military. It attempted to use the Sharia in a way which was reminiscent of communist states' use of Marxist-Leninist dogma to justify policy. The attempt at hegemony by the Muslims of the north over the mostly Christians and animists of the south has consistently been portrayed as that rare phenomenon in Africa, a religious war. Nevertheless, the true conflict is about Arab domination over non-Arabs, rather than about religion as such: once again, ethnic competition is the context. The Muslim Nuba, non-Arab Sudanese living in the area of the Nuba mountains in the north of the country, have been consistently victimized by Arabs as not being 'real' Muslims, when the real issue was in fact that they were *not* Arabs (Flint 1993b).

The main manifestations of organized traditional Sunni Islam in Sudan – the Khatmiyya (a Sufi order) and the various Ansar Sunna sects – also found themselves in conflict with the military government of President al-Bashir and the regime's Islamic allies, the National Islamic Front of Hassan Turabi (Flint 1993b). Sufi Islam has traditionally been strong in Sudan, where in addition to the Khatmiyya are to be found their arch-rivals, the Sammaniyya, along with the Sanusiyya, Qadiriyya, Shadhiliyya and Tijaniyya sects. There has never been a strong ulama class in Sudan, in marked contrast to neighbouring Egypt, because of the central role of Sufism in the spread of Islam in Sudan.

A millenarian Mahdist movement, the Mahdiyya (whose members are known as the Ansar, which is itself split into several factions), also exists as a significant religious force. Its political extension, the Umma Party (Hizb al-Umma), has been one of the main forces in Sudanese politics since independence in 1956, as has the Khatmiyya Sufi order which has worked through various political parties. Founded in 1954, Sudan's Muslim Brotherhood (Ikhwan al-Musilmin) soon also emerged as a powerful new religio-political force. Working with the military regime of General Omar Bashir through its political party, the National Islamic Front (NIF; Jabhat al-Mithaq), the Muslim Brotherhood stepped up its campaign for increased Islamization, and especially the introduction of Sharia law. The Ansar, for its part, issued a Ramadan call in March 1993 to the army and the NIF to revive democracy or face a campaign of civil opposition. In reply, the regime briefly detained Sadiq al-Mahdi (great grandson of the Mahdi who defeated General Gordon), leader of the Ansar and an outspoken critic of the regime, as well as dozens of his supporters. At the same time the Khatmiyya headquarters were taken over. In May 1993 the Ansar headquarters in Omdurman were similarly confiscated by the army.

Sudan's army rulers formed an alliance with the reformers of the NIF to build an Islamic state in Sudan along the lines of that existing in its closest ally, Iran. Even though the Sharia gives no clear or workable outline for such a state, especially not in the context of the technological, political and economic changes of the last 1,500 years, Sudan's modern version is notable for its repression, lack of human rights, political intolerance, policies of 'ethnic cleansing', and the creation of a regime which appears to negate the toleration with which Islam has traditionally been associated (Bernal 1994). Civil war in the south, which had already endured for twenty years by the mid-1990s, was probably the biggest stumbling block to the Arab north's bid for control of the polity. In the south, Islam has no more than a token presence, while its armed resistance, in two wings led by Colonel John Garang de Mabior and Riek Machar Teny-Dhurgon, can prevent northern hegemony but not defeat the regime. The result is stalemate and a proxy war between Iran (sponsors of al-Bashir's government) and the United States, which, covertly, backs Garang (*Africa Confidential* 1993d: 4, and 1993e: 8).

Conclusion

In this chapter I have examined the role played by leading religious organizations and by the state in a number of African countries. I argued that the normal role of mainstream religious hierarchies is to support the government of the day. Yet, as in Ghana and Zambia at periods when governments proclaimed, or appeared to adhere to, ideologies which apparently sought to downgrade religion's status, this may change under certain circumstances. The examples of Zambia and Ghana also indicated that it was highly important even for apparently stable regimes to have a reasonable working relationship with mainstream religious organizations, because otherwise the latter may form their own alliance with important interest groups to engineer a situation where the government finds itself under heavy pressure to amend its policies.

Governing regimes, for their part, and sometimes despite considerable misgivings, as in Angola and Mozambique and to a certain extent in Ethiopia, were often obliged to seek in turn the support of religious authorities, if only because of the educational and welfare goods under their control, even when they would perhaps rather rule without due concern for religious sensibilities. Because of the common shortages of resources in many African states and the ever-present possibility that state authorities will use force as a means of gaining compliance in the last resort, it is actually more rational for religious leaders to strike a working relationship with government both for personal and corporate reasons, rather than to set themselves up as leaders of the opposition to government. In Sudan the al-Bashir government and its religious allies each had particular reasons for their *de facto* coalition. The power of the former was greatly bolstered by the inclusion in government of powerful religious figures who could attract financial aid from, first, Saudi Arabia, and then Iran, which was crucial to the prosecution of the long-running, resource-draining civil war. For the religious figures, partnership with state power was a convenient way of installing their version of Islamic orthodoxy. In South Africa, on the other hand, de Klerk's regime found it highly advantageous to have the fulsome support of the NGK as a means of communicating with its main constituency, the Afrikaners.

What I have suggested, then, is that pragmatism dominates state-religious institution relations in Africa. The not especially surprising conclusion is that both religious and secular power-holders seek to manipulate political situations for personal and for corporate advantage. I have suggested that – most of the time – shared class concerns help to link religious and secular elites. From this it might initially appear surprising that some religious leaders – especially from the mainstream Protestant and Catholic churches – were in the forefront of the strong demands for democratic change which swept much of Africa in the early 1990s. In the next chapter, I examine the role of religious leaders in the period that saw Africa's most sustained political ferment since that which preceded independence in the late 1950s and early 1960s.

Note

1. The notion of theocratic government usually refers to a lack of separation between secular and religious power. I use quotation marks around the word 'theocratic' in relation to Sudan's government because it is unclear whether or not there is a separation between secular and religious power-holders. Nevertheless, it is unquestionable that some senior Muslims have an important voice in government.

4

Church, State and Democratic Change

The aim of this chapter is to examine the role of mainstream religious leaders in the recent democratization process in Africa. It will demonstrate that the leaders interact with the state to seek to achieve a hegemonic ideology that stresses the desirability of stability rather than progressive change. The concern with hegemony provides a framework of norms and values which helps to legitimize the policies and behaviour of the state elite by the development of regularized forms of mutually supportive action and expectation with leading religious figures. Senior religious figures usually seek to defuse, reduce and, when necessary, strive to help eliminate, serious political challenges to the status quo. Sometimes they forge relationships with international non-governmental organizations (NGOs) for mutual benefit. I will focus upon such issues especially in relation to the Roman Catholic Church and to Islam due to their great social, and often political, importance in many African states.

Passive Revolution

Africa has begun the final decade of the twentieth century with a wave of democratic movements that is sweeping away authoritarian regimes that had seemed firmly entrenched. At the *center* of *most* of these transformations and upheavals are religious leaders from a variety of Christian denominations. (Joseph 1993: 231: emphasis added)

Joseph's claim is superficially plausible: Christian church leaders generally assumed a central leadership role in the embryonic democratization movements in Africa by fearlessly focusing popular attention on pervasive conditions of injustice and misery, often becoming, as Fatton (1992: 78) puts it, the only 'legitimate interlocutors capable of mediating conflicts between government and citizens'. I want to argue that although some Christian leaders, especially in largely Catholic parts of Francophone West Africa, were clearly instrumental in helping to negotiate democratic transformations, they were not by any means always successful; when they were, it was due more to the prestige of the Catholic Church in certain countries, where it was strong enough institutionally to remain outside state control and where it was part of an international and transnational religio-political network, than to the democratic credentials of Christian leaders per se, or to the power of Christian churches more generally to force democratic change.

A second point is that even in those instances where democratic changes have been brought about in Africa in the 1990s they are, by and large, best understood as examples of successful 'passive revolutions', rather than as fundamental redistributions of power from one class or group to another. Passive revolution, according to Gramsci, denotes the necessity for any dominant socio-political group faced with a threat to its survival to effect some apparently fundamental change in its regime of power in order to preserve its hegemony. Passive revolution

> relates changes in politics, ideology and social relations to changes in the economy. [It indicates] the constant reorganization of state power and its relationship to society to preserve control by the few over the many, and maintains a traditional lack of real control by the mass of the population over the political and economic realms. (Showstack Sassoon 1982: 129)

Political society (that is, government plus the coercive apparatus, including police, armed forces and state-supported para-military formations like 'citizens' militias') often acts together with civil society to direct popular perceptions towards acceptance of the hegemony of a certain social stratum. In this sense, civil society is the counterpart rather than counterpoise of political society. Both 'organic' and 'traditional' intellectuals help to forge the climate of acceptance. The former are in the pocket of the regime because, as Femia (1975: 39) puts it, they are 'related to the economic and political structure, tied to the class they represent'. Traditional intellectuals, on the other hand, include religious leaders who may not necessarily share the world-view of the ruling group, but who, as a result of institutional pressures and financial inducements, tend to forge a *modus operandi* with it. The process is facilitated further by a perpetuation of ideals which serves to consolidate ruling class hegemony. In Africa, hegemonic ideology serves to bolster ruling-class dominance by extolling the virtues of national unity and by stressing the dangers to national progress of challenges to it.

Some recent examples might help to support the argument that recent democratic changes in Africa have not, by and large, been very deep or reforming of fundamentally non-democratic systems. In Senegal, the *de facto* one-party state system was transformed in the 1980s by leadership fiat into a liberal democracy where only extremist and sectarian parties (that is, Marxist, religious, ethnic) were banned (Fatton 1987: 53). In May 1993, Abdou Diouf was re-elected to the presidency, purportedly gaining about 70 per cent of the votes cast. This election seemed to characterize politics in the country: an immovable Parti Socialiste (PS) regime, notwithstanding the existence for years of a pluralist democracy and a decade of serious economic downturn (during the period 1980–91 annual growth of GDP per capita in Senegal was a derisory 0.1 per cent a year [Thomas et al. 1994: p. 76, Table 2]). One of the key reasons for the longevity of the PS government was that both religious and economic elites were integrated into the ruling structure; they obviously had much to lose if the complexion of power fundamentally changed. In other words, the proclamation of a multi-party system in Senegal was expressly designed to prevent the emergence of effective vehicles of change by allowing opposition groups to function while at the same time ensuring that the regime's hold on power remained tight.

Even when, in the case of Kenneth Kaunda's United National Independence Party (UNIP) government in Zambia in late 1991 following elections, an incumbent regime *was* ousted from power, the successor regime, the Movement for Multi-Party Democracy government led by Frederick Chiluba, showed by its speedy use of inherited state-of-emergency legislation, by its heavy-handed crushing of allegedly subversive dissent, and by its ludicrous raising of the spectre of Islamic fundamentalism (in a country with less than 0.1 per cent of the population Muslim), that the timbre of its democratic rule was rather reminiscent of the 'authoritarian' one-party UNIP government (*Africa Confidential* 1993a: 1–3).

Finally, in Benin, the regime of Nicéphore Soglo, elected in March 1991, showed itself to be uncomfortably similar to the ousted government of Mathieu Kérékou, where political power was largely a function of ethnic affiliation, with religious allegiance (Catholicism) also an important factor (Daloz 1992). A pertinent point is that leading figures of the main religious denominations in each of these three countries – Senegal, Zambia, Benin – found it expedient to work with ruling regimes whether their democratic credentials were good or not. In the next section I will focus on the role played by the Christian churches in the democratization processes in Africa in the 1990s, both because of their religious importance in many countries in the region and because of the claims referred to above regarding the churches' central position in the fight for democracy in Africa.

The Christian Churches and Democratic Reform in the 1990s

The stabilizing role played by many Christian leaders in the perpetuation of hegemony is rooted in their complementary relation to political society. Yet, in recent times such leaders have on occasion, in the absence of alternatives, become the focal point of opposition – the mouthpiece of public opinion, speaking on behalf of citizens who may well regard democratic change as a *sine qua non* for the achievement of both individual and collective material improvements. Although nothing should be taken away from the many courageous lower- and middle-ranking religious officials who oppose bad governments, it does appear nevertheless that senior religious figures have rarely been in the forefront of opposition to authoritarian and non-democratic governments in Africa from the outset of democratization campaigns.

The Catholic Church and democratic politics

As noted earlier, the Catholic Church is by far the largest in the region, with around 100 million baptized followers. In other words, nearly one-fifth of Africans claim to be Catholics – about one-eighth of the global total. The Church's well-developed institutional structure under the overall leadership of Rome – in effect, a transnational edifice with strong centralized control – led to it being perceived by some African political leaders as a vehicle of foreign interests. On occasions it was considered as a probable instrument of neo-colonialism. Suspicion of the church goes back to the beginning of the post-colonial era. Then, the church, with its foreign historical, institutional and financial links, was often regarded with a high degree of scepticism, especially by newly independent, politically radical regimes, such as that of Kwame Nkrumah in Ghana. Ironically, the gradual Africanization of the church's leadership in Africa led to the installation, by and large, of social conservatives at the pinnacle of the institutional pyramid. In Western Europe, on the other hand, Catholic officials in the 1960s often tended to be both socially progressive and relatively independent of Rome, to the extent that during periods of conflict with the Vatican over theological issues, religious officials might form a coherent oppositional force against the Pope's authority. In Africa, on the other hand, senior Catholic officials were 'rarely in conflict among themselves or with the Vatican; they tend[ed] to have a common, moderately conservative orientation...' (Vaillancourt 1980: 162–3). African Catholic leaders were often deemed to be both more conservative and more traditionalist in their religious beliefs than their European counterparts at the time (Vaillancourt 1980: 162). This was hardly surprising: the price of rapid promotion within the local hierarchy was unquestioning loyalty to the Pope.

More recently, the church has often been regarded as a champion of democratic values. This perception stems largely from its activist role in the democratization of Eastern Europe in the 1980s, led by a Polish pope. In the former Soviet satellites, unlike in Africa, the church was barely tolerated, much less a part of the nexus of power relations focused in the state. More generally, Witte (1993: 11) notes that 'twenty-four of the thirty-two new democracies born since 1973 are predominantly Roman Catholic in confession'. It is significant, however, that many of the examples of newly democratizing countries, he notes – Brazil, Chile, several in Central America, the Philippines, South Korea, Poland, Hungary and Lithuania – received a great deal of diplomatic and some-times material support from the United States for their democratization processes. It is not clear that the Catholic Church was on its own the instigator of democratic change rather than a part of the process, along with the United States government, once it had already begun as a result of popular pressure from below. In South Africa, for example, Ryall notes, neither Christianity as a faith nor the churches as 'faith communities' broke down apartheid. While some dedicated Christians were involved, the process was essentially and effectively dominated by political rather than church activists (Ryall 1994). It is noteworthy that in African countries where Catholicism is the leading faith – for example, Zaire, Togo and Rwanda – senior figures in the church were much less associated with democratization; those countries were, of course, by no means central to the United States' strategic interest in the same way as Eastern Europe, Central America or East Asia. In short, Africa rarely experienced prolonged American pressure for democratization in the early 1990s; stability, whether under a demo-cratic regime or not, quickly became the predominant goal of the United States and the West more generally, in the context of a worrying outbreak of civil conflicts – in Rwanda, Burundi, Liberia, Sierra Leone and elsewhere – which threatened to impinge upon Western commercial and strategic interests (Bratton 1994).

With regard to the role of the Catholic Church in Africa's recent democratization process however, it is beyond dispute that senior Roman Catholic figures were centrally involved in the national conferences on democracy in Benin, the Congo, Togo, Gabon and Zaire in the early 1990s (Gifford 1994). Furthermore, Monrovia's Catholic Archbishop Francis made a number of highly publicized comments on the political composition of Liberia's (abortive) transitional government in late 1993. It is significant, however, that the involvement of African Catholic figures in such issues coincided with the Pope's encyclical of January 1991 (Redemptoris Missio), which was centrally concerned with the Catholic Church's duty to help 'relieve poverty, counter political oppression and defend human rights' (Jenkins 1991: 6). Coming in the wake of the liberation of Eastern Europe from Communist rule and in the context of an apparently global move towards democracy, the thrust of such papal sentiments, coupled with the pre-existing social and religious standing of the Catholic Church in Benin and the other above-mentioned states, made local leaders the obvious choices to chair national conferences. The aim of the latter was to reach consensus between government and opposition over the democratic way forward.

This is not to suggest that leading figures in Catholic churches in Benin, Congo, Gabon, Zaire and Togo – respectively, Monsignors Isidore de Souza, Basile Mvé, Ernest Nkombo, Laurent Monsengwo, and Philippe Fanoko Kpodzro – were not serious about democratic change, or that they agreed to chair their country's national democracy conferences in order to try to control or manipulate the popular demands for reform. Rather, it is to note that their role is that expected of leaders of any socio-economic elite which is part of the status quo: to keep political and social change within manageable proportions – to seek to ensure that events do not spiral out of control. Unlike in Benin, Congo and Gabon, in Togo, Mgr Kpodzro was unable to lead his national conference to a democratic conclusion: President Eyadema was able to remain in power following a controversial election. In Zaire, President Mobutu made it only too plain that he alone had the ability to keep the country together: serious and growing inter-ethnic clashes from 1992, stimulated perhaps by skilful manipulation by the regime, raised the likelihood that the state would cease to remain unitary in the longer term.

Leaders of the Catholic Church were often persuaded to head democratization conferences. For, despite its often apparently close institutional relationship with many African governments, in popular conceptions the church was neither riven by overt ethnicity squabbles nor in obvious thrall to government. Rather, because of its widespread control of welfare provision, it enjoyed a high degree of economic independence. In addition, its provision of welfare functions – educational, health and developmental programmes – made it popular with many ordinary people, often encouraging them to be baptized in the church (Luneau 1987).

A second reason for at least some of the ambivalence felt by church leaders towards wholesale political change is that, generally speaking, Church and State have developed a relationship based on mutual tolerance, due in part to their hegemonic positions vis-à-vis society in Africa and in part to the state's propensity to deal with dissidents rather heavily. Over time, the Catholic Church – like other former mission churches – found itself on the horns of a dilemma in the post-colonial period: to what extent dare it criticize authoritarian governments even if they abuse power in ways that Christian morality generally finds unacceptable? There are two distinct, mutually exclusive options: to speak out whenever necessary and be damned in consequence by governments who, in many cases, already suspected their patriotism; or to keep publicly quiet and seek to change government policy by behind-the-scenes persuasion alone. The role of the church in relation to government in Africa, as elsewhere, is in theory a simple and clear one, and is well expressed in the following:

> [T]he limits of the state's sphere of action are set by the definition of 'temporal', that is, those activities of civilization that arise in the 'earthly' city … The church in no way limits the state's rights: church and state complement one another, each by working in its proper realm. (*Documents pour l'action 8*, March–April 1962, pp. 99–100, translated and quoted in Boyle 1992: 52)

Yet, as the cordial relations between Catholic Church leaders and the Mobutu regime in Zaire make plain, it was in the former's interests as much as Mobutu's for there to be stability, even if that was a stability arrived at through authoritarian means. As Joseph Malula, archbishop of Kinshasa, observed in 1965, in a message addressed to Mobutu: 'Mr President, the Church recognizes your authority, because authority comes from God. We will loyally apply the laws you establish. You can count on us in your work of restoring the peace toward which all so ardently aspire' (quoted in Boyle 1992: 49). Until 1992, the Catholic hierarchy was consistently hesitant to engage the regime in direct public confrontation; that is, until an unprecedented show of public displeasure

– significantly involving young priests and nuns – galvanized the
Catholic hierarchy into voice in the early 1990s. The point is that senior
figures in the Catholic Church were bought off by material inducements, while the institutional role of the church was seen as one which
ought to be supportive of the temporal regime – for, as Malula's quote
indicates, God is thought to give governments authority. Understandably,
Malula's church was anxious to re-establish a good working relationship with the state authorities, to resume the mutually supportive
arrangement which had typified the colonial period. Then, as Schatzberg (1988: 117) notes, '[o]ccasional differences [between the Catholic
and colonial authorities were] minimal in comparison to the numerous
issues on which church and state worked in concert.' Between 1965 and
1970, 'relations between church and state were generally good', and
from then only intermittently rocky (Schatzberg 1988: 118).

For church leaders more generally in Africa, silence in the face of
poor and corrupt government following independence reflected a
number of concerns: they themselves benefited materially from the status quo because they were inherently conservative; they believed that
governments, however bad, were exercising authority ordained by God;
and, finally, they recognized that their church's corporate position in a
country was in part dependent upon state acquiescence or support. In
Zaire, as Boyle (1992: 51) illustrates, the value of co-operation with civil
authorities for church leaders 'leads (them) to employ … indirect modes
of communication and influence in their relationship with society and
the political regime'. This is the idea of the 'two realms' of Church and
State, where the former may attempt to influence the latter by persuasion but has no other means at its disposal if it wishes to retain its
privileged position. In other words, normally the church hierarchy is
able to be no more than an interlocutor between state and society. As
the trajectory of Mobutu's rule has only too clearly shown, those who
gain a reputation for outspoken criticism tend to suffer for their bravery
(Schatzberg 1988: 30–51).

A further factor – apart from concern about stability and fear of
repercussions from openly challenging regimes – is that some Christian
leaders have been closely associated with ruling regimes, even to the
extent of holding political appointments. In Lesotho in the early 1970s,
for example 'the post-independence government of Chief Leabua
Jonathan and the National Party was predominantly Catholic in support
and conservative in policy', and as such was favoured by South Africa's
apartheid regime (Hastings 1979: 189). In Zaire, where political activists
of the ruling party, Le Mouvement Populaire de la Révolution (MPR),

and the ubiquitous secret police together dominate society, the church (with around 19 million followers in a population of some 37 million) has only a half-hearted desire to challenge Mobutu. This may be attributed in part to the fact that senior church figures have been well treated personally by Mobutu's regime: 'Cardinal Malula lived in a mansion that the President gave him [in 1974] ... [I]n 1978 or so the President gave a Mercedes to every bishop, Protestant or Catholic' (MacGaffey 1990: 261–2). The result is that Catholicism, in partnership with the independent, but powerful, Kimbanguist church, 'has assumed some of the functions of an ideology in the service of the dominant class' (ibid.). The position is similar in Togo: the ruling party, Le Rassemblement du Peuple Togolais, has a dominant position in the society analogous to that of the MPR in Zaire; the Catholic Church, with around 1.3 million of Togo's 3.7 million people, dominates spiritually. Together, Catholic and political elites consolidate a hegemonic grip on society. In addition, until 1985, the Catholic Archbishop of Kigali, Rwanda, was on the central committee of the single party, the Mouvement Révolutionnaire National pour le Développement. Furthermore, Bishop Mutale's membership of the commission responsible for instituting a one-party state in the 1970s in Zambia was a concrete manifestation of the empathy between State and Church in that country (Hastings 1979: 188).

When Christian leaders criticize governments outside the specific context of democratization, they tend to accuse them of violating fundamental moral values by their policies and actions. Church leaders unsurprisingly make it clear that they regard themselves as the principal guardians of morality, whereas (in pursuance of the 'two realms' idea noted in the quotation from Boyle above) government's job is concerned fundamentally with political issues.

The Catholic Archbishop of Monrovia, Michael Francis, a strong advocate of human rights and social justice in Liberia, was outspoken on such issues. He put forward several critiques of Liberia's sociopolitical situation from the mid-1970s (Gifford 1993: 72–3). In particular, he criticized three forms of corruption: 'social corruption' – 'unjust imprisonment, detention without charge or trial, inhuman and degrading prison conditions'; 'professional corruption' – the abuse by government officials of their positions, whether to make money or by employing individuals because they are of the same family or tribe or are girlfriends; and 'personal corruption' – 'the all-pervasive sexual immorality of the country' (ibid.: 73–83). A number of Catholic priests in Liberia followed Francis's lead; while he escaped governmental reprisals they were not so fortunate, suffering harassment by the state's security services as a consequence. The differing tactics of governments in Zaire and Liberia may be explained, in part, by demographic factors. Under 2 per cent of Liberians are Catholics – that is, about 50,000 out of a population of nearly 3 million. Some 33 per cent (1 million) follow official or independent Protestant churches; about 20 per cent (600,000) are Muslims. The bulk of the remainder – about 43 per cent (1.29 million) – are followers of African traditional religions (ibid.: 71–3). Given the limited importance of the Catholic Church in Liberia, it is perhaps understandable that Mgr Francis could criticize the government with a degree of impunity – in effect, become a social conscience – which leaders of larger Christian churches elsewhere in Africa might not dare to do.

It is likely that rank-and-file Christian officials will be the ones who become involved with opposition figures and their campaigns. Ordinary priests, as is the case in Eastern Europe and Latin America, tend to be more strongly opposed to a government (and perhaps to their ecclesiastic superiors who live in comparative luxury), because they are closer to the people who suffer from poor governmental policies (Luneau 1987: 164). A human-rights organization, Christians against Torture (CAT), was founded in Cameroon in the 1980s in response to the increasingly repressive measures used by the Biya government against opposition figures. CAT also has a Paris office and, along with universal-human-rights organizations like Amnesty International and Africa Watch, has been influential in helping to focus international attention on human-rights abuses in Cameroon (*Guardian* 1994). Sometimes priests support human-rights campaigns by allowing their churches to be used as meeting places by opposition movements. As church buildings are commonly regarded as sacrosanct, they may well be the only places outside of government or party control where people may gather legally in numbers. This gives priests a potentially central role, especially in the early stages of mobilizing opposition. Moreover, opposition movements will be based in the capital city, where the churches will also have their national headquarters: this will facilitate links both internally and with external allies, including foreign allied churches and NGOs.

In Kenya, opposition to one-party rule became a focus for rank-and-file discontent. Churchmen including Reverends David Gitari of Mount Kenya East, the late Alexander Kipsang Muge of Eldoret, Henry Okullu of Maseno South (all of the Anglican Church of the Province of Kenya) and Timothy Njoya of the Presbyterian Church of East Africa, helped to focus popular concern on the erosion of civil liberties, human-rights violations, the stifling of opposition, and the drift towards totalitarianism. They were all leading lights in the early 1990s' campaign by the Protestant churches' umbrella organization, National Christian Council of Kenya (NCCK), for political reforms. Later, more conservative church leaders, including the Anglican Archbishop Manasses Kuria and the country's eighteen-strong Catholic episcopate, added their voices to the campaign (Africa Watch 1991: 226–7, 232–3). Arap Moi's government used classic tactics of divide-and-rule in an attempt to blunt the NCCK's opposition, as it did later to blunt outbreaks of Islamic dissent. The NCCK highlighted the country's abysmal human-rights record in a report published shortly before the first multi-party parliamentary and presidential elections for twenty-six years in 1992. It reported that more than 50,000 Kenyans were in badly maintained internment camps, while more than 1,000 individuals had been executed by the state extra-juridically during 1992 (Simmons 1992). One of the government's critics, Reverend Muge, was killed in a crash in August 1990, when his car was hit by a lorry about 40 miles (65 kilometres) from the town of Eldoret in Busia province (Africa Watch 1991: 222). Many Kenyans thought that Muge had probably been assassinated by the government. Such fears were not fantasy: in neighbouring Malawi, leaders of the ruling Congress Party hatched a plot in late 1992 to kill the country's Catholic bishops because of their alleged involvement in a democracy campaign (*Africa Confidential* 1992: 7).

This discussion of the role of the Christian church in recent democratization initiatives has highlighted how ambivalent some of its senior figures were on the issue of fundamental political change. Apart from a tendency towards conservatism, which is of course a characteristic of the leaders of many large, powerful institutions, both religious and secular, there were also more material concerns at stake. In the next part of the discussion, I want to refer to the role of the church in development issues, before turning to a discussion of how a number of the church's professionals have carved out niches for themselves as entrepreneurs, businessmen, and so on, as a result of the secular decline of Africa's economic position. Sometimes they have become partners with international non-governmental organizations (NGOs) in welfare schemes.

The Church and Development

Control of education and of welfare in post-colonial Africa have sometimes been areas of contention between Church and State. This is because, in the case of education, it offers the controller the ability to instil one world-view at the expense of others. Sometimes government wants it both ways: for the church to provide education (at its expense), while following the state's ideological direction in its teachings. The radical Nkrumah government in Ghana (1957–66), for example, was keen to gain control of education from the church because the latter was perceived to be a conservative, and hence inappropriate, body; it wanted to take over the church's pivotal role.

During the colonial period the mission churches were in charge of education in many African colonies, which gave them both ideological and material power – the latter deriving from collection of school fees, grants, ownership of land and buildings, and so on. This was obviously of great importance. Government, freed from the restraints of the colonial system, could, as Nkrumah showed by the passing of the Preventive Detention Act of 1958, introduce legislation which aimed to deal with 'troublemakers', the church included if necessary. The educational and welfare roles of the churches were useful for bolstering what the state could provide; yet in the Gold Coast/Ghana the state nationalized the former in order to gain control of their operations for political purposes.

Nationalization of education was an issue of at least potential discord between Church and State around the time of independence. Then, however, the state was usually prepared to leave church control of education alone. Around ten years later – about 1970 – states became more concerned with ousting the church from control of education; the reason was that they had come to believe that education was a 'development good' which it was appropriate for the state to direct. At the same time, however, as Hastings notes, 'there was [often] more continuity than could be expected', in the sense that many Christian professionals, especially Catholics, did in fact – often quietly – retain their educational positions despite the often wholesale changes in education which many governments decreed (Hastings 1979: 189).

In other development fields there was a more overt continuation of the church's role. In relation to rural medical provision, for example, governments seemed less keen to replace the church; indeed, the 'institutional contribution of the churches' – especially during the time of cutbacks associated with Structural Adjustment Programmes in the 1980s and 1990s – continued to be 'massive' (Hastings 1979: 189).

This is not to suggest that control of development issues was always consensual. In Zaire, for example, as Schatzberg shows, during the period of 'authenticité' in the 1970s , the control of education was the main issue of contention between the main churches and the state

(Schatzberg 1988: 118–19). The Mobutu regime's nationalization of education early in the decade met strong opposition from the Catholic Church especially, which, although able to accept, for instance, the abolition of Christian names and the celebration of Christmas, was unwilling to cede this key province to the state. By the mid-1970s, the declining economic position and the inability of the state to run the education system provoked a scathing pastoral letter from the archbishop of Lubumbashi. In 1976, Mobutu handed back control of the country's educational establishments, including the university, to the Catholic, Protestant and Kimbanguist churches, ceding to them greater managerial control than they enjoyed formerly. As a result of the government's reversal of its diminution of the Catholic Church's influence, since the mid-1970s its fortunes have improved. It operated effectively throughout the country, while its economic position 'rose in importance', according to Schatzberg (1988: 122). It also provided 'certain facilities, credit, advice, and equipment which [were] … unavailable from any other source including the state' to aspiring entrepreneurs (ibid.). In effect, then, in Zaire, as the state withdrew from its responsibilities, the churches moved in to fill the gap. In Togo, following a similar period of 'authenticité' in the early 1970s, thy also regained their formerly pivotal role in education. In Tanzania, the ceding of control of the country's educational facilities to the churches in 1992, again because of the state's inability to continue providing a decent service, was one of the factors behind an outbreak of serious Islamic unrest (*Africa Confidential* 1994).

The issue of the church's role in education provision leads us to the issue of development more generally. In many African states, the church's often comprehensive structure of welfare provision had an important impact upon development provision. In remote areas especially – and once again Zaire is an archetypal example – the state virtually gave up its developmental role, passing it to the three official churches: Catholic, Protestant and Kimbanguist. Overtly 'apolitical' development issues were not, however, free of political connotations in reality. The existence of the church's autonomous structures beyond the state's control were increasingly regarded with both envy and suspicion by governments, despite or because of the fact that they were providing development goods which the state was unable or unwilling to supply. The very existence of such autonomous structures beyond the state's control was considered by some post-colonial African governments to be an unacceptable threat to their own monopolistic claims and their *amour propre*, despite the highly useful tasks that the churches' networks accomplished. Of necessity, the issue of church-based welfare networks brought the churches into areas of state policy, and thus controversy. The important role of the church in the provision of educational and other broadly welfare-oriented goods helps to explain why the Catholic ecclesiastical hierarchy often 'tends to exert a moderating influence on church involvement in opposition activities' (Johnston and Figa 1988: 42).

What developed in Africa in the post-colonial period, therefore, was a situation where for the churches to retain what they had, including a role in the provision of education, medical facilities and, more generally, social influence and material prosperity, it was usually both sensible and expedient not to challenge government policies in the open, but rather to choose the route of more or less discreet lobbying to effect desired changes of policy. This generally remained their preferred course of action until the recent widespread onset of democracy concerns thrust the churches to centre stage at the head of what were often popularly driven movements for fundamental change.

International NGOs and the rise of the religious entrepreneur

The context that shaped the growth in importance of both international NGOs and the religious professional as entrepreneur is the decline in the ability of the African state to fulfil its role as developmental agency. As the state's failure to lead Africa's development has become manifest, the role of the church and that of international NGOs has increased. It might well be that the church actually prefers a position where the state's power and ability to provide developmental goods is diminished, as this is likely to lead directly to an increase in the power of the church and that of its NGO partners. While NGOs are, of course, benevolent in their intentions, they may also conduct themselves in what Rossiter and Palmer (1991) describe as a 'neo-colonial style':

> The state is withering away [in several African countries] ... Whole districts ... are handed over for foreigners to run, especially in health and social services ... The more NGOs are prepared to move in the easier it becomes for governments to reduce support. NGOs ... have no legitimacy, authority or sovereignty ... they are self-selected and thus are not accountable.

International NGOs often work closely with Christian churches on the ground in Africa. As already noted, there is a long tradition of involvement by the Christian churches in education, health and literacy programmes which began in the colonial period. 'Parent' churches and NGOs provide the necessary funding for their African partners: the result has been the growth of NGO/church 'empires, with many departments, fleets of vehicles, [and] teams of employees' (Gifford 1993: 311). Between 1981 and 1985, French Catholic bodies sent some 340 million francs (about US$28 million) to African Catholic churches (Gaben 1989: 66–7). Other foreign NGOs channelled funds through church bodies rather than through state institutions, as the former were reckoned to be less corrupt. The result was that church leaders themselves became controllers of large foreign-exchange budgets: 'All Catholic bishops could count on some regular funds from abroad; a few could obtain very large sums indeed' (Hastings 1979: 238). According to Pénekou (1984: 29), African Catholic bishops have 'money, perhaps a lot of money, to feed and care for priests and nuns, to pay teachers and catechists, to help and "help out" those who solicit it; it is above all [the bishop] ... who[m] presidents and ministers turn to or grapple with if it's "hot" between church and state.'

It is sometimes suggested that the Catholic Church in Africa is run by people who understand their job in relation to three desirable goals: wealth, power and status (Bayart 1993b). The Catholic archbishop of Lomé, Mgr Dosseh, for example, has been described as 'tribalist, authoritarian and corrupt' (Toulabor 1991: 68). Often, it seems, church figures may be 'applauded for the amount of money they get for the church', not necessarily for their spiritual, social, or educational achievements alone (Ibrahim 1991: 126). Generally, the inflow of foreign funds enables bishops to dispense monies for several purposes; these include building up their own positions and authority within their institutions, and, more generally, rewarding clients, whether within their families and ethnic groups, or from their home regions (Gifford 1993: 312) . In short, some Christian welfare systems seem to have become prone to what Bayart (1993a) has called 'la politique du ventre' (the politics of the stomach), especially during the 1980s and 1990s, periods of extreme economic hardship which saw a growth in foreign funds, often channelled through the international NGOs. Ties of clientship are particularly functional in situations when society's formal institutional structure is lax and unable to ensure reasonable supplies of desirable things – goods and services – to all levels of society, from the top to the bottom. Those at the latter level will look to their contacts above them socially to fulfil their needs and desires.

What this suggests is that church leaders have often supported the 'big man'; that is, they have favoured personalist political rule because they themselves run their institutions like African states, where clientelism and corruption predominate. Due to the similarities in governing style, it has been relatively easy for the state to co-opt churches, encourage them to support the status quo by way of favours and privileges, or, if necessary, force them into line if prolonged resistance is displayed. Because religious institutions have been run in a non- or anti-democratic way, they have tended to be reluctant to criticize obvious abuses in society. As Gifford (1993: 312) notes, the churches can scarcely accuse politicians of '[t]ribalism, abuse of authority, misappropriation of funds, and so on, because the churches have been characterised by these evils themselves'.

While it may be easy to criticize religious figures for their human lapses, it is necessary to recall once again that, although they may be 'servants of God', they still have to live their mundane lives during a time of shortages of essential goods. In the common environment of shortages – of just about everything, from food to footwear to petrol – exacerbated by plummeting real prices for Africa's raw material exports and burgeoning population growth, many institutions (administrations, bureaucracies, ruling parties, the armed forces, and so forth), including on occasion the Christian churches, have functioned as repositories of groups of individuals with something to sell – people dominated by the struggle to obtain a sufficiency (or better) for themselves, their nuclear family and extended kin.

In many respects the accumulation of personal wealth – by virtually any means – is regarded as a sign of personal prowess. For example, Ivoriens tended not to criticize their late president, Felix Houphouet-Boigny, for amassing a huge fortune during his tenure as head of state. They did not ask themselves whether his salary was sufficient to pay for the US$100 million basilica he built at Yamossoukro. On the contrary, many thought it quite appropriate that political and economic power should be mutually supportive, reflecting 'le Vieux's' position as Côte d'Ivoire's national hero, as well as the shrewdest of political and economic players.

Developments in the church mirror what has been happening in many African societies over the last fifteen to twenty years. During this time the growth of second economies was prodigious, while the state's administrative capacity declined precipitously as the rent-seeking activities of state personnel expanded (MacGaffey 1991: 36). For example, two-thirds of Uganda's GDP emanates from the second economy, as does 75 per cent of the Central African Republic's, and at least one-third of both Tanzania's and Morocco's (ibid.: 15). On average, well over 50 per cent of productive activity in Africa is unregulated by the state (Mettelin 1984: 57). The second economy thus becomes the primary means of distributing goods and an important setting for both small-scale manufacturing and local agricultural production. Falling real wages and growing price inflation also fuel the growth of second economies. It is scarcely surprising, then, that some religious personnel seek to benefit from their positions personally. They have something to sell: spiritual solace and health. Priests, curés, mallams, sheikhs, catechists, bishops, archbishops and cardinals all need to live; in societies where practically everyone seeks or finds extra-legal or illicit means to gain additional income, it should come as no surprise that a proportion of religious personnel are also involved.

What this account suggests is that Christianity in Africa takes a specific form: that in the course of its development, it has adopted the characteristics of African societies. Bayart suggests

> conceptualizing the process of reappropriation of Christianity by African societies ... as a particular manifestation of the genesis of a more general 'governmentality', [which is] historically situated in the 'governmentality of the stomach' [la politique du ventre]. It involves the totality of strategies and of institutions working towards the advent of modern Africa, and, therefore, includes the Christian churches. (Bayart 1989b: 7–8)

This is not to suggest that there is a particular type of 'African Christianity' that exists in a clearly discernible spiritual sense, but rather that Christian leaders have used the power structures within their churches to gain personal benefit in the same way that individuals do in Africa when their social and employment positions permit. The tendency both to gain material possessions and to build grandiose religious buildings was evident right across the continent from the 1960s, as the Christian church hierarchies became Africanized (Hastings 1979).

Parallel to the growth of church 'big men' has been the phenomenon of religious official as entrepreneur: many different jobs are undertaken by religious professionals, in addition to spiritual ministering. There are

> priest-poultry farmers, priest-carpenters, priest-hunters, priest-transporters, priest-proprietors and priest-lessors who, by their own activities, seek to ensure their own well-being as well as to finance works in their parish or to supply [concrete] evidence of Christianity's contribution to the task of development ... Pastors, priests and bishops are religious, political and economic entrepreneurs... (Bayart 1989b: 12)

Grand occasions take place when a priest is practically 'crowned' as 'king' of a village or district (Bayart, 1989b: 12). As a consequence, the Christian churches have been affected by the same unfortunate developments as the institutions of the state: factional struggles exacerbate the question of succession, at both the parish and episcopal level. At stake is access to ecclesial resources:

> The economic activities of the churches and of their agents insert them into the rentier logic of the post-colonial state, according to which the holders of political power are 'in gear' with the channels of accumulation and strive to control them. For the churches, which claim to be in the service of the poor but which have inherited, from their collaboration with the colonizer, considerable land and buildings, the risks of compromise, individual or institutional, are real. (Bayart 1989b: 12–13)

Gifford argues that Catholic Church officials are, by and large, less involved in the misuse of funds from abroad, because they are, to a great extent, controlled from overseas: funds misused would simply be cut off, he alleges. Bishops are appointed from Rome, 'so the scope for manipulation and buying of votes and power struggles [is] minimised' (Gifford 1993: 312). There are three obvious problems with this. First, the level of corruption within a church is difficult to ascertain with any degree of precision. Those engaged in such activities are hardly likely to advertise the fact. Second, is sufficient Vatican control exercised over local representatives; and, if it is, would the Catholic hierarchy in Rome be more concerned with maintaining the status quo than with challenging abuses when found? Clearly, issues involving corruption would not only redound upon the individual(s) concerned but also upon the church as institution. The 'Milingo affair' in Zambia and scandals involving senior Catholic figures in, for example, Cameroon, Togo and Ireland, suggest that it is easy to underestimate the extent of the Catholic hierarchy's involvement in the covering up of various misdemeanours perpetrated by some Catholic professionals (Ter Haar 1992).

Third, the 'clean Catholic' argument is also problematic inasmuch as it assumes that there will be a universal mode of behaviour practised within the Catholic Church; whereas it is more realistic to locate each local church within its own cultural and social context. The former view reduces the complexity of African societies, overlooks the fact that the church may be either a minority or majority church, and gives too much influence to the institutional and transnational effects of supposed Catholic norms of behaviour.

In order to extend the analysis of the relationship between religious professionals and the state, I want to look next at a number of African states where Islam is the most significant religion. If it can be shown that the relationship of senior Muslims to the state is qualitatively different from that of their Christian counterparts, then it will enable us to shed some light on the important question of whether it is the religious characteristics of Islam and Christianity which determine the relationship of their senior figures with the state. Alternatively, should we seek to understand that relationship as a consequence of shared ideologies of domination which are themselves predicated upon a shared class position that allows joint domination over society in a context of serious shortages of disposable resources?

National Muslim Organizations and Political Change

In the final section of this chapter I want to look at the role of national Muslim organizations in the current phase of democratization in Sub-Saharan Africa. To this end I shall consider the situation in a number of countries, including Côte d'Ivoire, Mali, Niger, Uganda, Tanzania and Malawi. In each of these states Islam is an important majority or minority religion. I also focus upon Senegal, where, although there is no dominant Muslim national organization, Islam is nevertheless a highly significant factor in voting behaviour in national elections.

As noted earlier, since independence was achieved in those states where Islam is a substantial presence, governments have often been in close partnership with leading Muslims to perpetuate an ideology of domination based on a stated desire to reform traditional, usually Sufi, modes of Islam. As Bromley (1994: 42) notes, what he calls 'folk' Islam – that is, Sufi Islam – is often the religion of the majority of Muslims in a state; yet, because it is independent of the state, Islamic reformers in the national Muslim organizations seek to 'repress Sufi orders, seeing them as a threat to [their] own position'. In other words, Islamic reformers aim to bolster their own dominant position by systematizing their group values; that is, they seek to impose their Islamic ideology in a hegemonic fashion. The function of such an Islamic ideology is to concentrate belief in the values which are necessary for the domination of one group over others. Popular Islam – anti-orthodox Islam – is the ordinary people's response, and will be discussed in the next chapter. In the rest of the current chapter, I want to examine how regimes adopt 'Islamization': how they seek to force non- or nominal 'Muslims' either to convert to Islam or to adopt the reformers' version of the faith to enhance their religious 'purity'. The real aim, of course, is to bolster the hegemonic positions both of the reformers and of their secular allies in the state by manipulating national Muslim organizations for their own objectives.

National Muslim organizations, in the same way as many mainstream Christian churches, aim to fill the role of intermediary and interlocutor between state and umma. Senior Muslim figures thus claim to serve a dual role: to channel the state's orders and wishes downwards, while officially passing social concerns the other way. These organizations are not only found in Sub-Saharan African states where there are majorities of Muslims – such as Niger, Mali and Guinea – but also in others, including Tanzania, Malawi, Côte d'Ivoire and Uganda, where Muslims form substantial minorities. In these latter states, government, through its alliance with the national organization seeks to achieve control of Muslims, a potentially subversive group. Such organizations, then, function primarily as control and surveillance bodies, as 'a means of protection against the ... development of a militant Islam, uncontrolled and subversive' (Triaud 1982: 38). This recalls the way that, where possible, colonial administrations chose the 'big marabouts' as their interlocutors with Muslim society. The various national Christian church councils today fill something of a similar role to that of the state-level Muslim bodies. Because of international links with their former 'parent' churches, they are able to maintain a degree of financial independence; Muslim national associations may also receive funds from abroad – perhaps Iran or Saudi Arabia – although these foreign governments are just as likely to fund non-state Muslim organizations, especially in states where Muslims are in a minority, such as Kenya, Tanzania and Uganda. National Muslim organizations tend to be more quiescent politically than mainstream Christian churches, subservient in their relationship with the political rulers, and highly dependent on the latter's patronage.

The state, in partnership with senior Muslim figures possessing interests in the national organization, seeks to create hegemonic rule by exploiting the religious and moral prestige, cultural leadership, and ideological persuasiveness of the latter. As hegemony relates to the cultural leadership of a class in relation to society, so, in religious terms, does it refer to the significance of a leading religious institution (Islam) vis-à-vis ordinary believers.

Islamic members of the ruling establishment may themselves well have been challengers to colonial elites thirty or forty years ago; the aim then was to counter Western (Christian) colonial supremacy and to install themselves in positions of power. They often formed the leadership of Islamic renewal and reform movements – such as Wahhabiya – which aimed to give a new impulse to Islam by defining new modalities of both social organization and education, and to reform the

Sufi brotherhoods (Coulon 1983: 153). The reformers of forty years ago usually looked to Saudi Arabia or Egypt for their inspiration. Radical and reform movements – Wahhabists and groups linked to the Muslim Brotherhoods – spread their ideas to Africa, deriving inspiration from the works of, *inter alia*, Jamal Ad Din Al Afghani (1838–97), Muhammad Abduh (1849–1905), and Rashid Ridha (1865–1935) (Kane 1990: 7–8).

Reformers were also influenced by the Salafiyya, the Egyptian intellectual movement led by Muhammad Abdu (d. 1955), whose programme was concerned with a return to the fundamentals of Islam. This involved the renovation of Arabic as a religious language, Islamic education, and the development of modern Islamic scientific knowledge and technology in order to eschew dependence on the West. In the 1950s and 1960s, schools with curricula based on such ideals were founded by members of the Salafiyya in Guinea, Chad and Senegal (Coulon 1983: 153–4).

Governments were anxious to find common cause with Islamic reformers for two reasons: the first and obvious one is that regimes always wish to control any potential force of dissent or opposition; the second was that Islamic revival was deemed by black African leaders thirty years ago as little more than an Arab plot for control of Africa. Europeans were decolonizing; Arabs, it was thought, were seeking to step into the vacuum. African governments were determined to ensure that the Arabic roots of Muslim renewal were not utilized by Arab states as a means to gain undue influence with local reforming groups. While African regimes are naturally suspicious of their Muslim nationals' ties with the governments of foreign Muslim states, they are happy to use national Muslim organizations to help regularize cultural and religious contacts with the Arab world, and to entice Arab development capital. It is not unusual for their leaders to be included in diplomatic missions or to be named as ambassadors to Muslim countries outside of Africa.

What this suggests is that black African governments are often ambivalent about Islam, especially when it is not the religion of the majority: whereas its value as social cement is welcomed, historical ties between Muslims in North Africa and elsewhere in the continent predate the drawing of modern state boundaries, which obviously threatens the modern masters of the post-colonial state. For example, the Libyan Sanusiyya has widespread links with Muslims in West Africa. This helped to facilitate Qaddafi's (ultimately futile) expansionist dreams in the region in the 1970s and 1980s. Followers of Sanusiyya in Chad, a state dominated by southern Sara Christians, appeared for a time to have more in common with their co-religionists over the country's northern border than with 'Christian' state leaders. Yet eventually Qaddafi's expansionist foreign policies served to unite Chad's competing factions (albeit temporarily) from the mid-1980s (Kelley 1987).

Islamic reformers are closely linked to modernizing secular power-holders; they are part of the elite, and target traditionalists. Formally and ostensibly they seek a return to the original principles of Islam, as related by God to the Prophet Muhammad. By treating the Sharia as an ideological reference book, reformers seek to use it as a blueprint for reorganizing society to solve present social, moral, economic and political dislocations.

Muslim reformers, despite their predilection for the revival of a 'pure' (or purist) version of Islam, nevertheless find it expedient to borrow from the West's organizational models, including the formation of bureaucracies and management systems (Cruise O'Brien 1986: 78). Using modern methods, they collect and collate useful political information through networks of appointees and confer upon their state's Muslims the feeling that they have a national body working for their interests. Members of the Muslim national organizations receive salaries from the state, have the ear of governments, and are important in the maintenance of political order. They aid the creation of a Muslim political allegiance to the state in a way which is far more complete and systematic than that achieved by the mainstream Christian religious bodies. Even though ulama may sometimes lead popular protests when religious concerns are at issue, they must play a shrewd and skilful game to appear to be all things to all people – oppositionist enough to lead discontented Muslims when necessary, quiescent enough to maintain their relationship with state rulers.

Côte d'Ivoire, Mali and Niger

The influence and political significance of Muslim reformers appears generally to have grown over the last three decades of African independence. They have been notably successful in Côte d'Ivoire, where Muslim reformers – Wahhabists – are integral components of the state itself. The position of Wahhabiya as a solidifying force among the country's Muslims was facilitated by the patchy presence of Islam in the country. Around one-quarter of Côte d'Ivoire's 13 million people are Sunni Muslims of the Maliki school, concentrated in the north-west of the country amongst the Mandinka, Dyula and Kono. Conversion to Islam has been swift since the first decade of the twentieth century, at which time only about 7 per cent of those living within modern Côte d'Ivoire's borders were Muslims. Three Sufi brotherhoods (Qadiriyyah, Tijaniyyah, Sanusiyyah) are to be found.

In neighbouring Mali, Wahhabist ideas began to circulate from the 1920s, spread by local Muslim traders returning from the hajj. Wahhabist reformers came into conflict both with the marabouts and with the French colonial administrators, who had made political alliances with the marabouts. As in Côte d'Ivoire, Wahhabists gave their political support to nationalist politicians. They built their own mosques and schools, and challenged the marabouts to religious disputation. Support for the Wahhabiya grew steadily from 1945. Following Mali's independence in 1960, Wahhabist reformers, 'in political terms ... constituted an indispensable element in the support base of the military rulers of Mali' (Cruise O'Brien 1986: 79). Support was institutionalized by the formation of the Association Malien pour l'Unité et la Progrès de l'Islam (AMUPI) in 1981. AMUPI was formed, at least in part, in response to a perceived threat from an Islam newly radicalized at the time by the event of the Iranian Revolution and by Libya's activist foreign policy in West Africa (Haynes 1993a: 129–32). The national leader, General Moussa Traoré, and the ruling Mali People's Democratic Union government were overthrown ten years later in March 1991, following a military coup. His successor, Alpha Oumar Konare, was as concerned as his predecessor to keep opposition Islamic groups under close supervision by AMUPI.

In neighbouring Niger a similar kind of neo-traditional corporatism, with Islam as an ideological component, was also created after independence. Seyni Kountché's military-dominated regime founded the Association Islamique du Niger (AIN) in 1974 for six interrelated purposes: to unite Niger's ethnic groups politically within their common Islamic culture; to serve as a focus of Islam in Niger in order to attract foreign aid from wealthy Arab states, such as Saudi Arabia; to apply Islamic ideology to all areas of national life; to help spread Arabic as a lingua franca; to serve as a means of combating Libyan-inspired radicalism; and, finally, to form a focal point for Niger in international Islamic bodies (Triaud 1982: 37). AIN sought to perform the task of interlocutor between state and society, and to serve as an insurance against Qaddafi-inspired subversive Islamism. Marabouts were attacked by AIN's zealots. In sum, AIN represented the religious side of the alliance between state power and the reformist cadres who were united against the alleged obscurantism and self-serving tactics of both traditional Islam (marabouts and the Sufi orders) and the threat of radical

Islamism (Lapidus 1988: 851). What this amounted to was that Wahhabist reformers had official sanction for their campaign for Islamic purification and restoration, which was aimed at their competitors for popular allegiance, the 'petits marabouts charlatans' (Clévenot 1987: 215–16).

Uganda, Tanzania and Malawi

National Muslim organizations are not necessarily under the control of members of the ulama, especially where a state contains only a minority of Muslims among the population. When the latter is the case, the organizations will be dominated by Muslims who hold powerful secular positions in the state apparatus; their objective is to facilitate control of Muslims and obtain their loyalty to the state, rather than to reform spiritual behaviour. For example, in the Uganda Muslim Supreme Council, created by Idi Amin Dada in the early 1970s, five of the thirteen members (38 per cent) were senior figures in the police or armed forces (Coulon 1983: 163). In Tanzania – approximately one-third Muslim, concentrated in coastal groups – the single party, Chama Cha Mapinduzi, recognized the fact that the traditional power structure was too strongly entrenched to be pre-empted by its *arriviste* socialist ideology. Traditional leaders, including where appropriate Islamic authorities, were inducted into the party's official leadership structure. A National Muslim Council of Tanzania was formed to supervise Islamic affairs on the mainland, the leading figures of which comprised Muslims with stature in society. The Mosque Council of Zanzibar, founded in 1981 and led by Shaikh Ameir Tajo Ameir, fulfilled a similar role in Zanzibar. In Malawi, in areas where Islam predominates, officials of the former dominant party, the Malawi Congress Party, were nearly always Muslims. Malawi's state Muslim body, the National Muslim Association (NMA), was actively involved in the provision of mosques and madrasas (Islamic schools) to enable state appointees to control religious education and worship. It was also useful in providing sine-cures to state employees of the NMA (Bone 1982: 134). These examples suggest that the national organizations will contain a variety of Muslims, whose common characteristic is that they are all allies of the ruling regime.

What this account of various national Muslim organizations has underlined is that one of their chief purposes, in addition to seeking to purify Muslim practices, is to control local Muslims for the benefit of the state. They 'accomplish this work of encadrement with all the more zeal as they are themselves much more dependent on the state than the "traditional" Muslim leaders' (Coulon 1983: 164).

African regimes, when possible, seek to utilize Islam as a component of national identity and state power, and to bolster autonomy and influence in the international Muslim community. The state aims to dominate all international Muslim transactions; it strives to be the interlocutor, the negotiator and the beneficiary of all relations and communications that its national Muslim community maintains with the wider Islamic world. The state seeks to make use of Islam as an ideology of national unity. National Muslim organizations channel the faith of the Prophet into specific organizations, offering material rewards in order to integrate any putative Islamic counter-elite into the state-controlled Muslim framework (Bayart 1993a: 190). While the national organizations have often been successful, nevertheless in recent times a number of oppositional popular Islamic groups have emerged, either because of state attacks against Muslim minorities – as in Tanzania and Kenya – or because of self-proclaimed revolutionary regimes' apparent intention of diminishing Islam's cultural role, as in Burkina Faso. Fuller examination of these issues will be found in Chapter 5.

Senegal

I want to focus next upon the role of Islam in Senegal – demographically predominantly Muslim – where, unusually, Sufi leaders have forged a tight, mutually advantageous relationship with the state which has endured since independence in 1964. This illustrates that it is not necessarily Islamic reformers who achieve the dominant role in the Islamic hierarchy in an African state; what the Senegal nationalist leaders discovered was that the support of the powerful Sufi brotherhoods was integral to the perpetuation of their own position. Consequently, state officials work closely with brotherhood leaders.

Nonetheless, in Senegal the equanimity of the state, dominated since independence by the Parti Socialiste (PS), has been shaken recently by evident popular resentment at economic hardship; this was reflected in the reduced (although still substantial) proportion of the votes cast for the PS at the most recent national elections in 1993. Although the ruling regime has never lost power in an election since the country's independence in 1964, it is generally agreed that this has been due in part to the state's ability to strike a *modus operandi* with the main Sufi brotherhood, the Muridiyya (Fatton 1992; Coulon 1983; Cruise O'Brien 1986).

Recently, as the PS government has struggled to retain its pre-eminent position, there have been signs that a loss of faith in the regime by some marabouts has led to a decline in the vote it receives among ordinary Senegalese.

Around 90 per cent of Senegalese are Muslims; marabouts (Muslim holy men), leaders of the Sufi brotherhoods, have filled the role of interlocutor between state and the bulk of society since independence in 1964. In the early days of colonialism – the first decade of the twentieth century – marabouts often sought to build messianic communities, counter-societies, away from the control of the Christian French colonial administration. Eventually, however, they forged a *modus vivendi* with the French which led, as planned, to mutual benefits: economic rewards and social cohesion for the marabouts, political consensus and at least quiescence in colonial rule for the French. During colonialism, and extending into the post-independence period, maraboutic social control developed into an apparatus which exercised substantive hegemonic control over a civil society at the behest of the state authorities (Coulon 1985: 364).

The alliance between the marabouts and the state is virtually synonymous with Senegalese society, except in the region of the Casamance, separated from the rest of the country by the Gambia, where Christians and Muslims reside in rough equality of numbers (Bayart 1993a: 189). As is the case elsewhere in Africa, such political intermediaries shield their peasant clients from the more onerous of state demands – such as taxes – while simultaneously depending on the state for the resources necessary to build up their clientelistic networks. The marabouts in Senegal exemplify the role of intermediary between state and subordinate classes. As Fatton (1992: 81) notes, they 'help the state penetrate the countryside, but they mold that penetration and indeed manipulate it to their own advantages'. The marabouts embody a class of *courtiers politiques* engaged in permanent negotiations of dependence and authority between their patron state and peasant clientele. In a period of normality or limited crisis, they will collaborate with the state openly. During periods of serious economic dislocation, however, they may be openly critical of the regime; in other words, they will attempt to reject the state's influence when necessary (Coulon 1979). A particular strength of Islam is its ability to exercise political and social control; it is therefore especially useful in helping to maintain the status quo. In return for electoral favours – that is, in ordering their disciples to vote for President Abdou Diouf and the PS – marabouts have been able to command governmental favours, including grants of land and preferential import licences. The Niassist Tijaniyya brotherhood has especially enjoyed commercial success, establishing international trading links with Europe and North America (Cruise O'Brien 1988).

Radical Islam as a putative mould-breaker arrived in Senegal in 1979, the year of Iran's successful revolution. Abdullah 'Khalifa' Niass, a radical and maverick, attempted to follow the example of the Iranian Revolution when he declared Senegal an 'Islamic state'. Although a member of the important Niass family, Khalifa nevertheless found neither his call to *jihad* nor his Iranian-backed party, Hizboulahi (Party of God), in favour among ordinary Senegalese. What is more, his personal standing was undermined by allegations of financial corruption. Ostracized by his family and with only minimal popular support, Niass was imprisoned in 1981. Other initiatives that derived from the Iranian example included a number of newspapers, such as *Wal Fidjri* (The Dawn) and *Djamra* (Islamic Review), which campaigned against the secular state in Senegal (Magassouba 1985). Such developments, rather than suggesting the possibility of a mould-breaking realignment in Senegal, reflected instead a growing resentment against the Diouf regime. On the other hand, Abdou Diouf was able to emphasize his government's *de facto* pro-Islam position as he was head of state when Senegal hosted the December 1991 Sixth Heads of State summit of the Islamic Conference Organization. He also enjoyed close links with the Muridiyya brotherhood, whose influence and numbers burgeoned following the accession to leadership of Abdul Lahat M'Backe.

Despite these developments, there were signs that the political stranglehold of the marabouts was weakening. In the most recent presidential elections in February 1993, President Diouf seemed, whether through force of habit or some other factor, to be 'able to mobilise voters in rural areas, and this time without the express instructions' (i.e. the *ndiguel* [instruction]) from the big marabouts (*West Africa* 1993a: 455). Despite such evidence that the marabouts' hold on their rural followers may be diminishing, other accounts of the growth of urban brotherhoods indicate that the role of the marabouts may be developing into a new form of community solidarity in the urban centre of Dakar and elsewhere in the country (Cruise O'Brien 1988).

In the legislative elections of May 1993, Diouf's Parti Socialiste (PS) won 70 of the 120 seats (58 per cent). Diouf's chief rival, Abdoullahi Wade's Parti Démocratique Sénégalais (PDS) won 40, and four other parties won 10 between them. Once again the *ndiguel* was absent.

Formerly, the Khalifa-General of the powerful Muridiyya brotherhood publicly backed the PS; on this occasion the endorsement was absent. In the past, the bond between marabouts and disciples, which had the effect of binding the latter to the former unconditionally, was no doubt worth thousands, perhaps hundreds of thousands, of votes for PS candidates. The Sufi brotherhoods (Muridiyya, accounting for 25 per cent of Senegalese; Tijaniyya, 50 per cent; Qadiriyya, 15 per cent) have a reputation for promoting conservatism and sectarianism. Traditionally, the Muridiyya chiefs control groundnut production, and engage in religious rivalries with their main competitors, the Tijaniyya. During the late 1980s and early 1990s, the guaranteed price paid by the state for groundnuts fell considerably. Many Muridiyya disciples drew a distinction between two categories of instruction from their chief – in effect, two sorts of *ndiguel:* one was the electoral instruction to vote for the government, which could be disobeyed by the disciple; the second, an *ndiguel* 'for the brotherhood', retained its customary authoritative character. In 1993 there was no 'electoral' *ndiguel,* as the marabouts ran the risk of provoking the desertion of their disciples should they attempt to push them too hard into voting for Diouf and the PS (Cruise O'Brien 1993).

Electoral malpractice, including the issuing of bogus voters' cards by both the PS and the PDS (especially to an Islamic group, Moustachidines Wal Moustachidates) was recorded in the 1993 elections. This was a new departure in so far as in the past the PS appeared to have a near-monopoly on the distribution of bogus voters' cards – which enabled the recipients to vote more than once. Notwithstanding from the effects of ballot-rigging, which aided the PS and the PDS alike, the high proportion of votes which Diouf and PS candidates apparently received probably reflected the conservatism of ordinary Senegalese as much as it indicated an abiding affection for the government. Followers of the brotherhoods were to be found among supporters of the PDS, with their slogan of *Sopi!* (Change!), while voting for the PS by brotherhood followers did not necessarily reflect a knee-jerk reaction to the wishes of the marabouts. Economic motivations were uppermost; the PS probably gained the benefit of the doubt in 1993. Such an outcome cannot be guaranteed in the future.

Conclusion

In this chapter we have examined the role of the leaders of the Catholic Church, as well as that of national Muslim organizations and other important Muslim factors, in the context of recent moves towards democratization in Africa. A feature shared by the two groups was that senior religious figures forged close relationships with the state; this often made them rather ambivalent towards the notion of fundamental political change. Where senior Islamic figures were concerned, with the exception of Senegal, the aim was to seek to undermine and belittle the traditional expositors of Islam – the Sufi brotherhoods – in order to replace their rather eclectic variant of Muslim belief with an 'Arabized' version which sought, literally, to do things Islamic 'by the book'. Nevertheless, the goal of religious reform either coexisted with or took second place to a more material concern on the part of Muslim elites to enjoy the political and economic advantages of leadership positions in national Muslim organizations. Secular leaders found it advantageous to endorse the climate of reform which national Muslim organizations sought to perpetuate because it enabled the latter to gain control over local Muslims, to make them feel that someone was looking after their interests. In recent times, however, in the context of economic downturn and democratic aspirations, the partnership between national Muslim organization and state entered a period of strain. Whereas liberal democracy per se was not necessarily of major concern to Muslims – believing as many do in a continuity of religion and politics which makes strictly secular goals of deeper democratization somewhat irrelevant – it was the case that reform of Islamic practice and of the forms of control which it represented became increasingly questioned.

I argued in the case of the mainstream Christian churches that their leaders were generally involved in a similar kind of relationship as their Muslim counterparts: they sought to prosper, both religiously and materially, within the context of their relationship with the state. The peculiarities of Africa's economic downturn, coupled with authoritarian rule, acted to push popular demands for political reform to the top of the agenda. Roman Catholic leaders tended to be ambivalent about the concept of fundamental political reform because they feared emphatic change every bit as much as did the entrenched political elites. Although on occasions they headed conferences, it was not at all clear that they wished actually to endorse the demands for change until the groundswell of public opinion was such that not to do so would emphatically link them with the secular political elites at a time when demands for change focused on the latter's role. However, even when regimes were replaced by new ones, the political change represented passive revolution rather than anything more fundamental.

In the next part of the book, comprising Chapters 5–7, I want to focus upon the burgeoning examples of popular religion in Africa which, despite their great differences in a number of respects, nevertheless have something important in common: a political or politicized orientation engendered or galvanized by a realization that the best way to achieve individual and collective benefits was by practising methods of self-help. In other words, popular religious groups were often founded on the premiss that mainstream religious organizations were not always able to advance the spiritual and material interests of co-religionists. Modern popular religious groups in black Africa, it will be argued, often represent a turning away from mainstream religious groups to more community-centred, solidarity-enhancing local-level groups during a time of considerable socio-economic and political flux; this, for many people, has been a defining characteristic of the post-colonial period in Africa below the Sahara.

PART III

Popular Religion and Politics in Africa Today

5

Popular Religion and the State

The idea which galvanizes the idea of 'politics from below' is that analysis of state–society relations in Africa has been overconcerned with traditional political actors that have been of singular importance in such relations in the West; for example, states, governments, parties, institutions. In Africa, while such actors are certainly significant, they are nevertheless often accorded too central a role, which leads to a loss of analytical clarity. To understand the role of African popular religion in social and political change it is necessary to address an issue often overlooked in comparative political analysis: how do popular religious beliefs stimulate and affect political developments? To pose the question in this way is to deploy the state as a unit of analysis, which may or may not be wholly appropriate; for one of the most significant factors concerning popular religious movements is that many have international or transnational links with other groups. For example, some popular religious groups, such as Sufi brotherhoods, militant Islamist groups and Protestant evangelical sects, are generally not 'constrained' by supposedly 'hard' state boundaries. Governments often claim that such groups are *controlled* (rather than merely encouraged or partially funded) by foreign regimes – the United States, Iran, Saudi Arabia, Libya, and so on; this gives such governments a justification to vilify or clamp down on the groups. Leaders of the mainstream or 'orthodox' religions, for their part, also weigh in with their criticisms of such 'foreign controlled' religious movements: they are alleged to be Trojan horses of outside interests.

Virtually every Sub-Saharan African state has a fair number, and sometimes very many, religious faiths and sects, often characterized by a mixture of Islam, Christianity and indigenous religions; often orthodox

137

Christian churches compete with Protestant fundamentalist and independent churches. Popular – usually Sufi – Islam competes with the orthodoxy championed by the ulama. Leaders of the hegemonic religions often appear unwilling to accept that such groups are nearly always rooted in ordinary people's concerns, and therefore closer to social, community and material issues than the former. Leaders of such groups *may* be self-serving; after all, leadership of a religious community is often lucrative. On the other hand, they may be individuals incensed by corruption or the subservient position of certain groups in society. They are close to the people, being involved in religious issues at community level; they find themselves responding to popular pressures for change which may cut across horizontal class stratifications, vertical ethnic or regional differences, or the urban–rural divide.

Popular Religion in Africa in Comparative Perspective

For many ordinary Africans, 'politics' is something to be kept at arm's length whenever possible. It is something rather unsavoury, denoting the often dubious goings on between elite groups (Molutsi and Holm 1990). Nevertheless, it is undeniable that many ordinary people took to the streets in the early 1990s to protest against political decisions which had affected their lives deleteriously. The dividing line between politics and other social activity is clear cut from the perspective of the social sciences. What are often rather arbitrary disciplinary divisions between politics, sociology and economics lead us to assume that reality may be divided so neatly. However, it is not quite so easy to put 'messy' reality into such discrete categories. In accounts of African politics it has traditionally been considered rather difficult to pigeonhole individuals in terms of their social class, because the usual Marxist categories are deemed less useful than in some other contexts. In the same way, the relationship between religion and politics among the lower classes is usually dealt with by seeking to explain popular religious movements by reference to their sometimes 'hidden' political objectives (see, for example, Buijtenhuis 1985). Yet this approach is problematic. Not least of the problems is that it is difficult to be sure where 'religion' ends and 'politics' begins. During the colonial period, for instance, religious movements were often actually both anti-colonial and concerned with internal socio-cultural reform (Ranger 1986). The point is that it is not analytically necessary or always possible to ascertain whether religious, political or social objectives are paramount. It is more productive to understand such movements as often involving a combination of motivations which defy easy, and precise, pigeonholing.

Most Africans regard themselves as religious people, believing in a God (or gods) who overlooks them and what they do. Many believe that religious worship is a means to improve their mundane position. In other words, it is actually rather difficult to tell when an individual's motivations are 'religious' or 'political'. Schatzberg (1988: 11) argues that social dynamics in Africa are best viewed as a 'triple-stranded helix of state, class, and ethnicity'. The metaphor of the triple strand is also useful in understanding the role of popular religion. In my account, the triple helix comprises religion, ethnicity and politics. Each is present within an individual's world-view; and in certain situations, at certain times, one element will dominate. Sometimes religion serves to form the context for political action; that is, political concerns will be imbued with religious notions which help to determine the nature of a group's collective response. Examples include recent political developments in Nigeria and Sudan. What I am getting at is that spiritual and material concerns interact within very fluid boundaries in a context where many Africans relate to religion as a means of solving a number of personal problems, some of which concern material issues.

As noted earlier, in order to perpetuate hegemony successfully it is necessary for the dominant stratum to maintain a more or less consensual moral order which has the status of common sense. Subordinate classes accept such a moral order, according to materialist analysis, out of 'false consciousness'. This allows the ruling elite to rule through consent rather than relying too heavily upon coercion. Yet this should not be taken too far in the African context: hegemony is rarely achieved on the basis of social and popular consent alone; coercion is always a highly useful option for the authorities to maintain social control. The false consciousness argument is not a convincing explanation as to why subordinate-class Africans obey the authorities (when they do, which is by no means all of the time); obeisance (or at least the apparent or outward manifestations of compliance) is undoubtedly as often due in part to a well-founded fear of the consequences of not toeing the line. Due partly to the apparent passivity produced by this fear and partly to the social divisions that exist in most African societies, it is usually difficult to identify unified political actions undertaken by subordinate classes in pursuit of their class interests. It is by no means clear whether subordinate-class Africans perceive their interests to be best pursued by class action or by 'plugging in' to the networks of reciprocity and the creation of popular – including religious – vehicles of mobilization.

I understand a popular religion to be one which serves as a community expression of a group desire to achieve a religious satisfaction that is not forthcoming from a mainstream religion. Both Marx and Weber stress how the 'contingent nature of the relationship between the content of an ideology and the social position of the group who are its "carriers" is of fundamental importance in understanding the social role of the ideology' (Giddens 1971: 211–12). What this suggests in relation to the hegemonic religions is that their leaders will be concerned with perpetuating and promulgating a version of religion which is also an ideology of domination, which aims to strengthen and bolster their own social and theological position.

Popular religions are the ordinary person's way of cocking a snook at authority, Bayart (1993a: 256–8) contends. Mbembe argues that 'the current explosion of religious revivalism in Africa is another ruse by the common man to create a counter-ideology and alternative political space in response to the totalitarian ambitions of African dictators' (Mbembe 1988: 96). Popular religion may be a potent and overt symbol of political opposition, yet this is not to claim that all popular religion is politically oriented. Spiritual benefits are also an important factor in an individual's choice of religion. Nevertheless, what is often of most importance is how the state perceives the popular religion's aims. For example, as Fields (1985) notes, the Watchtower sect in Central Africa was regarded by the colonial authorities in the early years of the twentieth century as a politically revolutionary movement masquerading as a religious group. Similarly, in the post-colonial era orthodox Islam has done its best to dominate its myriad Sufi rivals – thirty Sufi sects in Sudan alone – because Sufism has often been a leading force in societal opposition to the status quo. The point is that the state in Africa may often make great efforts to dominate popular religious sects to ensure that they operate according to the official rules laid down by the state's politico-administrative framework (Forrest 1988: 428). Any apparently substantive manifestations of anti-regime opposition will be taken very seriously indeed. The ramifications of this are clear: regimes must do all they can to reduce challenges to a minimum; one effective way is to bring real or imagined dissidents into the state nexus. If this is not possible, they must be neutralized.

As already suggested, religion is a force which may have significant political implications for ruler and ruled alike. Within Christianity there thrives a multiplicity of conceptions concealed behind an often spurious religious unity – one which, for example, may seek to establish the efficacy of liberation theology amongst all Third World Catholics regardless of differences in culture, tradition, history and political structures. What is more, every supposedly universal religion is in fact host to a plurality of forms of religious belief which correspond to the classes and strata which use it. There is, for example, a 'Catholicism of the petit bourgeoisie and of city workers, a women's Catholicism, an intellectual's Catholicism equally varied and disconnected' (Gramsci 1971: 419–20). This is not to argue that there is one religious orthodoxy which somehow mutates according to social or class context, but rather that there are many different 'Catholicisms' of which the hegemonic, orthodox version is but one. The same goes for Protestantism, which does not even lay claim to the same degree of uniformity as Catholicism. Within Islam, for instance, there are at least four separate conceptions of the faith, each of which corresponds to a specific socio-cultural context. First, there is the culturally dominant, strongly patrimonial Islam of northern Nigeria, northern Chad, and northern Cameroon. It is inextricably linked to notions of social hierarchy and political power. Second, there is the Sufi Islam of the marabouts, which may itself be divided into so-called 'pure' and 'corrupt' forms (Cruise O'Brien 1988). Third, there is the Islam of discrete ethnic groups in societies controlled by Christian leaders, which carries with it much cultural and racial baggage. Finally, there is the type of fundamentalist Islam associated especially with the radical higher-education student (who may wish to re-create Saudi Arabia's or Iran's nonsecular states). Such categorizations by no means exhaust all the extant types of popular religious belief, of course, but hopefully the point has been made: popular religion, in all its manifestations, relates to the perceptions, ethics and conventions of various groups, divided as they are by occupation, class and gender, expressed through religious practices and terminology.

In Africa, reflecting an often bleakly unpromising economic and political reality, popular religions often express themselves in terms of the apparent hopelessness, reflecting the lack of expectations, of the mass of the people, where religious faith is regarded as the key to this worldly material favour:

> Africa at prayer looks for a miracle, it is a daily appeal for the ultimate solution to illness, poverty, and misery. That is Africa of the night, of Saturdays and Sundays. Africa of the week and of the day 'manages', and corrupt and corrupting individuals die between the two worlds, struggling to survive. (Kabongo 1982: 18)

Popular religion is basically materialist, in the sense of being grounded in the material, and is therefore quite distinct from the more idealist speculations of Weber's 'genteel intellectuals' (Giddens 1971: 211). A materialist conception of popular religion relates to particular forms of ordering and organizing within religious communities. It is, then, rather surprising how resolutely opposed otherwise 'radical' scholars are to the idea that religious beliefs may contain progressive ideas. In a recent volume entitled *New Social Movements in the South*, Wignaraja argues that people 'withdraw' into religion as 'the anarchy in their lives develops'. The withdrawal (presumably from the 'real' world of class conflict) is then, apparently, 'used by vested interests and immature political leaders to manipulate the people' (Wignaraja 1993: 33). In another contribution to the same volume, Kothari (1993: 68) claims that those who look for religious solutions to their material and social problems are duped by the 'ruling class [which] has set in motion a completely new canard ... to distract attention from the socio-economic sphere ... releasing strong regional, linguistic and cultural sentiments...' The writer of another chapter in the book, Samir Amin (1993: 77), explains the *raison d'être* of popular religious groups in the following way: they are movements of 'religious revival' which appeal to the 'heritage of the past' overlain by the 'modern world'; they are symptomatic of 'crisis ... products of disillusionment. They will eventually lose steam as they reveal their powerlessness in the face of the real challenge' – how to build socialism. Thus, according to these accounts, those who belong to popular religious groups in the Third World are, with the exception of those motivated by liberation theology, duped either by opposition politicians (Wignaraja), by the ruling class (Kothari) or by appeals to a (probably mythical) 'golden age' (Amin).

Amin, Kothari and Wignaraja fail to give credit where it is due: class organizations often seem to appeal rather minimally to many people in the Third World; religion, on the other hand, appears to offer an ideological belief system which has spiritual, material and community benefits, and which, in some cases, will appeal to people across otherwise prominent social divisions such as ethnicity or class. It will hopefully suffice for now to make the point that not all popular religious groups pursue goals which can clearly be described as political, yet some do. In the current chapter the popular religions with political goals that I focus upon are largely urban-based. I leave the important question regarding the motivations and goals of 'new religious movements' in Sub-Saharan Africa to Chapter 6, and that of religious fundamentalist groups to Chapter 7, as I believe both require close individual examination.

Amin is surely right to stress how 'modernization' has brought a state of crisis for many people in the Third World; he is wrong, though, to claim that they are passive in the face of it. Throughout the Third World, with the important exception of post-revolutionary states such as Iran and China, modernization is regarded as symptomatic of Westernization. The growth of formal political organizations (for example, political parties) and procedures (such as 'the rule of law') would in the process, it was thought, reduce the central role of clientelism and patronage. In short, the advent of social change leading to modernization would result in a jettisoning of older, traditional values and the adoption of other, initially alien though actually more 'rational', more 'realistic' social and political practices. In many respects, however, the adoption of Western ways in many African states is really only skin deep: at the personal level, Western-style suits for men rather than traditional dress, and skin-lightening cream for women; at the level of symbols of national unity, the trappings of statehood – such as flag, constitution, legislature, at the level of social intercourse, a European lingua franca, and so on. Yet, change as a result of modernization is not evenly distributed throughout African societies; social, ethnic and political conflicts are common owing to the patchy, partial adoption of modern practices which coexist with 'traditional' (that is, premodern) ways of doing things. Social change destabilizes, creating a dichotomy between those who benefit from change and those who do not. New social strata arise, the position of which in the new order is decidedly ambiguous, such as the twentieth-century phenomenon of rural-to-urban migrants in Africa who find themselves between two worlds, often without an effective or appropriate set of anchoring values. Such people will be likely to join popular religious groups. On the other hand, membership of such groups is by no means confined to the alienated: members of the middle class may also find in them something lacking in the mainstream, orthodox religions. As we shall see later, elements of both individualistic and community concern are present in the motivations of those who join Christian fundamentalist churches in Africa.

As noted earlier, popular religions deviate from mainstream religious orthodoxies inasmuch as the former offer something of value to many ordinary people which the latter apparently do not. Within African Islam, Ibrahim (1989) notes, current conventional wisdom concerning popular Islam is largely coloured by Trimingham's nearly fifty-year-old account of the faith of the Prophet in Sudan (Trimingham 1949). Trimingham, originally a Christian missionary, regarded what he perceived as 'unorthodox' versions of Islam to be debased, somewhat primitive types of 'real' Muslim belief – that is, ulama-led orthodoxy. He regarded Islam in the Sudan as polarized between 'popular' and 'orthodox' versions. Popular Islam is Sufi Islam. Yet Sufi Islam is itself divided between a 'pure' version – akin to ulama orthodoxy – which appeals predominantly to the educated (as Cruise O'Brien [1988] relates in the context of current day Senegal), and a traditional Sufism where worship of saints is an integral part of belief and which is followed by ordinary people. The thrust of Trimingham's argument is that by mixing orthodox Islam with local customs, Sudanese – and by extension many other Africans – ended up with an *inferior* version of the faith.

Perhaps the most serious limitation of such a polarized view is the assumption that Islamic phenomena can be graded in relation to ortho-dox norms. For what is orthodox in Saudi Arabia may not be so in Indonesia or Afghanistan. The point is that Islam adapts itself to con-form to local needs. The ulama claim the institutions of Islam as their own personal property; their version of 'orthodox' Islam becomes the conventional form of the faith. As we saw in Chapter 4, in order to guard against any insurrections or other outbreaks of mass disobedience led by the Sufi brotherhoods, the ulama and their allies must have control of national Muslim organizations. In this way, the ulama achieve political power in tandem with secular rulers.

Sufi saints have much more relevance to many ordinary Muslims in Sub-Saharan Africa than the ulama's orthodox Islam or that of Islamic reformers more generally. As we shall see in Chapter 7, this is one reason why Islamic fundamentalism has enjoyed comparatively little success in Africa below the Sahara as compared to parts of North Africa, notably Algeria. What is clear is that normative tenets operate in popular Islam which mould religious orthopraxy. In other words, Muslims will adhere to a correct model of behaviour according to their own conception of what is right and proper. Certainly, the orthodoxy of the ulama is not the only version of Islam which is regarded as spiritually correct. The point is that popular Islam in many African countries fulfils many people's religious *and* material needs, including medical and social problems. For example, as Last shows in northern Nigeria, Sufi shaykhs (preachers) are probably in just as great demand for their perceived powers of healing as for their purely religious teachings. Their 'medicine' – which may comprise verses of the Quran written on a blackboard which is then washed down by water and the resultant mixture drunk – is sought by rich and poor alike. According to Last, Islamic power (*baraka*) is considered 'particularly efficacious despite the range of other therapies available' (1988: 199). People seek out medicine as aid for their social problems as well as purely medical complaints.

There are parallels with popular Christian sects with regard to the goals that religion may serve. Peel (1993: 88) divides popular or unorthodox Christian sects into two categories, the 'instrumental' and the 'expressive'. He relates the emergence of popular Christian sects in Africa to the way that 'the synchronization of two epochal processes ... the adoption of a world religion and the religious expression of modernity' did not, as in Western Europe, take a thousand years, but rather was practically simultaneous. He sees secularization as 'the interplay of two strands: a decline in the prestige and influences of institutions, personnel, and activities identified as religious; and a change in the overall character of human thought and action, such that it becomes less governed by mystical or transcendental criteria' (Peel 1993: 89). The first strand of secularization occurred in the context of a process by which religious institutions became differentiated and went on to acquire some hegemonic force in society. Yet, while the orthodox versions of both Christianity and Islam have undoubtedly worked to desacralize African life in some respects – especially, for example, in the Christian notion of separating out the religious from the temporal – they have also interacted with African social forms and traditional beliefs, as we saw above in relation to popular Islam, to produce specific forms of the world religions with a high degree of relevance to many Africans.

The point is that popular religion in Africa may be predominantly 'instrumental' – that is, pertaining to material concerns – or predominantly 'expressive' – relating to ritual. Generally, however, popular religion in Africa combines elements of both. Peel argues that such concerns are especially salient in 'primitive' religions such as the Pacific Cargo Cults. He claims that 'our problem is to explain how people whose traditional religion was importantly concerned with securing health, fertility, prosperity, guidance, and so on, responded to unprecedentedly difficult and perplexing circumstances' associated with the effects of modernization (Peel 1993: 89). It seems to me that one way people deal with such problems is to adopt religious beliefs which offer them both instrumental and expressive benefits. During Africa's modernization people flocked to the new population centres. Traditional religious arrangements were transformed into new forms which offered people multiple benefits in their changed circumstances. As a result, popular urban religious groups sometimes developed into self-sustaining communities which offered a range of benefits – both spiritual and material – for group members.

Popular Religious Groups

Five categories of popular religious group are to be found in Africa: development-oriented, ethno-religious, gender-oriented, fundamentalist and syncretistic. They are all community-oriented, yet each serves its followers in somewhat different ways. Development-oriented groups, such as the basic Christian communities found throughout many parts of Africa, are organizations which form largely as a result of two imperatives: a lack of religious professionals and poor living conditions. Ethno-religious groups, in contrast, emerge when a community, possessing both a religious and ethnic identity, perceives itself as an increasingly powerless and repressed minority within a state dominated by 'outsiders', often those of different ethnic or religious affiliation. The mobilization of the opposition group's culture (of which religion is an important part) is directed towards achieving self-control, autonomy or self-government. Examples include southern Sudanese Christian peoples (such as the Dinka and the Nuer fighting both Islamization and Arabization) and Muslim groups in both Kenya and Tanzania, which we shall say more about below. In each case, the minority group's religion provides part of the ideological basis for action against representatives of a dominant culture whom the minority perceives are striving to undermine or to eliminate their individuality. Gender-oriented groups, our third category, seek to use religion as a weapon of liberation: to challenge those with a particular perception of a faith – namely, that it is God's will that women should be second-class citizens. In this regard, I consider below Muslim gender-oriented groups, and in Chapter 7 the role of women in the fast-growing Protestant evangelical groups.

The fourth category consists of those religious groups that are often labelled 'fundamentalist'. The problem with the use of the term 'fundamentalism' is that it tends to suggest that all who can be labelled in this way are simply atavistic: they feel their traditional way of life to be under serious threat. As a result such groups aim to transform an increasingly areligious, amoral society in accordance with their religious tenets; that is, they wish to change the laws, morality, social norms and sometimes the political culture of their country. In short, the idea is that fundamentalists wish to (re-)create a tradition-oriented, less modern(ized) society. There are, however, at least two broad subcategories of 'fundamentalism' existent in Africa. In the north – that is, in the Arabized region bordering the Mediterranean – fundamentalist Islamic opposition groups, such as the Front Islamique de

Salut (Algeria) and An-Nahda (Tunisia), do indeed wish to return religion and society to a purer, less corrupt golden age. Islamic activists fight against governments because the jurisdiction of the latter encompasses spheres which the former hold as integral to the building of an appropriate society; these include education, employment policy (of men rather than women), and the nature of society's moral climate. In Sudan, on the other hand, fundamentalists control government, using reform of religion as a means to attack the non-Arabized or non-Islamic peoples of the country. Below the Sahara, opposition groups styling themselves as Islamic fundamentalists are generally less politically significant, tending instead to be rather marginal groups comprising chiefly higher-education students and other intellectuals who may be galvanized by the idea of an Islamic state along the lines of Iran's. In Nigeria, on the other hand, Islamic fundamentalism defines itself in the context of rivalry with Christians; religion is used as a surrogate for unresolved political issues which centre on power and control of the state.

The fifth category of popular religious group is that of the highly diverse syncretistic bodies; they may be linked with either Christianity or Islam, and may be either urban or rural. We shall examine them in Chapter 6 when we look at African new religious movements. During the colonial period many syncretistic cults arose in response to the social changes which accompanied the entry of European administrations. After colonialism, similar cults continued to appear: clearly their existence could not be adequately explained by the stresses and strains occasioned by colonial rule. What seems clear is that such movements were not merely a reaction either to colonialism or to discrete post-colonial political developments. Rather, they were concerned with cultural, ethnic, political and economic tensions which existed before colonialism (and which the latter helped to politicize), and which resurfaced in the post-colonial epoch when one group sought to achieve hegemony over others. Groups that have resorted to religious symbolism as political ideology are generally those that not only feel they have been mistreated or abandoned by government, but that have also traditionally been marginalizd by both colonial and post-colonial political and economic structures and processes.

I want next to illustrate the theoretical discussion above with some empirical examples of popular religious groups, both Christian and Muslim, the experiences and goals of which help to illustrate and exemplify the points already made.

Basic Christian Communities and Liberation Theology in South Africa

I want to start by looking at a type of popular religious organization – the basic Christian community – which is found in many parts of Africa, including, *inter alia*, South Africa. Such groups are oriented towards increasing the capacity of communities to make beneficial changes to members' lives through the application of group effort. They are by no means solely an African phenomenon. Usually Catholic in religious orientation, they are found in many Catholic societies in Latin America, as well as in Haiti and the Philippines among others (Haynes 1993a: 95–121). Basic Christian communities are popular in the sense that they are usually run by the people who form their membership, often with only intermittent assistance from religious professionals.

I will begin the account of basic Christian communities in Africa by surveying the background to their development in the region where they first grew, Latin America, before proceeding to the African context, with a focus upon South Africa. It was an essentially biblical radicalism, often melded with elements of Marxism-Leninism, which stimulated a number of Catholic priests in the 1960s to champion the concerns of the poor in Third World Catholic environments. The development of liberation theology became a widespread feature of socio-political division and struggle in Latin America. Liberation theology is an intensely political phenomenon, a response to poor socio-economic conditions. Central to the concept is the notion of dependence and underdevelopment; the use of a class-struggle perspective to explain social conflict and justify political action; and the exercising of a political role to achieve both religious and political goals. In Latin America, the church was radicalized both by certain theologians and thinkers – such as Gutierrez and Freire – and by many younger priests, who collectively helped to develop a socially progressive Catholicism. Basic Christian communities were the most concrete sign of the spread of liberation theology.

Despite the growth of evangelical Protestantism in Latin America over the last few decades, Latin America remains both culturally and (largely) religiously Catholic (Martin 1990). This was a result of the first wave of European imperial expansion led by Spain and Portugal from the fifteenth century. In contrast, the Catholic Church in Africa derives from the second wave of European expansion in the late nineteenth century. This later evangelical wave involved a greater – although by no means complete – differentiation between imperialistic (political) and missionary (religious) penetration than was the case with the earlier colonization. The important social and political result in Latin America was that in Spanish and Portuguese colonies Catholicism created a singular world-view marked by a particular perspective on ordinary people. The later emphasis on liberation centred on the claim that it was first necessary to be 'humanized' (that is, released from degradation and poverty) before becoming a religious Christian. Since this involved comprehension of the conditions which historically created the phenomenon of 'the man who is not a man' (to use the phrase of liberation theologian Gustavo Gutierrez), the process could not be simply one of spiritualization; it also had to involve a socio-political 'conscientization' which reflected the wide gulf between 'haves' and 'have nots'.

Basic Christian communities were introduced into Sub-Saharan Africa from the late 1960s, just after they first appeared in Latin America. In Africa, however, they were not generally formed in response to calls from radical priests for ordinary Catholics to organize themselves to fight what were essentially socio-political injustices – the exception being in South Africa, where the particular conditions of apartheid society led to radicalized basic Christian communities (Walshe 1991) – but for a rather more prosaic reason: to bring collective help to deprived communities experiencing spiritual and material problems. In the spiritual realm, the communities were necessary because of the decline in the numbers of ordained priests working at community level in Africa (Gray 1986). Some idea of the problem may be gauged by observing the drop in numbers of priests after 1960, the *annus mirabilis* of African independence. In 1960, the ratio of Catholic priests to baptized Catholics in Africa was 1:1,652; by 1980, this had increased to 1:3,659; and by 1984, it was estimated that Africa's 90 million or so Catholics were being ministered to by only 17,402 priests (Luneau 1987: 105) – a ratio of 1:5,172. Of these only 6,813 were African, while 10,589 were non-African. By the year 2000 the ratio is expected to have risen considerably higher with the proportion of African to foreign priests falling below the current 3:5.

The shortage of priests on the ground, and the resulting 'Eucharistic starvation', led the various local Catholic hierarchies in Africa to push for the development of basic Christian communities as organizations which would continue to exist even if there was no priest. To help overcome the shortage of priests and to prevent the loss of the faithful to other Christian faiths, the church placed lay ministers, or 'guides' with several years' training, in charge of parishes in a number of countries where priests were in short supply; these included Zaire, Cameroon, Congo, Central African Republic, Chad, Angola, Mozambique, Burkina Faso, Zambia and Senegal (Boillot 1994: 7–8). Such men and women were empowered to conduct all pastoral services except ministration of the sacraments and to preside over local Christian communities' activities. The latter generally include groups which meet fortnightly or perhaps monthly in order to study the Bible, discuss problems of daily life and how to deal with them, catechize children, organize help for the poor and needy, undertake funeral ceremonies, and maintain collective responsibility for the locality (Bavarel 1983: 36–44).

It will be seen that the main reason for the spread of basic Christian communities in Africa was a shortfall of priests, which in effect compelled some religious communities to seek survival through self-help efforts. In South Africa, on the other hand, a radical Christian theological interpretation gained ground in the 1970s and 1980s which had significant political ramifications. The Institute for Contextual Theology (ICT) declared in 1984 that it sought to promote the formation of basic Christian communities because it perceived them as vehicles of conscientization. To advance toward this goal, it worked to develop 'contextual theology' – liberation theology – programmes for study by South Africa's emergent Christian communities. Father Albert Nolan, a member of the ICT staff in 1984, published a book with Richard Broderick which quickly became known in South Africa as a 'manual for contextual theology' (Nolan and Broderick 1987). Members of Christian communities were encouraged to interpret the Bible with a stress on what it says about political oppression and liberation; to seek conscientization through social analysis; and to arrive at an understanding of the need for major structural changes in society. What this amounted to was the application of Latin-American-style liberation theology to the South African context in order to further the chances of political liberation. In South Africa, liberation theology is usually known as 'Black theology' or 'contextual theology' in order to differentiate the country's particularistic political environment – its specific type of race and class exploitation; the wide range of Christian, Islamic and traditional religious cultures – from that of Latin America. The new theology contained within it the seeds of political liberation, beginning from an awareness of, and a positive approach to, what it meant to be a black African living under apartheid. The political effects of liberation theology in Latin America are widely believed to have contributed to the process of democratization in the region that began in the 1970s (Haynes 1993a: 95–109). In South Africa, socially progressive Christians, both black and white, were also galvanized by their own radicalized Christian ideology of liberation.

Black theology identifies 'the concept of salvation with liberation, which leads [it] to justify and support active struggle by [Christian] believers against social exploitation and oppression', involving, when appropriate, class-based political struggle (Schoffeleers 1988: 186). More generally, the social polarizations that apartheid rule entailed convinced many ordinary Christians in South Africa that the struggle against it was necessarily both theological and political in thrust. Ryall (1994) notes that, in effect, the mainstream Christian churches had been absorbed into the structures of white dominance during the decades of apartheid rule. None offered a lead to those striving for liberation. Gradually, however, more and more Christian professionals emerged from a state of conformity to the norms of apartheid culture; thus, for a long time they were 'not so much the servants of God as of temporal power' (Walshe 1991: 33). Nevertheless, several Anglican priests, including Trevor Huddleston and Michael Scott, campaigned vigorously against apartheid; the former was recalled to England, the latter imprisoned and subsequently expelled from South Africa.

Black theology originated at the 1960 Cottesloe Conference of the World Council of Churches, which condemned apartheid as an evil system that had led to such atrocities as the Sharpeville massacre. Over the next twenty years, opposition to the racist government grew steadily at home and worldwide. Within South Africa itself, the focal points of opposition were the township councils, formed explicitly to control and tax urban blacks; and the tricameral, racially based constitution of 1983, which sought to divide and rule non-whites – to separate 'Indians' and 'Coloureds' from blacks by giving the two former groups limited representation while denying it to the latter. This was the political context that led to the growth of Black theology, which served as an ideology of support for blacks' political struggles.

By the mid-1980s, things began to change with increasing pace: the South African Council of Churches came under black leadership and became an ecumenical vanguard for the articulation of Black theology. The best-known expression of radical Christian concerns was the Kairos document, which included a social and political-contextual analysis to describe the struggle for salvation from public sin. The importance of Christian opposition to white minority rule became clear by the end of the 1980s, when premises of leading church organizations were destroyed by right-wing groups (Moore 1989: 244–5). The weight of the churches was of significance in helping to persuade the de Klerk regime of the necessity of 'transforming' South Africa's political system by top-down reforms (Huntington 1991: 113–14). As was the case with other one-party states, the collapse of Communism also had a direct bearing on the de Klerk government's decision to democratize the country's political system.

In sum, basic Christian communities in Africa, like their counter-parts in Latin America, function as popular religious vehicles which aim to bolster both the spiritual and material aspects of members' lives, and, in the case of South Africa, may also serve as vehicles of political liberation. They share common ground with our second example of African popular religious movements, Islamic women's groups, in that these are not concerned exclusively with gender-specific issues, but are also highly politically motivated in trying to change the attitudes of men towards women in order for the latter to achieve personal and group liberation.

Islamic Women's Groups

It is a truism that Islam is as concerned with politics as it is with spiritual issues. Muslims deny the existence of separate sacred and secular realms. Yet, for many Muslim women, Islam is a religion which, purposively or not, belittles them and undermines their attempts at progress in rapidly changing societies in Africa and elsewhere. In the Third World, generally speaking, indices of modernization in society – for example, formal Western education and economic growth towards 'modern' economies – usually appear to favour men over women. Accounts of African political and economic development invariably stress how women as a group have been systematically disadvantaged over time. In the colonial period, for example, prevailing Victorian attitudes towards women – that their place was in the home as wives and mothers – meant that most African women had no access to Western education and its associated material benefits. As Parpart notes:

> for most African women ... the colonial period was characterized by signifi-cant losses in both power and authority. Colonial officials accepted Western gender stereotypes which assigned women to the domestic domain, leaving economic and political matters to men. (Parpart 1988: 210)

In the post-colonial era African men enthusiastically continued the stratification of society based on their dominance. African women have been prevented from developing their full potential by restricted eco-nomic opportunities. Few women hold important economic positions in

African societies. As Parpart relates, in both Kenya and Nigeria in the mid-1970s far fewer than 10 per cent of lawyers, engineers and medical doctors in Kenya were female, while in Nigeria only about 6 per cent of academic staff were women (Parpart 1988: 217). Informal economic activities are open to women, and many – especially in parts of West Africa – make a resounding success of trading – though it is usually men who own the more profit-intensive shops. In Muslim contexts the position of women is often lower than that of females in Christian societies: Islamic societies, 'though guaranteeing women certain inheritance rights, constrain[...] many female economic and political activities through purdah or ritual seclusion' (Parpart 1988: 209). Women rarely hold public positions of authority and are prohibited from holding religious offices. In general, in Muslim societies in Africa, as Reveyrand-Coulon (1993: 97) relates, 'women in Islamic societies considered here [Nigeria and Senegal] constitute a subordinated group'.

In the post-colonial period, various types of women's socio-economic organization have been formed in most parts of Sub-Saharan Africa. First, there are the official women's organizations, whose position tends to reflect that of the governing regime which supports them. Second, there are women's organizations concerned with employment, trading, farming, and so on. Third, there are the grassroots women's organizations, which may be centred on the church or mosque; they provide services for women and furnish support networks. Finally, there are the radical feminist groups, where highly educated women band together to press for basic changes in social attitudes towards their gender. Such groups are often to be found in modernizing Muslim societies where orthodox religious norms and beliefs conspire to belittle women's attempts to improve their socio-economic status.

Several of the feminist groups are organizations of educated women who seek to change their societies by campaigning for the reform of Islamic cultural norms. In Nigeria, the Federation of Muslim Women's Associations of Nigeria (FOMWAN) is concerned with 'mobilizing Muslim women in support of liberal interpretations of Islamic teaching' (Callaway and Creevey 1994: 156). By keeping within already 'legitimated boundaries FOMWAN gains both support and material resources'. The organization's focus is on women's rights in Islam, particularly those rights denied to women in Hausa culture, such as inheritance rights and the right to gain custody of children upon divorce. In Senegal, there is an active and vocal feminist group called Yewwu Yewwi ('raise consciousness for liberation'). Its goal is to liberate women – of whatever religious persuasion – by creating a 'crisis of conscience and a mobilization to transform the situation of women and the relations between them and men' (Callaway and Creevey 1994: 166). Yewwi Yewwu, unlike FOMWAN, is not a mass organization but one that appeals to a fairly small group of educated Senegalese women. Neither is Yewwi Yewwu supported by the maraboutic clans, and certainly not by the fundamentalist groups. The latter see the women of Yewwi Yewwu as thoroughly corrupted by their contacts with foreign feminists, especially those from the United States and Europe (Callaway and Creevey 1994: 166). In Sudan, on the other hand, an organization calling itself the Muslim Sisters is highly visible in public and may be engaged in creating new kinds of political role for women. This, as Bernal (1994: 61) suggests, is because in Sudan the growth of Islamic fundamentalism is not a reflection of traditionalism; rather, it is a form of modernity which looks towards the Arab countries – and especially Saudi Arabia – for its inspiration. What these three examples indicate about women's religious movements that are not simply attached to mosques and churches as gender-oriented voluntary movements is that their role and orientation are contextualized by the nature of the societies which produce them.

The role of women in the Sufi brotherhoods in Senegal is a good example. Women cannot technically become talibes – that is, full members of any of the brotherhoods (Cruise O'Brien 1981); yet they certainly participate in the activities of the brotherhoods. Although women seldom hold leadership or administrative positions, they do take part in the important community groups, the dahira, which have both religious and social goals. The most important function of the dahira is to raise funds for their marabout or for some other brotherhood cause. It is debatable whether women's involvement in the dahira is a sign of modernization. Women are not, of course, usually allowed to take part in Muslim religious events on a par with men. On the one hand, it may be that the marabouts cleverly exploit the propensity of women to involve themselves in the activities of the brotherhoods for the former's benefit; on the other hand, women's involvement may be a sign that the brotherhoods 'offer a particularly female religious path by deemphasizing the strict code of orthodox Islam (Callaway and Creevey 1994: 49). The point is that each of these examples of Muslim women's self-help groups indicates that females who feel themselves individually and collectively repressed within male-dominated societies are seeking to use vehicles of popular Islam to increase their status and prestige vis-à-vis men.

Ethno-religious Groups, Sufi Brotherhoods and State Power in Africa

The third example of popular religious groups that I want to examine are those bodies – usually, but not exclusively, Islamic – which function as vehicles of community resistance to what is perceived as the oppressive use of state power in the hands of outsiders. They are the ethno-religious groups and Sufi brotherhoods that are common in Africa. Examples will be drawn from Uganda, Ghana, Burkina Faso, Kenya, Tanzania and the Casamance region of Senegal.

The first type of popular religious group we will consider is the Sufi brotherhoods, which we have already referred to in Chapter 2, with regard to their growth and economic strength during the colonial period. Many of Africa's Sufi brotherhoods have their headquarters in the Middle East or North Africa: for example, the Alawiyya in South Yemen; the Qadiriyya in Iraq; the Sanussiyah in Libya. This suggests that the Sufi mystical tradition, and one of its principal strengths, is that the brotherhoods often function as transnational movements which are able to ignore modern international state boundaries, as well as the domestic divisions between urban and rural life that have been so important in governments' divide-and-rule strategies (Cruise O'Brien 1986). The flexibility that Sufi brotherhoods have developed has often enabled them to defeat the state's attempts to control them. Brotherhoods have been an important force among African Muslims for at least two hundred years, often taking on the work of mass proselytization and organization. The brotherhoods are not normally closely associated with the state, except in a few countries, notably Senegal. In order to try to dominate the brotherhoods, national Muslim organizations, as we saw in Chapter 4, are headed by 'reformers' who seek to control their power and influence in the name of Islamic orthodoxy. Another reason that the brotherhoods find themselves under attack by Muslim reformers is that the latter wish to control their economic power. The Tijaniyya and Qadiriyya in northern Nigeria (with the latter particularly influential amongst the Hausa) and the Sufi brotherhoods of Senegal have particularly significant political, social, cultural and economic importance. In Sudan, one of the main targets of the Islamic reformers, apart from seeking to dominate Southern non-Muslims, was to take power from the hands of the Sufi brotherhoods in the north itself and to place it in their own.

With regard to the second type of popular vehicle we are concerned with in this section, ethno-religious groups, it is of course often possible to discern close links between religion and ethnicity, not only in Africa but also elsewhere. Sometimes, indeed, it is practically impossible to separate out the specific characteristics of a group's cultural composition when religious belief is an integral facet of an overall concept of ethnicity: both are highly important components of a people's self-identity. Ethnic groups which share a religion often perceive themselves as culturally distinctive enough to be attacked by a dominant group. When, on the other hand, government is dominated by Muslims, ethno-religious opposition may emanate from groups which perceive themselves as culturally different; this is the case in both Sudan and Senegal. While in the former the al-Bashir government rules in partnership with Islamic reformers, in Senegal an ethno-religious struggle against the Diouf regime is being waged by the Diola of Casamance – whose population is approximately 45 per cent Catholic and generally economically disadvantaged; in Senegal overall about 90 per cent of the population are Muslim (Callaway and Creevey 1994: 127).

Encarnacion and Tadem (1993) indicate how in Burma, Indonesia, Thailand and the Philippines minority ethnic groups seek to achieve increased autonomy or even independence in states run by a dominant ethnic or religious group. This suggests that the development of minority ethnic challenges to central government is a common phenomenon in those parts of the Third World where Western colonizers attempted to force together disparate cultural groups into unitary states. Yet, recent developments in Bosnia-Herzegovina suggest that it is not, as it were, the 'third-worldness' of states which is the chief cause of religious, ethnic and cultural rivalry; rather, the incomplete nature of state formation and modernization which should be regarded as the chief cause.

A common feature of ethno-religious mobilizing ideology is that groups motivated by such calls to collective action almost always perceive themselves as either marginalized or under threat of attack from outside forces, very often the state itself. In this respect, the emergence of putative unitary states in Africa as a result of decolonization is closely linked to the process of modernization, which implies, among other things, the development of strongly centralized government, generally along the lines bequeathed by former colonial administrations. Since then, as developments in Sudan for example indicate, the consequent centralized government, often dominated by ethnic, cultural, religious or other particularistic groups, serves to exacerbate previously latent tensions and produce overt conflict. Modernization is regarded as a threat to culturalist and religious differentiation; thus, the tendency since

1955 has been periodic eruption of civil war between different ethno-religious groups.

In Sudan, for example, southern Sudanese non-Muslim peoples, including the Dinka and the Nuer, have fought a recurrent civil war against northern Sudanese Muslims, who dominate the state. The aim of Islamic reformers, realized in 1988, was to establish an Islamic state. Even though the government indicated that Islamic (Sharia) law would not be introduced in non-Muslim areas of the country, it became clear that their aim, involving forced conversion of non-Muslims to Islam, was eventually to 'Arabize' the entire country in a form of 'ethnic cleansing'. Obviously, culturally and religiously distinct southern Sudanese would regard such an objective as tantamount to an assault upon their way of life, even perhaps to their collective survival.

Financial aid to prosecute the civil war was granted to Sudan's rulers first by Saudi Arabia and then by Iran. If the impact of Islam as a political force in Africa is at times dependent upon the relationship of Muslims with central government, a catalyst towards increased Islamic awareness has been the efforts of some Arab states and of Iran to seek to achieve foreign-policy goals through an application of Islamic dogma to pre-existing social tension. In addition, the significant yet un-quantifiable impact of the 1978–80 Iranian Revolution, and more recently the thwarted electoral ambitions of the Algerian Front Islamique de Salut, built upon the impact of oil-rich Muslim states' funds applied to co-religionists' disillusionment with the course and content of secular rule. Iran and Saudi Arabia's use of Islamic dogma to help achieve foreign-policy goals has been influential, notably in Sudan but also in a number of other black African states. This develop-ment is best seen in the context of the broader impact of Islamic and Christian 'fundamentalism' in Africa below the Sahara, a discussion which forms part of Chapter 7.

It would be wrong to assume, however, that popular Islamic vehicles in black Africa are the direct consequence of efforts by certain govern-ments in the Middle East to gain foreign-policy advantages (Haynes 1993a). Of major significance to the development of popular Islamic opposition to the state has been the failure of modernization to achieve discernible improvements in the mass of people's lives in many African countries. Etienne and Tozy (1981: 251) argue that Islamic resurgence in Morocco carries within it 'the disillusionment with progress and the disenchantments of the first 20 years of independence'. However, in-creased reliance on religion is not attributable merely to disillusionment with 'progress'; for this would imply that there was once a clearly discernible secular route to societal improvement which has, for some reason, been thwarted. Manifestations of popular Islam are not only symptomatic of the failure of governments to improve people's living standards; they also express the desire of many ordinary African Muslims to escape the control of religious elites, who are often perceived to have much more in common with secular rulers than with ordinary believers. In other words, popular Islam is a vehicle of opposition to the power of religious elites as much as it is a defensive response resulting from disillusionment at the failure of modernization to deliver the development 'goods'. Faced with state power which seeks to destroy or control the former communitarian structures and replace them with the idea of a 'national citizenry' based on a social link between state and individual, popular Islam emerges as a vehicle of solidarity and mobilization, invariably with political aspirations. The popular Muslim appeal should be understood in terms of its *capacity to oppose* the state (Coulon 1983: 49).

Sometimes, however, the capacity to oppose the state is not realized; it may be more rational in certain circumstances for marginalized Muslims to seek to use the political structure for their own ends. Next we shall look at some examples of marginal ethno-religious groups which seek to use the prevailing power structure to pursue their objectives, before turning to a further group which has become convinced that anti-state activity is the most rational course of action to achieve collective advancement. Marginalized Muslim groups are commonly found in those Sub-Saharan African states which have a fairly substantial proportion of Muslims in the population (between, say, 5 and 35 per cent), but split between a number of ethnic groups; this serves to reduce their collective strength vis-à-vis the state.

Along the East African littoral, for example, Islam is by and large the religion of discrete ethnic groups usually all but excluded from the exercise of state power. Islam has, as a result, periodically assumed the mantle of mobilizing ideology of resistance to a central rule which is seen as operating exclusively in the interests of certain (usually Christian) groups. In extreme circumstances various sectarian forms of Islam, such as that of the Asian Ismailis, have found themselves the focal point of what can only be described as 'ethnic cleansing'. This occurred in 1972 in Uganda when the former president, Idi Amin Dada, himself a Muslim, expelled the Asian Ismailis at very short notice and without compensation for their assets, which they were forced to leave behind. The motivation was in no way political; rather, it was racial and economic. Amin and his cronies were able to enjoy the confiscated land

and property at no cost, in a move which was politically popular with some Ugandans.

Where Islam is a significant but not dominant, religion – for example, in Uganda (where Muslims form 7 per cent of the population), Ghana (16 per cent), Burkina Faso (30 per cent), Kenya (10 per cent), and Tanzania (30 per cent) – Muslims often face concerted attempts by state authorities either to marginalize them politically or to coerce them into the nexus of power at the state level. Such pressure serves to produce forms of popular Islam which are commonly defensive and related to ethnicity. Below we look at the situation in each of the countries named above in order to see how state and Muslims joust with each other in a struggle for influence and power. By way of comparison, we shall also refer to the region of the Casamance in Senegal, where Christians are as plentiful as Muslims. Many Christians in Casamance – predominantly Dyola – feel themselves economically and politically dominated by Muslims, and as a result have joined ethnoreligious opposition groups.

Ghana

Relatively few Ghanaians belong to Sufi brotherhoods. Often members of different ethnic groups join particular brotherhoods, which serves to create tension between brotherhoods. Muslims in Ghana are also divided between orthodox followers of the Maliki rites (that is, not members of Sufi brotherhoods) and followers of the unorthodox (some say heretical) Islamic sect, Ahmadiyya, which claims the allegiance of about one-twelfth (some 200,000 people) of the country's Muslims, many of them Fante. Orthodox and Ahmadiyya Muslims tend to regard each other with mutual hostility. Over and above tensions arising from different interpretations of Islam, there exist ethnically based divisions, especially in the main cities. In Accra, for example, Hausa and Zabrama immigrants (the latter originally from Burkina Faso) vie for control of the city's Muslim organizations and mosques; in the central city of Kumasi, the competition for religious control is between Hausa and Gao, originally from Mali. The point is that 'Islam' becomes an emblem of confrontation and ethnic differentiation where material control of religious buildings reflects the wider superiority of one group over another.

It should be noted that intra-Muslim disputes in Ghana are not solely a result of the stresses and strains of modernization. Over forty years ago, around the time of the beginning of Ghana's struggle for independence (which was gained in 1957), an intra-Muslim dispute focused on local Ashanti Muslims' unwillingness to cede control of the central mosque in Kumasi to *arriviste* Hausas. Concurrently, societal disputes centring on Islam, ethnicity and political rivalry were paralleled at the centre in national issues involving Kwame Nkrumah's Convention People's Party (CPP) and its rival, the National Association of Liberals based in Kumasi, the Ashanti capital. Each group attempted to control Ghana's national Muslim organization, the Gold Coast Muslim Association (GCMA). The pro-CCP faction of the GCMA split off to become a rival body, the Gold Coast Muslim Council, which was controlled as an arm of the CPP by Nkrumah's political allies (Pobee 1992: 107).

In 1954 the GCMA metamorphosed into the Muslim Association Party, based in Kumasi and largely concerned with defence of the (orthodox) Muslim minority and with the status of Ashanti Muslim traders in relation to their Hausa rivals in Kumasi. In local elections at the time, in both Kumasi and in the southern port of Sekondi-Takoradi, Muslim candidates, standing officially as candidates of the mainstream parties, in fact sought to appeal to fellow Muslims in a display of religious solidarity rather than for the programmes of the parties. As Pobee (1992: 107) puts it: 'People were asked to vote for a candidate because he was a Muslim and there was much vitriolic attack across the platforms, resulting in breaches of the peace.'

Further evidence of the volatility of the 'Muslim issue' in Ghana's politics was exemplified in the 1960s. In Tamale, capital of the Northern region, intra-Muslim tensions also reflected ethnic division. About two-thirds (500,000) of the inhabitants of Tamale are Dagomba, of whom about three-quarters are Muslim, organized in the Anbariyya sect. Most non-Dagomba Muslims (mostly Hausa) in Tamale are either Tijaniyya, or Ahmadiyya. Violent clashes occurred between the Tijaniyya and the Anbariyya intermittently during the 1960s and later. Differences between them centred on apparently relatively trivial issues, such as the orthodox Anbariyya's rejection of the Tijiniyya's veneration of certain Sufi saints. Also, in contrast to the Sufi traditions, mystic routes to God through trance and ecstatic singing and dancing were declared invalid by the more austere, or purist, Anbariyya sect. The division between Anbariyya and Tijiniyya was also manifested in their support for different political parties in the 1969 general election: followers of Tijaniyya (Hausas) were overwhelmingly for the Progress Party (PP) of Kofi Busia, while Anbariyya supporters (mostly Dagomba) supported K. A. Gbedemah's National Association of Liberals. Progress Party victory in Tamale was due to the block vote of the Dagomba Anbariyya. Anbariyya Dagomba leaders were duly rewarded with state positions in the 1969–72 PP government. Anbariyya support for the status quo was evidenced in the 1978 referendum on the continuation of military-dominated government; the Anbariyya were 'clearly identified with the Yes-Vote, [in support of] General Acheampong, the military strongman of the time' (Pobee 1992: 110).

This account of Ghana's intra-Muslim disputes not only shows how membership of different Sufi brotherhoods is largely a function of ethnic membership, and that political parties sought to exploit those divisions for their own ends; it also demonstrates how Muslims believed that the best way to achieve political (and, by extension, economic) power was to throw in their lot with one of the national political parties – obviously the one they believed would win elections. This underlines an important point about the role of Muslims in many Sub-Saharan African states where they are a minority of the population: state control will nearly always be in the hands of Christians; it is therefore in the Muslims' best interests, divided as they are, to throw in their political lot with one of the contending factions in order to achieve a measure of power.

Uganda

Whereas some of Ghana's Muslim leaders found their way into the framework of state power, in Uganda their counterparts' experience was different, reflective of another combination of ethnic and religious tensions. Religious rivalries between Catholics (around half the population), Anglicans (about one-quarter) and Muslims (about 7 per cent) were exacerbated by the division between the black African south and the more Arabized north of the country. As in Ghana, religious establishments, whether Christian or Muslim, were manoeuvred and controlled by the ruling group to ensure that its grasp on power remained firm. One year after independence from colonial rule in 1964 the National Association for the Advancement of Muslims (NAAM) was founded. It was led by Adoko Nekyon, a cousin and close confidante of Milton Obote. As in Ghana, Uganda's Muslims were divided between two competing national bodies. The NAAM was controlled by non-Bugandan Muslims; while the Uganda Muslim Community (UMC) was led by Kakungulu, an uncle of the Kabaka (king) of Buganda. The government regarded those Muslims not belonging to the NAAM (that is, Bugandans) as 'disloyal to the state' (Mutibwa 1992: 68). Nevertheless, the state found it impossible to control its 'dissident' Bugandan Muslims, who, for their part, were unable to influence state policies. UMC leaders were used as intermediaries between the state and the Bugandan Muslims although no *rapprochement* was created. Under Amin's rule (1971–78), prominent Muslims, whether Baganda or non-Baganda, found themselves targeted as putative recipients of Arab financial largesse. Rich Arab states – especially Libya and Saudi Arabia – believed that it was incumbent upon them to proselytize on behalf of Islam in Africa, and especially in a country like Uganda, which was so centrally placed in the region. Qaddafi, who appeared to believe that as many as 70 per cent of Ugandans were Muslims, condemned Christianity as an agent of imperialism, in a speech at Makerere University in March 1974 (Mutibwa 1992: 109–10). Qaddafi's visit to Uganda led directly, it is alleged, to the murder of Michael Ondoga, the Foreign Minister, and Charles Arube, a prominent Christian Kakwa (Pirouet 1980: 19). Since Amin's political demise Uganda's Muslims have been politically marginalized, as in the eyes of the non-Muslim population they were intimately associated with Amin's excesses. The examples of Muslims' experiences in Ghana and Uganda indicate that, whereas colonial authorities had generally allowed Islamic community groups to function in order to encourage Muslims' political and economic development, during the post-colonial period they were more likely to be used as elements in politicians' plans to achieve power. In addition, latent ethnic tensions, apparently subdued in the colonial era, resurfaced to provide a dimension of social conflict.

Burkina Faso

Whereas during the 1960s and 1970s regimes successfully suppressed ordinary Muslims' concerns by helping to exacerbate religious–ethnic divisions, by the 1980s increasing economic decline, growing political repression and authoritarianism combined with international moves towards democratization and growing universal Muslim assertiveness to produce a number of popular Islamic groups. These confronted orthodox religious leaders and their temporal rulers alike. In Burkina Faso, Kenya and Tanzania popular Islamic groups led opposition to one-party states when the systems they represented were beginning to fracture as a result of both domestic and international pressures.

In Burkina Faso the catalyst for Muslim opposition was the self-styled revolutionary military government of Captain Thomas Sankara which grabbed power in a military coup in 1983. Muslims, about 30 per cent of the country's population, were galvanized into confrontation with the state in response to attempts to diminish the social and political status of Islam during a period of putative revolutionary transformation.

In the mid-1980s Sankara's revolutionary government co-ordinated attacks against Islamic institutions by radical secular groups who argued that Islam was a barrier to modernization of the country. As a result several mosques were destroyed, while revisions in family law (to ease the process of divorce for women, for example) were mooted. Muslim defence campaigns were led and articulated by the Association des Etudiants Musulmans de Burkina (AEMB), aided and inspired by Libyan money, by Iran's theocracy, and by the local Islamic schools (*medresas*). Leaders of Muslim community groups sought to gain public support for their campaign by stressing the cultural and educational benefits of Muslim institutions – an exercise made necessary by the country's high degree of ethnic diversity. The population of around 10 million includes the predominant Muslim Fulani and Mandingo, as well as the mostly non-Muslim Mossi, Lobo, Dagari, Senoufo, Gouronisi, Bissa and Gourma. The AEMB, on the other hand, was dominated by an 'Arabized' counter-elite whose cultural and ideological preferences differed significantly from those of the pre-existing Westernized (that is, French-oriented) political elite and from the newly dominant group of revolutionary cadres. After Sankara's assassination in 1987, his successor as head of state, Blaise Compaore, toned down the attacks on Muslim interests, and as a result rather shrewdly collected large amounts of aid from Libya, as well as gaining the support of the militants of the AEMB. Over the last few years, Burkina Faso has undergone a Wahhabist-inspired reform of Islam. This has targeted the local Sufi brotherhoods because of their 'traditionalism'; sought to introduce Sharia law into the country's Westernized legal system, a legacy of French colonialism; attempted to diminish the status of women; and aimed to introduce Arabic as the country's first language and as the medium used in schools (Otayek 1989: 25).

Kenya

In Kenya, opposition to single-party rule among the 10 per cent Muslim population which is concentrated in the coastal, north-eastern and eastern provinces has been linked to some groups' perceived economic marginalization. Certain non-Muslim ethnic groups – for example, the Luhya, Kamba and Kalenjin – have commonly been regarded as having benefited disproportionately during the rule of the Kenya African

National Union (KANU). The legalization of political activity in December 1991 was the catalyst for the emergence of popular Islam groups with strong ethnic connections. In February 1992, a senior KANU official warned mosque guardians not to allow their premises to be used for political meetings, as this would be illegal. Religious parties were not allowed to register for the 1992 elections, which prevented the newly formed Islamic Party of Kenya (IPK), led by Khalid Salim Ahmed Balala, from competing. The IPK had its power base in Mombasa and in Lamu, a centre of the Yemeni Alawiyya brotherhood. It was founded by a group of Asian intellectuals and businessmen to tap popular Muslim discontent on two main issues. The first was the question of the introduction of Sharia law for the country's Muslim population, who felt discriminated against by the wholesale application of 'Christian' (that is, European-derived) law; the second was economic resentment on the part of coastal Muslims over land issues (*Africa Confidential* 1993d). Many Mombasans objected to the fact that local land was being bought up by outsiders, including whites and Kikuyus; this served to focus pre-existing resentment about economic matters, deriving from the perception that Kenya's Muslims were discriminated against. A KANU-sponsored Muslim movement, the United Muslims of Africa (UMA), was created to counter the IPK, whose political muscle was evidenced by a series of riots in Mombasa, Voi and several other coastal cities during 1992. The aim of UMA was to split the Muslim constituency along ethnic lines in order to diminish its political impact. Young black Kenyan Muslims were encouraged by Abdullahai Kiptonui, a Muslim and prominent KANU figure, to fight for their ethnic and religious rights by targeting in particular Asian co-religionists. The resentment felt by some Muslims at being both politically and economically discriminated against by the country's mostly Christian rulers was also a feature of Muslim discontent in neighbouring Tanzania.

Tanzania

About one-third of mainland Tanzania's population is Muslim. There is in general a high degree of demographic dispersal in a country consisting of numerous ethnic groups, although Muslim concentrations are found in the coastal areas. Some 97 per cent of the island of Zanzibar's population (about 650,000 people) are Muslim. As in Kenya, the general context for the emergence of Islamic-based opposition was the fracturing of the one-party system and the tentative beginnings of political pluralism. And again, Tanzania's Muslims argued that they were discriminated against economically. Yet, until recently, there appeared to be little tension between Tanzania's Muslim communities and the government, no doubt in part because Muslims enjoyed senior political positions, or between Muslims and Christians, a reflection of the almost unique social consensus achieved under Julius Nyerere. The catalyst for the emergence of opposition Muslim groups was the announcement by the government in early 1992 that, in order to reduce public spending, it would transfer the country's health and education system to the control of the country's powerful Catholic Church. This fuelled an outburst of resentment from a new, radical Islamic group, the Council for the Propagation of the Quran in Tanzania (CPQT – Balukta), which quickly rose to prominence as a fierce critic of the Muslim religious establishment that dominated the national Muslim organization, Baraza Kuu ya Waislamu wa Tanzania (Bakwata), and of the Catholic Church – accused by Balukta of seeking to build a religious empire. Balukta radicals accused Bakwata representatives of self-serving, corrupt practices, and denigrated its attempts to promote Islam. In an attempt to take over Bakwata, Balukta militants occupied its headquarters until ousted by order of President Mwinyi. Bakwata's resentment against Christians was made plain in a series of inflammatory sermons broadcast from Dar's central mosque in March 1992; this action triggered street battles in the capital between Christian and Muslim youths (Shaikh 1992: 240). Balakta was banned in April 1993, following a riot during which it was alleged that its supporters went on the rampage in Dar es Salaam, attacking shops which sold pork (*Guardian* 1993). Two years after elections in 1992, which Chama cha Mapinduzi comfortably won, Muslim-oriented opposition parties, led by the Civic United Front based on the islands of Zanzibar and Pemba, publicly raised the issue of separation from the mainland in a move that reflected continuing resentment on the part of the islands' Muslims to mainland domination of the union (*Africa Confidential* 1994).

The Casamance (Senegal)

In Kenya, Burkina Faso and Tanzania, the anti-government and anti-Christian sentiment felt by many Muslims was fuelled by frustration arising from their minority status and a potent mixture of ethnic, economic and religious concerns. In Senegal – over 90 per cent Muslim – on the other hand, a partly Christian group, the Diola of Casamance, expressed resentment at the way they were economically dominated by

Muslims. This shows, in effect, how any minority religious group may fuel its discontent by reference to either its ethnic or religious distinctiveness.

The southern Casamance region in Senegal is separated from the rest of the country by the state of the Gambia, a physical separation that helps emphasize the region's 'apartness'. A political militancy fuelled by Catholic separatism has underpinned a long-running civil war between Casamance and the rest of the country. The Diola group of peoples of Casamance – about 45 per cent Catholic, with the rest either Muslim or pagan – have been mobilized to oppose what they see as foreign invasion by the Mouvements des Forces Démocratiques de la Casamance (MFDC), led by a Catholic priest, Father Augustine Diamacoune Senghor. Diamacoune was arrested in 1983 after political disturbances, and released in May 1991 following a partial amnesty between the government and the leaders of the MFDC (Geschiere and van der Klei 1988: 214, 220). The MFDC campaign has economic, ethnic and cultural roots, although it is religious concerns that have served to focus discontent. Since the early 1970s, the Diola have felt that they have been 'colonized' by 'fishermen, peasants and traders from the much poorer North, such as the Sereres, Toucouleurs and Wolof Muslims' (Smith 1993). Recently, and reflecting increasing pessimism among the MFDC that armed struggle could ever liberate Casamance, the movement split into two: the 'Northern Front' led by Sidy Badji the MFDC's commander in chief, and the more radical 'Southern Front' headed by Father Diamacoune. Like the al-Bashir regime in Sudan, which managed to drive a wedge between different ethnic factions of the Christian-dominated Sudan People's Liberation Army, the Diouf government managed to split the MFDC in two. Badji's group agreed to negotiate with Diouf; Diamacoune's initially refused, although later admitted that liberation of Casamance by force was probably impossible (Smith 1993). Diola resentment at what they see as foreign invasion with economic and religious objectives parallels the situation in Kenya, where coastal Muslims regard outsiders as exerting disproportionate economic influence in their country, and in Tanzania, where minority Muslims see the Catholic Church as attempting to raise its profile at their expense. The point is that in each of these examples popular religion, closely linked with ethnicity concerns, was the main symbol of opposition to the state and its allies in their attempts to strengthen their domination over their subordinate opponents.

Conclusion

This chapter has sought to account for a variety of African popular religious groups, both Christian and Muslim, which share the desire to utilize collective community strengths to overcome what are felt to be positions of marginality or disadvantage. It has described how over the last twenty years or so various types of popular religious group have had considerable impact upon socio-political issues in many parts of Africa below the Sahara. Two broad trends were examined: (1) religion as a vehicle or ideology of opposition; and (2) religion as the basis of a growth of community self-interest with both spiritual and material aspects. I argued that the basic Christian communities were founded in a number of African countries largely in response to a shortage of religious professionals. They subsequently developed as popular vehicles for community aspirations. This was especially the case in South Africa, where the ideas of liberation theology made a strong impression on many Christians. Islamic women's groups, on the other hand, were motivated more by a feeling of disadvantage vis-à-vis men in cultural and religious contexts which served to enhance men's status and prestige over that of women. Muslim women sought to improve their position in societies which were not only dominated by men but also by what women often perceived as unduly onerous social controls, legitimized by religious belief.

The chapter also examined two other manifestations of popular religion, Sufi and ethno-religious groups, which share the desire to enhance the position of those who consider themselves unable to control their own lives owing to the state's oppressive power – that is, the prevailing structure of power relations often serves to prevent or diminish such subordinate groups' socio-economic progress. Ethno-religious vehicles of opposition to what were regarded as inappropriate or unacceptable state policies were discussed in the context both of Kenya and of Tanzania, while in Burkina Faso many ordinary Muslims were seen to have mobilized themselves in opposition to the demands of an unwelcome radicalization and secularization of political issues. In Ghana and Uganda, on the other hand, Muslims have attempted, sometimes without success, to use the prevailing power structure to their own advantage by involving themselves in political jockeying. Finally, in the Casamance region of Senegal, it was shown how the religious affiliation of marginalized groups may be less important than a feeling of marginality when it comes to opposing the state. This chapter has shown that not all manifestations of popular religion are necessarily 'political';

although much depends on whether it is considered analytically possible to separate the temporal and the sacred in accounts of religion and politics in Africa. What seems clear, however, is that popular religious vehicles function as manifestations of community solidarity in the face of unwelcome aspects of modernization. In the next chapter I want to take this concern further in order to examine the range of new religious movements in Africa which have emerged during the twentieth century in response to pressures associated with modernization.

6

New Religious Movements and Political Change

In this chapter I am concerned with what are commonly, if rather loosely, termed 'new religious movements'. This designation denotes several attributes. First, it is the label conventionally applied to religious groups that have their roots in either Islam or Christianity but additionally adopt characteristics derived from the culture in which they develop. Many new religious movements in Africa are overtly syncretistic. Nevertheless, this is not necessarily their defining characteristic; for, as I have already suggested, both Islam and Christianity, introduced over time from outside, became more or less thoroughly indigenized in the region. In fact, it might be argued that the very use of the term 'syncretistic' reflects an ethnocentric certainty that one interpretation of a faith – whether Christianity or Islam – is merely that of the dominant orthodoxy, whether it derives from Rome, Canterbury, Saudi Arabia or Iran. I shall nevertheless retain the use of the term 'syncretistic' in the current chapter as a means of defining certain new movements in relation to their 'orthodox' roots.

Second, new religious movements in Africa, like the various 'fundamentalist' religious vehicles that we shall examine in the next chapter, have grown as a result of the destabilizing effects of colonially induced modernization, including the socio-economic consequences of state centralization and rural-to-urban migrations. In other words, the development of the new movements, like that of other popular religious vehicles, reflects the attempt of ordinary people to come to terms with socio-economic environments which have changed massively within one or two generations, and with the effects of a centralization of power that has led to many feeling both marginal and impotent in the face of state dominance.

The current chapter is structured as follows. The first section examines the development of new religious movements in Africa in global and historical context, and suggests that their growth and development is largely due to the effects of modernization which have by and large enveloped all parts of the world over the last three-quarters of a century. The second section shifts the focus to the growth of Christian new movements in Africa during and since the colonial period. It suggests that the growth of independent African churches should be seen as a response to a number of developments associated with the impact of colonial and post-colonial governments. The third section moves on to consider rural Christian new movements, arguing that in both colonial and post-colonial periods such groups were not necessarily covert vehicles of nationalist aspiration, as is sometimes alleged, but more often vehicles of community aspiration which sought to deal with threats to the community by strengthening the bonds of solidarity with religious symbolism and example. The fourth section extends the analysis to Islamic new religious movements. It argues these have generally served as manifestations of group solidarity and of material interests in the context of Muslim marginality in non-Muslim dominated societies, a trait of popular Muslim groups more generally, as we saw in Chapter 5. The conclusion underlines how the new movements in Africa are popular religious organizations that fulfil a number of functions for their followers, some of which may be political.

New Religious Movements in Africa: Genesis and Objectives

Between the world wars, various manifestations of mission Christianity tended to appeal, more or less exclusively, to certain distinct African class constituencies: pentecostalism to the lower classes and mainstream mission Christianity to the emerging middle classes. Differences in social status were also shown among independent Christian churches and syncretistic Christianized bodies, such as the Zionist churches of South Africa and the syncretistic Aladura churches of West Africa. Each recruited members largely from among those of low social standing (Peel 1984: 184). Others, such as the Harrist church in West Africa, were self-consciously modernist in their thrust: they focused explicitly on the ending of the worship of traditional deities and the adoption of a single God (Ranger 1986: 29–30). In effect, the Harrist movement was a response to the ineffectuality of separate religious cults, of which there was a plethora. The adoption of the Harrist faith was a more or less conscious move towards modernization by Africans, in the same way that conversion to the controversial Ahmadiyya Muslim sect was for the Africans who joined that sect, as we shall see below.

Religious beliefs began to change in response to developments in African society, catalysed by Western penetration and colonization. The result was that, for followers of Harris and of Ahmadiyya, religion became an autonomous or discrete part of life, rather than something that was indistinguishable from other social practices. Such religious developments were not only a response to colonialism of a spiritual kind; they also represented opportunities for wealth accumulation by their leaders. Like their mainstream counterparts, the new religious movements generated power and status, materially expressed via flows of patronage that were to be fought over (Ranger 1986: 31).

The emergence of Africa's new religious movements during the twentieth century, and especially since World War II, reflects a continued popular adherence to traditional religious ideas, symbols and rituals, juxtaposed with modernist accretions from outside the region. The results are more or less hybrid faiths which may become routinized into formal organizational structures, just like other, earlier, religions such as mission Christianity (Ranger 1986: 1). The emergence of the new movements is a further indication that sets of religious beliefs continually develop over time, melding religious and cultural resources in response to changing socio-political and economic conditions. A particularly important factor in the appeal of any religion in Africa is that it functions as both a material and a spiritual-healing force. Peel (1984: 184) argues that 'the most tenacious elements of "traditional" religion, the most likely to survive migration to towns, were those that touched a common bedrock of African traditional religions: the individual's concern for divinatory and magico-medical assistance.'

Despite the clear connection between the development of religious vehicles and both spiritual and material concerns, the emergence of African new religious movements in the pre-independence period – especially during the 1940s and 1950s – was often explained in terms of the unique pressures and transformations associated with colonialism. Commonly regarded thirty or forty years ago (see, for example, Lanternari [1963], and Balandier [1955]) as forerunners of nationalist political parties, the continued existence and further development of the movements *after* colonialism was later explained as a result of the 'cultural and psychological tensions ... [which] deepened with the rapid modernizations' of independence-era Africa (Ranger 1986: 2).

In fact, the very diversity of Africa's 20,000 new religious movements – with, between them, over 30 million followers – makes attempts
at classification difficult and unrewarding (Turner 1988: 950; Oosthuizen
1985: 71). Attempts to categorize the new movements by their origins –
such as local and externally derived traditions and psychological roots
– tend to be of little general analytical use because such classifications
provide only a limited or partial indication as to the nature of their
organizational structures and sources of support. Wallis (1984) argues
that a useful way of categorizing new religious movements is in terms
of their orientation to the world around them. Without, unfortunately,
focusing on Africa, he separates out three trends of analytical salience.
These are: world-denying (Hare Krishna, Moonies, Children of God);
world-affirming (Church of Scientology and followers of transcendental
meditation); and world-accommodating (charismatic renewal movements). Wallis's tripartite division is analytically problematic because it
says too little about the emergence of the new movements – information that is of importance in quantifying and understanding their
political impact. In Africa, new religious movements are often highly
syncretistic and millenarian, aspects which make it difficult to classify
them in terms of their orientation towards the outside world.

It is not possible to point to a convenient group of factors that African
new movements have in common. An imprecise, though common, way
to categorize them is to relate their religious beliefs to those of the
world religions. Thus five types of new religious movement in Africa
may be identified: (1) Traditionalist: a return to spirit-mediumship; for
example, the Zezeru of Zimbabwe. (2) Neo-primal/revitalization: close
to traditionalist but adopts some characteristics of imported faiths; for
example, Godianism of east Nigeria, Bori cults among Hausa women
in Nigeria, and spirit-possession movement among Lebu females in
Senegal. (3) Syncretist/synthetist: Spiritual and prophet-healing
churches; for example, Aladura and Musama Disco Christo church (the
Aladura churches are syncretistic churches which combine elements of
traditional belief with conventional Christian dogma). (4) Messianist;
for example, L'Eglise de Notre Seigneur Jesus-Christ sur terre of Simao
Toko in Angola, Kimbanguist church in Zaire. (5) Millenarian; for
example, Maitatsine movement in northern Nigeria (Turner 1988: 945–
6; Lewis 1986; Jules-Rosette 1979).

The chief problem with such a typology is that it seeks to locate
disparate religious movements in a neat system based on their relation
to Christianity or Islam, but fails to consider relevant social or political
factors. Looked at from a social perspective, eight factors tend to be of

importance, although not all will be relevant to the emergence of every movement: (1) racial, political or class discrimination (leading for example, to the establishment of Ethiopian churches and the Maitatsine maverick-Muslim group); (2) social and cultural upheaval; (3) historical background (for example, land grabbing by colonists in southern and East Africa); (4) denominational rivalries between mainstream sects; (5) religious concerns (for example, traditional religious desire for a religion 'to feel comfortable with'); (6) ethnic exclusiveness (new movements may be vehicles for ethnicity: for example, conflict between Xhosa and Fingo in South Africa, or between Digo and Kikuyu against Kalenjin in Kenya); (7) ecclesiastical shortages (few religious professionals on the ground); and, (8) for leaders, economic imperatives – 'Some establish churches in order to collect money which they utilise for themselves' (Oosthuizen 1985: 77).

What emerges is that African new religious movements usually evolve in response to some kind of social crisis, and are often founded by someone who claims to have had a mystical experience and who henceforward is regarded as an authentic prophet. Reflecting this, each movement has clear millenarian hopes, which include the belief that the divinity will help its followers. Adherents do not recognize all aspects of established authority. There is a selective rejection of traditional culture; the rejection–retention balance corresponds to popular demands, with the emphasis on more satisfying forms of worship. Social solidarity expresses itself in membership of the religious community, which also offers healing and other, more material, advantages. Reflecting the tendency towards counter-culture, followers of new movements see themselves as possessing moral purity. If the new religious movement becomes institutionalized, there will be expansion by concerted missionary activity (Turner 1988: 948–9). This is not to argue that new movements dominate the religious scene everywhere in Africa: even in those countries most prone to religious independency there have always been at least an equal number of (mainstream) Christian Zulu, Luo, Yoruba or Kongo who equally suffered at the hands of colonialism but who stayed in the mission bodies. One obvious reason people shift their loyalty to new movements is the poor quality and doubtful relevance of mission Christianity (Hastings 1979: 255–6).

The once common idea that new religious movements in Africa arose solely in reaction to colonial oppression was shown to be wrong when their numbers burgeoned after independence. In the post-colonial environment, economic variables (particularly in relation to *la politique du ventre*) and political tensions occasioned by ethnic groups competing for power are of fundamental importance in understanding how African politics works. The same factors are of great analytical value when thinking about the new movements. As with the conventional, mainstream faiths, the development of the new religious movements has gone through a succession of phases, and in the process its relation to larger political and social contexts has also changed. For example, in regard to the urban fundamentalist churches of south-west Nigeria it will be noted that the status of women has generally improved (see Chapter 7). There are a number of other examples among both Islam-oriented and Christian-related new movements of similar enhancement of women's status. Recent and contemporary female prophets, such as Gaudencia Aoko (Maria Legio in Kenya), Alice Lenshina (Lumpa Church of Zambia), and Alice Lakwena (Holy Spirit Church in Uganda) have used the vehicle of religion to enhance their own personal – and, by extension, their sex's – social position in one of the only ways available in male-dominated societies. The use of religion as a means of social enhancement for women is not new: Dona Beatrice, alleged incarnation of Saint Anthony, was burnt to death at Mbanza Congo (present-day Angola) as a heretic at the beginning of the eighteenth century by the Portuguese. Her crime was to preach an Africanized Christianity, which later led to her being proclaimed a national heroine during the anti-colonial war (Parpart 1988).

There is no doubt that social change plays a very significant role in the formation of new religious movements. With the decline in the ability of the post-colonial African state to provide adequate social services, religious movements offer both spiritual and material benefits (such as health-care delivery systems and employment opportunities), which it is obviously quite rational for followers to seek. It is wrong to assume that only poor, disorientated, former peasants join the syncretistic spiritualist churches (Lanternari 1985). Rather, they attract followers from all walks of society, including the middle classes and the politico-economic elite, although it may be necessary for the latter to be secret members (Mbon 1987).

In common with other popular religious groups, as we saw in Chapter 5, new religious movements may fulfil a role as a vehicle of ethnic solidarity. For example, Simon Kimbangu's messianic church in Zaire in the 1930s was particularly attractive to his fellow Bakongo; later it developed political links with the ABAKO party. The breakaway Roman Catholic sect Maria Legio found most of its devotees amongst the Luo after Kenya's independence; while among the Chunya of Tanzania, the Religion of Jehovah and Michael (characterized as 'a Protestant response to TANU "Catholicism'"), evolved after independence as a response to the authoritarianism of local TANU (Tanganyikan African National Union) party officials (Welbourne 1968: 133). Additionally, the Lumpa Church of northern Zambia, the Holy Spirit Church among the Acholi in northern Uganda, the followers of Manuel Antonio in north-east Mozambique, the Ovimbundu Church of Christ in the Bush in southern Angola, Dini ya Msambwa among the Bukusu of western Kenya led by Elijah Masinde, and the Jehovah's Witnesses in Malawi were all focused on certain ethnic groups, though not always exclusively. In short, there are often connections between African new religious movements and specific ethnic communities.

It is sometimes argued, on the other hand, that Catholics have less propensity to break away from the established church than Protestants, because of the 'protesting' nature of the latter; yet this is in fact an almost wholly spurious claim, reflecting unsupported ethnocentric certainties (Welbourne 1968: 137–8). Africans generally do not recognize the finer points concerning the doctrinal divisions which separate the Protestant and Catholic churches. There is little difference between the two broad sets of religious belief in most Africans' eyes: both denominations were brought to Africa by European colonists, both are often felt to be Eurocentric, and both worship the same God. Even when supposedly ideologically radical regimes take power, such as that in, until recently, 'Marxist' Congo, where Catholicism is common, leaders are pragmatic enough to work out a *modus vivendi* with local sects and decidedly non-Marxist traditional healers (Gruénais and Mayala 1988).

Some African new religious movements have derived from predominantly Catholic constituencies. For example, Le Mouvement Croix-Koma (literally, the Nailed to the Cross Movement) was founded in 1964 in the Congo by a Roman Catholic layman, Ta Malanda. Croix-Koma is thought to have attracted, at one time or another, some 400,000 Congolese (20 per cent of the population) to its main pilgrimage site at Kankata. Its chief aim was to get Congolese to renounce their fetishes, and more generally to function as an anti-witchcraft movement, ostensibly *within* the Catholic Church yet clearly not straightforwardly *of* it. It is not without coincidence that there was a diminution (although not eradication) in the social standing of traditional religious figures, and a corresponding rise in the position of Croix-Koma. Since the death of Ta Malanda in 1971, and following the creation of a 'Marxist' regime in the Congo in 1970, the price of (often at best tacit) support for the regime from the Catholic hierarchy was the excision of Ta Malanda's sect from the body of the church. This reflected both the Vatican's desire to keep deep Africanization at bay, and its fear at the spectre of Catholic-oriented independents. Apart from Croix-Koma, other breakaway Catholic-oriented new movements include: Maria Legio of Kenya; the Church of the Sacred Heart in Zambia; the Jamaa sect in Zaire; and Simao Toko's Church of Our Lord Jesus Christ on Earth in Angola, as well as numerous others in Central Africa (Dirven 1970; Hastings 1979: 116–18; *Marchés Tropicaux* 1987). This section has suggested that African Christian new religious movements have emerged during the twentieth century in response to the stresses and strains of modernization, exacerbated initially by colonialism and then by independence. Politicization of the movements has been partial and intermittent; they are not political vehicles masquerading as religious bodies.

Christian New Religious Movements and Political Activism

Neither the Catholic- nor the Protestant-derived new religious movements have a clear-cut political role. During the colonial era, as previously mentioned, the breakaway Christian churches were deemed to be substitutes for political parties. It was argued that whether a given church was or was not politically acquiescent was related to the nature of colonialism in a particular colony. If colonialism resulted in wide-spread land acquisition by Europeans, then breakaway churches, it was argued, were politically active and radical. If, on the other hand, colonialism was not associated with land expropriation, then break-aways were politically acquiescent, and regarded Western civilization as a role model (Lanternari 1985). Examples of the former were the Aladura and Harrist churches of West Africa; and of the latter, South Africa's Zionist churches. The Aladura churches generally, and the Church of the Cherubim and the Seraphim in particular, Lanternari argues, were 'in no way concerned with social and political affairs' (ibid.: 138–9). In South Africa, on the other hand, it has been asserted that the indigenous churches 'have a more radical doctrine, ideology and cultural bias' than those of West Africa, and that 'the relationship with missions being similar or equal, clear patterns of difference between emancipationist [for example, Isaiah Shembe's Nazareth Church] and integrative [for example, Aladura, Harrist] churches are to be related to the nature of cultural and socio-economic relations between native society and colonizers' (ibid.: 140–42).

The problem with the claimed polarization between 'integrative' and 'emancipationist' churches is obvious: South African independent churches are usually just as politically acquiescent as those of West Africa. Shembe, leader of the Nazareth Church, actually 'opposed any form of anti-white or anti-governmental activity' (Ray 1976: 201). Moreover, many of South Africa's Zionist churches – including the biggest, the 2-million-strong Zion Christian Church – have been criticized for their political acquiescence to the status quo, even to the point of tolerating, apparently comfortably, apartheid. The point is that the leaders of these churches – Harrist, Aladura or Zionist – usually fit neatly into the same role as that identified earlier in the case of the chief officers of mainstream Islamic and Christian organizations in Africa: they are part of the status quo, benefiting from political and social stability. Because they are members of the socio-economic elite, the position of their religious organization as either 'independent' or 'establishment' is entirely irrelevant for an appreciation of their political role.

A second argument concerning South Africa's independent churches is that they attract those for whom the experience of colonialism has been a time of 'cultural upheaval and social destruction'. Such churches form counter-societies, a haven for those seeking a refuge from a 'hostile environment'. Political parties, on the other hand, attract those who are reacting to 'political and economic oppression' and seek to capture political power (Buijtenhuis 1985: 323). This is a satisfyingly clear-cut argument, which apparently accounts for those who choose one of two distinctive options: church or politics. The problem with it though is, first, that it is not possible to tell where 'political and economic oppression' ends and 'cultural upheaval and social destruction' begin, and, second, that we now know that very few, if any, of Africa's mass parties, were actually popularly based. The 'counter-society versus political activism' argument demonstrates some of the difficulties of attempting to dichotomize between religious movements whose real differences may be much smaller than those 'discovered' by Western analysts. Much is often made of the claimed distinction between Ethiopian and Zionist churches, which centres on their different relationships with nationalist parties, post-colonial governments and political movements. Ethiopian churches are aggressive and contentious, with a tendency to enter into conflict with representatives of the established order; they are religious counterparts of secular nationalist movements. Both, it is argued, have as a primary aim the ousting of establishment authorities (whether religious or political) in order to assume power themselves (Buijtenhuis 1985: 336–7). Zionist churches, on the other hand, are 'escapist' or 'retreatist' counter-societies, cut off from global society (which only the most ambitious seek to alter through the influence of their example); they have neither political strategy nor analysis. As a result, 'they do not correctly perceive the real mechanisms of colonial domination or political exploitation in general' (ibid.: 338).

Zionist churches in South Africa are well known for their co-operation or collaboration with the former apartheid authorities. In 1985, the largest of South Africa's independent churches, the Zion Christian Church (ZCC), invited the then state president, P.W. Botha, to address 2 million followers at the annual Easter gathering at Mount Moria in the Transvaal (Tingle 1992: 95). Even though most of the country's independent churches are recognized as politically 'moderate' or 'conservative', Botha's invitation reflected the affinity that existed between 'Christian' institutions. South Africa's apartheid government portrayed itself as a Christian regime, while its main political foe, the African National Congress (ANC), was stigmatized for its extremist, 'communist' stance. It may or may not be of relevance that the ZCC leader lives in a luxury house in Zion City behind 'gold gates', and enjoys massive personal wealth (Channel 4: 1993). He would, perhaps, be anxious to maintain the status quo for personal reasons as much as for the corporate good of his church.

As the anti-apartheid struggle gained pace in the mid-1980s, leaders of the Zionist churches proclaimed that 'members were free to join political parties, and that it was not the task of the Church to engage in politics' (Schoffeleers 1991: 9). This announcement was significant for two reasons: first, it indicated that Zion church followers were at least tacitly encouraged to enter politics as individuals; second, it suggested that church leaders had political opinions which needed a secular institutional vehicle for their expression, rather than the church itself. It soon became clear just what the trigger was for certain Zionist leaders' political involvement: the issue was the ANC's 'communism'. As Tingle notes: 'In 1991 there were rumours that one of the Zionist leaders might set up his own political party which would be prepared to enter into a "Christian Democratic Alliance" with other moderate [sic] parties' (Tingle 1992: 96). As with fundamentalist Christians in Nigeria, fighting what they saw as creeping Islamization (see Chapter 7), it was the fear of an unwelcome take-over of power by ideological foes which impelled hitherto non-political Christian leaders towards political activism.

It seems clear that leaders of churches such as the ZCC have as much to lose from an overturning of the status quo as the white political elite. People join urban-based 'healing' churches such as the ZCC for four main reasons: to get closer to God; to deal with their medical ailments in the absence of affordable scientific health care; for community feeling; and for the enhanced job chances which may result. ZCC converts must wear their uniforms, which are available exclusively from church headquarters in Zion City. To wear the uniform is to advertise oneself as a virtuous, trustworthy, Christian person; it greatly enhances job prospects in an economy in which there is a chronic shortage of employment opportunities (Channel 4 1993).

What spiritualist and other independent churches have in common is their important role in healing. Health has, of course, always been the central focus of the independent churches, indeed their major attraction. As Sundkler (1961: 220) notes: 'what sacraments are for Catholics and the word for Protestants, healing is for Zionists.' The healing churches are completely non-revolutionary, inasmuch as it is not so much the political structure which is considered to cause 'a person's sufferings but that person's own failings or the failings of some personalised agency' (Schoffeleers 1991: 15). Illness is seen in terms of social deviancy; the patient is under scrutiny, if not suspicion, and healing involves a process of resocialization. Generally in Africa healing practices restore personal order to a sufferer, which in turn is significant for the continuation of societal stability.

The more society breaks down, the more new religious movements flourish. In civil-war-ravaged Liberia, for example, independent churches provided an alternative community for those cut off from family links and surrounded by signs of social breakdown, such as 'sickness, crime, alcoholism, violence, prostitution, drug addiction' and poverty. The churches also function in Liberia, and more generally, as entrepreneurial vehicles for leaders. Those with leadership qualities found churches as a means to make an income and gain social status in the absence of alternatives. To head an independent church offers a rare opportunity to develop leadership and organizational skills. Whereas the mission churches required priests to undergo years of training, the independent churches offered social status and an (often substantial) income sometimes without any instruction (Gifford 1993: 289).

The example of South Africa – with 6 million followers belonging to over three thousand independent churches – suggests that the growth of such churches is not necessarily a sign that followers wish to withdraw from the state's jurisdiction. It is, rather, an alternative means of re-creating community solidarity in urban areas where people come together from a number of diverse backgrounds and find their traditional social networks either destroyed or seriously curtailed. Most independent churches sit quite comfortably with the status quo, with leaders happy to find a source of monetary income and social status, and followers benefiting from both spiritual and material opportunities. In other words, they rarely, explicitly 'subvert the space of the State' (Bayart 1993a: 256–7). At the same time, it is argued, the churches hardly sit comfortably with the authorities: for they are loath to pay taxes or parrot the official ideology relating to development and national unity. Moreover, because they provide material services to their clients, they may undermine the statist system by creating their own solidarity and material networks. According to Bayart, 'rivalry [between new religious movements and the state] is all the more formidable because it makes conflict inevitable' (ibid.: 257). While the idea of political conflict between new religious movement and state may be attractive to those who wish to see in the former at least a latent political radicalism, in reality very few new movements aggressively seek the withdrawal option or confront the state. The state is actually quite happy for the movements to offer services which it cannot supply, as this will help to soak up discontent and allow the political elites to concentrate on the accumulation of personal wealth.

Leaders of new religious movements in Africa, like practically every other organization, religious and secular, quickly realized the necessity of cultivating close links with political leaders in the post-colonial era; *mange d'abord* (eat first) propelled them into the hurly-burly of political competition. For example, independent churches in Ghana are usually patronized by low-income groups, uprooted urban dwellers, especially women; most churches offer healing and exorcism as material services, and many leaders enjoy close personal relations with political bigmen (Pobee 1992: 76–7). The Musama Disco Christo Church of Jehu Appiah, for instance, was very close to Kwame Nkrumah, leader of Ghana between 1957 and 1966; followers apparently 'deluged' Appiah with requests as to how they should vote in elections. They wanted to know whether Nkrumah was the envisaged prophet (Baeta 1962: 62). The Church of Africa was also close to senior figures in Nkrumah's Convention People's Party (CPP) government. The F'Eden Church, for its part, taught the virtue of obedience to those in both secular and religious authority, counting among its followers Mrs Regina Asomaning, MP for Akim Oda; Mr Inkumsah, minister of state; and Kobina Owusu, director of State Distilleries (a political appointment). The church's leader, Reverend Brother Yeboa-Korie, was asked by Nkrumah in 1965 to seek election as a CPP member of parliament. This led to the former falling out with anti-Nkrumah CPP factions and, as a result, being attacked in the quasi-party paper, the *Evening News*. Despite this, Yeboa-Korie showed himself to be a skilful political operator: following Nkrumah's downfall, he remained in favour with Prime Minister Busia (1969–72), and then with the military dictator General Acheampong (1972–78) (Pobee 1992: 83). Although independent church leaders often have a high social and political standing, educated and wealthy Africans often profess to regard such churches as not quite respectable. Bigmen often attend services in secret. Membership of mainstream churches is regarded as a mark of civilization and respectability; for healing and exorcism, the spiritual churches tended to be consulted by the 'great and the good'.

Spiritual and other independent churches in Ghana do not necessarily seek a role in institutional politics, but are nevertheless political players at the personal level and within the elite network. Nigeria has literally thousands of new religious movements; as was the case with foreign-influenced 'fundamentalist' churches, to be examined in Chapter 7, they grew in the post-independence era in response to crisis, whether individual (sickness, bereavement, financial hardship) or community (economic regression, social upheaval as a result of the civil war and urbanization) (Hackett 1987: 237). Generally speaking, Nigerians – whether Christian, Muslim or pagan – perceive their personal problems, as well as those of their society, in terms of religious explanations, and seek redemption, through religious fervour, as a palliative and counteraction to disorder. People freely move from one religious faith to another (for example, from mainstream to spiritualist church and back) in search of satisfaction. Religious organizations have a multiple impact upon people's lives, whether by dealing with illness through prayer, helping people to find employment, or providing help to those accused of witchcraft (Hackett 1987: 239–40).

One of the biggest of Africa's independent churches is the Aladura (Yoruba, 'owners of prayer') movement. The Aladura churches are syncretic churches which combine elements of traditional belief with conventional Christian dogma. They date from the end of World War I in Nigeria (Peel 1968). Expansion of the Aladura was facilitated by Joseph Babalola's healing movement in the 1930s, the growth of which was itself a product of the economic uncertainty and social dislocation occasioned by economic depression. Aladura gained in respectability and size following Nigeria's independence in 1960. 'Aladura' is a generic term for a number of churches, including the Celestial Church of Christ, the Brotherhood of the Cross and Star, and the multitudinous Cherubim and Seraphim societies; the latter has branches in West Africa, Europe and the United States. Membership of the Brotherhood of the Cross and Star alone was estimated at 600,000 in the 1980s, with followers organized in 2,000 branches worldwide. In total, the Aladura movement now has more than 1 million members. The Church of the Lord (Aladura) is affiliated to the World Council of Churches. Links with Western pentecostal churches are common. Aladura churches generally steer clear of institutional political activities and involvement (Lanternari 1985: 138–9; Hackett 1987: 239).

Reflecting its Yoruba origins, until recently most recruits to Aladura were drawn from former mission churches in the south of the country. The growth of the Aladura churches was, in effect, a reaction: a spiritual renaissance in the face of 'cold' Western-style, mission-oriented religion. Converts were attracted by the less elitist nature of Aladura, which offered scope for the religious and social advancement of members, especially women. Claimed benefits of Aladura membership include: recovery from apparently incurable ailments; deliverance from fatal accidents by way of some *deus ex machina*; victory in court cases; fertility of women and potency of men; 'a sense of security, of belonging, and of being loved and appreciated as persons in the movements'; success in business undertakings; promotion at work; finding a job; gaining entrance to university, and so on (Mbon 1987: 213–14). Individual success is attributed to the spiritual power of the founder or leader of the movement and to the convert's own intensity of faith.

In recent times, Nigerians at all social levels have joined Aladura churches. Senior figures, such as state governors, university professors and top civil servants have sometimes become Aladura converts secretly, even though such people have nearly always been baptized as Christians in mainstream churches and may still attend their services (Mbon 1987: 214). The point is that membership of the Aladura churches is held to be a boon for those seeking spiritual and material advance. If the churches themselves are not active as institutional political players, this is hardly surprising given that Nigeria has been under military rule for all but ten years of its thirty-five-year existence. Moreover, in Africa it is relatively uncommon to try to achieve political goals openly and above board; much more may be accomplished by behind-the-scenes persuasion, arm-twisting and negotiation. Yet, when there is a trigger issue – communism, Islamic resurgence, institutional corruption – then religious actors may take overt political action. In this respect, then, Aladura churches, like other religious institutions in Africa – whether in South Africa, Ghana, or elsewhere – aim to achieve political goals without overt political involvement whenever possible, but will use other means as and when necessary.

Rural Christian New Religious Movements and Politics

I want to turn the spotlight next on rural Christian new religious movements in order to underline how widespread such religious organizations are in Africa. Unlike some of their urban counterparts, the rural organizations do not seek to gain the ear of important political figures in order to achieve group benefits. Rural Christian movements tend to be more insular, concerned primarily with community solidarity, the aim of which is to keep powerful outside forces – perhaps the state, perhaps anti-state guerrillas – at bay by invoking religious symbols, while persuading potential followers of the collective benefits of membership. Such groups have flourished during both the colonial and post-colonial eras in many parts of Africa.

During the colonial era it was in the rural areas that anti-colonial religious movements flourished. Numerous accounts relate their rise to dissatisfaction with aspects of colonial rule (see, for example, Ranger 1986; Fields 1985). In *Revolt in Southern Rhodesia*, Ranger (1967) illustrates how erstwhile foes – the Shona and the Ndebele – combined to resist British hegemony in the late nineteenth century. Spirit mediums used medicines to enhance warriors' martial efforts. They created a national network of shrines to provide an agency for the transmission and coordination of information and activities, a structure which was reestablished during the independence war of the 1970s (Fields 1985: 260–61; Ranger 1985; Lan 1985). The use of medicine also helped galvanize the anti-colonial Maji-Maji rebellion of 1905–07 in German-controlled Tanganyika. Then, the diviner and prophet Kinjikitili gave his followers medicine which was supposed to render them invulnerable to bullets. He anointed local leaders with the *maji* (water), which helped to create solidarity amongst some twenty different ethnic groups and encouraged them to fight together in a common anti-European cause (Ranger 1986). In northern Uganda, the cult of Yakan, which also centred on the use of magic medicine, galvanized the Lugbara in their short war against Europeans in 1919 (Allen 1991: 379–80). Other instances of such religio-political movements could be enumerated. The point, however, should be clear: many cults arose, led by prophets, stimulated by colonialism and emergent social change. They employed local religious beliefs as a basis for anti-European protest and opposition.

After colonialism, similar cults continued to appear: clearly their existence could not be explained solely by the stresses and strains occasioned by colonial rule. For example, the beliefs associated with the followers of Alice Lenshina and Joseph Kony in Zambia in the 1950s and 1960s, and the violence these beliefs engendered, should be located within the general context of upheaval that resulted from the ending of colonial rule (Allen 1991: 379). They can be explained as a response to extreme social trauma, a manifestation of collective despair at an unwelcome political outcome. Lenshina's sect was established amongst the northern Bemba people, and in many respects was an ethnic vehicle of opposition to rule by the southern-dominated United National Independence Party government. Other instances of collective opposition in the post-colonial era also possessed an ethnic or regional dimension – for example, in northern Uganda and northern Mozambique.

In north-eastern Mozambique, a 25,000-strong pro-government militia, known as napramas (spirit warriors), was formed in 1990 among the Makua people of the Zambesia and Nampula provinces. It was led by Manuel Antonio until his death in 1992. Antonio was a young man who claimed to have died at the age of twelve and been resurrected in order to end the civil war between Renamo rebels and the Frelimo government. Antonio 'vaccinated' his followers against Renamo bullets with the ash of a sacred bush, which led them to often foolhardy feats of courage in the face of Renamo firepower. Many Renamo soldiers came from the Ndau-speaking people of central Mozambique. They counted upon the support of local Ndau chiefs and of the spirit mediums who provided the blessing of the ancestors. Initially, Renamo soldiers ran from the practically unarmed napramas, before later rallying. The slaying of Antonio by Renamo troops led to the collapse of the napramas movement (Wang 1992). The Frelimo government was forced to recognize the political power of traditional culture as a result of the napramas' short-lived opposition to Renamo. Having done much to destroy rural organizational structures in an attempt to impose party rule in the country, it was somewhat ironic that Frelimo claimed to welcome Antonio's 'spirit warriors' as manifesting 'a return to traditional sources of peasant strength, abandoned in the rush to modernisation' (Brittain 1991). What the example of Antonio and, before him, Lenshina and Kony suggest, is that in rural areas of Africa threatened by crisis and profound social instability, provided there is a sufficient degree of communal solidarity, prophet-led resistance, whether to colonial or post-colonial state or rebel attack, will succeed in organizing communities in self-defence. They will use a combination of premodern and European-introduced beliefs to oppose aggressors. In each of these examples, oppressed and defeated peoples turned to the metaphysical in pursuit of their cause against technically superior military forces, believing themselves immune from harm during combat.

A further example of a syncretistic politico-religious movement which opposed outside control was the Holy Spirit movement in Uganda, led by Alice Lakwena. While strongest among the Acholi, its appeal also spanned the Lango, and Teso people (Behrend 1991; Omara-Otunnu 1992). In the mid-1980s, troops led by Lakwena and purportedly protected by magic medicine, engaged the dominant National Resistance Army (NRA) in Uganda in a series of battles. Many of Lakwena's followers were former Acholi soldiers of Milton Obote's Uganda National Liberation Army. In a bid to gain the upper hand against the rampant NRA, the defeated rebels desperately sought a religious messiah who could dispense magic medicine to aid soldiers in their battles. Mamdani (1988: 1170–71) argues that what distinguished Lakwena's Holy Spirit movement from other rebel groups in Uganda during the 1980s was that its leadership came not from the middle class but from within peasant society. According to him, Lakwena's organizational successes amongst the Acholi and other people resulted from the local peasantry's loss of confidence in traditional leaders and from the inability of Yoweri Museveni's National Resistance Movement government to arrive at a viable political programme in the area. To view Lakwena's revolt as simply a manifestation of class-consciousness is to miss the point that rural people gain solidarity and effectiveness from the use of community-strengthening beliefs against outside attack. In addition, it is stretching a point to call former soldiers 'peasants'. There was also a strong element of ethno-regional solidarity in the fact of the Acholi and geographically related northern peoples being organized by Lakwena against southern attack. Once again, the strongest explanation is that Lakwena's movement represented a social response to serious upheaval and external attack in a situation where the state was unable to establish an effective administrative structure.

Mamdani's resort to a class-based argument is an example of the way religion is often perceived by neo-Marxists and others as little more than 'false consciousness'. It is not conceptually persuasive, however, to regard religion in African rural societies merely as something which serves only to obscure the 'real' issue, that of class. Many Africans find in religion a means of altering their situation and even of 'reversing their status in both symbolic and social terms' (Ranger 1986: 9). What our examples of rural new religious movements have in common is that all play the role of mediator during conditions of rapid and uneven transformation. During the colonial period, religio-political movements were regarded with a high degree of suspicion by colonial administrators: some viewed them as allies of Islam; others saw them as organizations bent on agitation, fuelled by German money; still others saw them as African revolutionaries hiding behind religious camouflage. In the post-colonial period, official comprehension of the movements did not advance much. A senior figure in the National Resistance Movement government, for example, referred to Alice Lakwena in 1991 as that 'lunatic prostitute of Gulu town turned witch' (Behrend 1991: 162). Head of state Yoweri Museveni, for his part, called the rebels 'culturally backward' and welcomed the clash between the Holy Spirit warriors and the NRA as a necessary development to ensure the dominance of the forces of patriotism and modernization over the 'remnants of colonialism and backwardness' (Omara-Otunnu 1992: 457).

What seems clear is that rural Christian new religious movements cannot be viewed as merely a reaction either to colonialism or to discrete post-colonial political developments. Indeed, many such movements have been concerned with cultural, regional, ethnic, political and economic tensions which existed before colonialism (and which the latter helped to politicize), and which resurfaced in the post-colonial epoch when one group sought to achieve hegemony over others. People who resort to religious symbolism as political ideology are generally those who have not only been mistreated or abandoned by government but also traditionally marginalized by both colonial and post-colonial political and economic structures and processes. Although these movements have mostly arisen in response to the post-colonial state, their opposition is culturally based, with clear historical roots, and has been a potential threat to incumbent regimes. In Kenya during most of the post-colonial period, government was usually more preoccupied with monitoring the main church bodies than with small sects and the growing number of breakaway churches. It regarded the latter's schisms as instrumental in helping to perpetuate the political system – part of the divide-and-rule strategy (Africa Watch 1991: 227; *Africa Confidential* 1992). During the pro-democracy agitation of the early 1990s, Kenya's government began to regard ethno-religions with intense suspicion. Whether it was the Digo people seeking self-improvement through Islam, or the Kikuyu striving to express ethnic solidarity through a revival of their traditional religious beliefs, the government sought to curtail them. A Kikuyu church, the Tent of the Living God, which melded traditional practices with Christian belief, was banned in

February 1990 and its leader, Ngaruro, arrested. The government justified the church's closure on the grounds that it was allegedly being used by Kikuyu opposition politicians as a front for their illegal (because based on 'tribalism') opposition campaign (Africa Watch 1991: 227).

New Islamic Movements

So far the discussion in this chapter has been concerned with Christian new religious movements. It would be wrong to assume this is because there are no religious groups which might be described as Islamic new religious movements. In fact, there are a number of such movements which have grown from Muslim roots.

Two of particular note will be examined in the next section: the radical, anti-establishment Maitatsine movement of Kano, northern Nigeria, active from the late 1970s; and the revisionist Ahmadiyya movement, active throughout much of Africa as well as elsewhere in the Muslim world, the main purpose of which has been to develop a network of fellow religionists for both spiritual and commercial reasons.

While the Muslim faith ostensibly allows no reinterpretations of the fundamental tenets of belief, especially the precepts that Muhammad was the prophet of God and that there is but one God, in reality many Muslims worldwide interpret Islam through a prism of traditional belief. At the same time, however, with the exception of Shiism, very few breakaway groups have challenged the authority of the Arab-derived Sunni interpretation of Islam. The Sunni–Shia division is, of course, both religious and political; yet each interpretation regards the message of Islam somewhat differently. In Africa, the schism between Shia and Sunni is not of religious or political significance, because virtually all African Muslims are Sunnis. On the other hand, African Islam is always more or less syncretistic. The Bori cult amongst the Hausa, for example, worship some two hundred different spirits, each of which is held to be connected with a different ailment. The cult is predominantly a women's organization, giving followers enhanced status within their male-dominated societies. The Mossi, for their part, believe that conversion to Islam will end barrenness amongst pagan women; while the Giriama of Kenya often convert to Islam because of the protection from illness it is said to offer (Lewis 1986: 97–8). The partially Islamized Berti of northern Dar Fur (Sudan) have Islamic leaders who write verses from the Quran on slates; the slates are then washed off and the resulting mixture drunk by clients, with apparently efficacious results (Stewart 1985: 365). Lewis notes the 'symbiotic relationships that appear to function between cults often labelled "pre-Islamic" and mainstream Islamic practice.' What he is pointing out is that between traditional and modern religious beliefs there is always 'a continuous process of reactive counter-diffusion in which, as the spirit of Islam flows in one direction, other spirits return the compliment' (Lewis 1986: 105).

Islamic revivalist movements have always sought to revitalize and renew their faith through the application of fundamentalist doctrines; by drawing on local initiative, needs, forms and symbols; and by the importing of exogenous religious ideas and structures. Young people may be particularly attracted to the revivalists because of their fervour and commitment to a radical vision of Islam. Those possessing charismatic gifts and spiritual powers may face a problem within mainstream Islam as there is no acceptable way for them to proclaim their special prophetic powers without appearing apostatical; they are therefore drawn to the new movements. More generally, the nature of the economic and social upheaval in recent times in Africa seems highly likely to generate a strong sense of dissatisfaction with the status quo, which religious leaders may exploit for their own spiritual and probably commercial advantage. One of the most notorious instances of the latter in recent times was the Cameroonian Muhammadu Marwa, known as the Maitatsine, who was active in Kano, Nigeria in the late 1970s and early 1980s.

The Maitatsine movement in Nigeria

The unorthodox religious character of the Maitatsine movement – led by a man who claimed to be a new prophet of Islam – was grounded in a social and political radicalism which rejected authority, whether of mainstream Islamic preachers, politicians or the Kano State government, and counted upon the support of the urban poor of northern Nigeria (Kastfelt 1989: 84). About five thousand people died in December 1980 during eleven days of rioting in Kano involving Marwa's supporters. Further outbreaks of Maitatsine-inspired violence subsequently broke out in 1982 in Bulunkutu in Borno State, and in 1984–85 in various parts of Bauchi State, Gongola State, and Kaduna City. Whereas some interpretations see Marwa as the leader of a popular, millennialist Islamic ideology, others focus upon the micro- and macroeconomic factors which are said to have precipitated the birth of his movement (Clarke 1988; Lubeck 1985). Lubeck (1985) notes, for example, an intensifying division between the mass of under-employed, poverty-stricken Quranic students in Kano and those who had personally benefited materially from the city's sudden economic transformation as a result of the country's oil boom. Maitatsine's followers were, according to Lubeck, a 'lumpenproletariat': products of an Islamic education system which appeared to be increasingly anachronistic in the context of Kano's rapid modernization. They had contempt for the materialism of Kano's new middle classes and demonstrated their class antagonism by taking to the streets to destroy the symbols of ungodliness – shops, banks and Christian churches – and to attack ordinary Muslims.

Initially, the movement was relatively introverted, aiming only to advance Maitatsine's claims to prophethood. The turn of the Muslim millennium in A.H. 1400 (1979) coincided with the rise to power of Ayatollah Khomeini and the establishment of his theocratic government, and appeared to offer Marwa an exemplar. As was the case in Algeria and Egypt, the radical attack on the status quo by Maitatsine was in part a function of the lack of employment opportunities for local youths. In Egypt, there are more than 3 million unemployed graduates of universities and high schools; they are the main source of recruits for radical Islamist movements, such as Gama'at al-Islamiya. As in Nigeria, the effects of an International Monetary Fund sponsored economic restructuring programme, involving the planned large-scale privatization of state industries, would throw hundreds of thousands more out of work. People's hardships are more difficult to bear because of the obvious corruption of the government, the bureaucracy and the military elite, and the ostentatious wealth of the *arriviste* middle classes. Together they are increasingly coming to represent a repugnant mixture of old-and new-rich. In Egypt, Gama'at is popular because it targets such people for attack. Maitatsine, on the other hand, reviled ordinary, lower class, Muslims; this casts doubt on the 'class' explanation offered by Lubeck. The Maitatsine movement was actually reminiscent of a strain of millenarianism, exemplified by the attempt of a Nejdi-led band of armed and highly trained men to seize the Grand Mosque in Mecca in 1979 in order to proclaim the advent of a new Messiah (Dorr 1993).

Marwa was by no means a conventional follower of Islam: he had an allegedly 'excessive belief in fetishism'; the Imam of Marwa declared him an infidel; and his wife thought he was a magician (Birai 1993: 197). While his sect exhibited aspects of millenarian radicalism, using Islam as a tool of socio-political protest, it was not generally regarded by local people as part of the Muslim community, because of its members' beliefs and its leader's claims to prophethood. Riots in late 1982 in Bauchi, during which more than 450 people were reportedly killed, were sparked off 'by followers of Maitatsine preaching publicly in Buluntuku (near Maiduguri, Borno State), urging people to refrain even from mentioning the name of Muhammad whom they called "an Arab"' (Clarke 1987: 94).

The interesting aspect of the Marwa phenomenon is not so much its radicalism, which is quite common historically in northern Nigeria, or its only partial location within the accepted corpus of Islam. Rather, it is the highly ambivalent position which Marwa – probably an apostate – enjoyed amongst many prominent figures in Nigeria. Such people purchased from him charms and other concrete signs of spiritual power to help advance their careers and personal lives, and to avoid such misfortunes as illness, road accidents and early death. The result was that Marwa became renowned as an important dispenser of protection, enjoying the company of significant politicians, business people and senior state bureaucrats, and as a result believed that he had immunity from authority's challenge. He believed that people in high places would intervene if there was a significant risk that he or his followers would be apprehended. In the words of the official report published after his death at the hands of the state: 'The material concerns of the elites who sought spiritual assistance from him helped Marwa to flourish ('Official Report on the Maitatsine Riots', quoted in Clarke: 1987 109–10).

There is, of course, nothing unusual in the African context in individuals, preoccupied with personal and business problems, resorting to holy men of the different religious traditions for advice and aid. For example, Tuareg visitors to Nigeria's northern states sell amulets and potions on the basis of the supposed mystical powers conferred by the Tuaregs' nomadic and desert existence. Another case is that of the Muslim businessmen who pay Muslim clerics to pray for them five times a day because they are too busy to do it themselves. Muslim spiritual advisers, the marabouts, may be descendants of holy men, intellectuals, or – like Marwa – neither academic nor even literate. One of the most politically significant instances was that of Oumaruo Amadou 'Bonkano', close adviser to the late president of Niger, Seyni Kountché. He was so influential that Kountché appointed him head of the security service. After Bonkano fell out of favour in 1983, Kountché's subsequent illness and death was blamed by many on his curse (Diallo 1988). The former leader of Benin, Mathieu Kérékou, also had a Malian marabout, Mamadou Cissé – 'Djiné', the Devil – who was also in charge of security. He held this job because it was thought he could see into the future to identify plotters and other enemies. Before Kérékou, Djiné was employed by President Mobutu. A third Malian, M'Baba Cissoko, held a position of power in the household of Gabon's president, Omar Bongo (*Africa Confidential* 1987b).

What this demonstrates is that the conjunction of political and spiritual power are commonplace in Muslim and Muslim-influenced Africa. The link between Maitatsine and sections of the economic and political elite led many people to assume that the authorities did nothing to suppress the Maitatsine movement, either because they were afraid of Muhammadu Marwa's spiritual powers or, more prosaically, because they had been bought off by him. Such views indicate a 'deep distrust of the authorities and simultaneously and implicitly formulate a specific view of the nature of political power' in Africa (Kastfelt 1989: 88). Whatever else it was, the Maitatsine movement was not a clear-cut manifestation of Islamic fundamentalism: after all, Marwa proclaimed himself a prophet and denigrated Muhammad, and attacked ordinary Muslims as well as Christians; indeed, some accounts claim that his followers at Yan Awaki in Kano City slaughtered people 'by the neck as if they were rams or goats' (Birai 1993: 198). Another interpretation of the Maitatsine movement maintains that it represented primarily a political attack upon the entrenched Muslim elite in northern Nigeria. Such religious 'new men' as Maitatsine in regions of entrenched Islam are fundamentally out of sympathy with the Islam mediated by the traditional clerics, whether of the reformist or maraboutic type. As the limited popular support for Muhammadu Marwa indicated, however, such a reaction affects only a small number, often the Islamically educated yet jobless, without convincing ordinary people more widely of the movement's virtues.

In areas where Islam itself is a relatively new religion – that is, in those areas of Africa to which it has spread over the last hundred years – its cultural impact has been modified by the countervailing attractions of Western modernization. To neophytes, Islam is seen not as a religious culture, as in northern Nigeria, but rather as a rationalistic religion in the Western sense. In this perception, religion is but one, albeit significant, part of an individual's set of beliefs in which all spheres of life are autonomous. In the past, one could not 'adopt' Islam in areas where it was not traditionally part of the socio-cultural make-up, because it could not be separated from other aspects of culture. People affected by both Islam and Westernism, like the Yoruba, absorbed elements from both simultaneously; some became Muslims, some mainstream Christians, others followers of Aladura or of born-again American-style fundamentalist churches. The point is that religious fanaticism was stymied, with individuals following the religion of their choice rather than of cultural necessity; this allowed them to transfer from faith to faith as they deemed it necessary.

The Ahmadiyya sect

The Ahmadiyya sect is the most recently evolved Muslim faction. It was founded by Mirza Ghulam Ahmad (1835–1908), who was born at Qadian in the (then) Indian Punjab. His followers claim that he was the Mahdi; his denigrators that he was nothing but a false prophet whose claims thrust him beyond the religious pale. Ahmadis do not consider themselves a sect, but rather followers of a contemporary interpretation of Sunni Islam, as pronounced by their founder. Some Ahmadis claim that Ahmad was a true prophet: that Muhammad was the giver of perfect law, but that Ahmad was the greatest interpreter of the law. Most mainstream Muslims consider the followers of Ahmadiyya heretics. Ahmadiyya in Pakistan, the birthplace of the group, has an especially large following, with devotees often enjoying solid political and economic positions. Despite (or perhaps because of) this, anti-Ahmadiyya riots were a frequent occurrence in (West) Pakistan between the early 1950s and mid-1970s. The cause was ostensibly religious, but was also rooted in the fact that Ahmadis tended to enjoy disproportionately greater economic and social prominence than many non-Ahmadi Pakistanis. As a result of the riots, the National Assembly of Pakistan amended the constitution in 1974 to provide that, for purposes of law, Ahmadis are not Muslim. This official sign of displeasure did not, however, alter the ability of Ahmadiyya to gain recruits (Weekes 1978).

Ahmadiyya is often regarded with ambivalence by Muslims because of the seeming contradictions in its beliefs: some see it as nothing more than a heretical, non-Muslim sect, while others regard it as a modernist movement within Islam, the followers of which frequently achieve high social status. The movement's leaders are educated and enterprising; its followers seek modern, secular education, while piously accepting the basic duties of Islam. It is active throughout the world, and, rather like the American-style born-again churches with their particular interpretation of Christianity, is especially prominent in West Africa. The non-conformism of Ahmadiyya followers is exemplified by their refusal to pray behind a non-Ahmadi imam and by allowing women to enter their mosques (Trimingham 1980: 80–81). On the other hand, Ahmadi missions contributed to a regeneration of Islam in colonial Africa between the world wars, finding outlet in the growing political consciousness of many Muslim communities. Many converts were attracted to Ahmadiyya because of its political awareness and as a result of its challenge to the traditionalist ulama.

There are said to be around half a million Ahmadis in Sub-Saharan Africa (Shaikh 1992: 62, 214). The largest single group, which numbered about 30,000 in the mid-1970s, is to be found among the Fante of Ghana's Central Region (Owusu 1978). Ahmadis in Ghana adopt modernist social characteristics: women may pray with men, and brides may or may not give consent at their wedding. In addition to the different forms of religious behaviour practised by Ahmadiyya and orthodox Muslim in Ghana, other distinctions rest on the cultural division between (orthodox) Hausa and (Ahmadiyya) Akan – between what the latter regard as lower-status, 'inferior' northern immigrant pepefo cultures (mainly Hausa, but also Zambrama, Gonja, Mossi and Kotokoli), and the often higher-status, Westernized Ahmadiyya Fante and Ashanti. Orthodox Muslims tend to resist modernizing influences, and particularly Western-style secular education. By the end of the 1970s, on the other hand, Ahmadiyya converts had built more than 150 mosques and established numerous schools at junior and secondary level throughout much of Ghana. As in Pakistan, Ahmadiyya converts are to be found particularly amongst educated and literate Muslims in Ghana, including commercial and government clerks, and some university graduates (Owusu 1978).

What this amounts to is that Ahmadiyyah regularly recruits from amongst the *evolué* class. Politically, the Ahmadis have a tradition of supporting the established authority, not only in Ghana but also elsewhere in Africa. This is pragmatic: because of their – at best tenuous – status within Islam, passive support for governments has been necessary to ensure the movement's continued existence. For, until 1950 the Ahmadiyya movement in Ghana was subjected to constant persecution from orthodox Muslims (Pobee 1992: 109). Yet this conservatism cannot be ascribed solely to religious intolerance; it is due also to the fact that many benefit economically from the status quo. In West Africa the movement tends not to ally itself overtly with the aims of any one party, instead leaving followers (in the manner of the South African Zionist churches) to follow their own inclinations so long as no overriding issue necessitates corporate action. This contrasts with an earlier period in Ghana's political history when, from the early 1920s, in the coastal region, Ahmadiyya exercised a certain political influence on the autochthonous elite, which led them to seek a political vehicle for their aspirations (Nicholas 1981: 234). The result was that in 1939, southern Muslims, supported by Ahmadiyya, founded a Muslim party, the Muslim Association Party, which initially was a religious ginger group; later in the 1950s it evolved into an Islamic party led mostly by Ashantis in opposition to Kwame Nkrumah's Convention People's Party. In the first post-colonial National Assembly in 1957 there were seventeen Muslim representatives, including two Ahmadis (ibid.: 235). In 1978, Ahmadis, in common with other religious groups, were courted by General Acheampong at the time of his attempt to push through a socially unpopular governmental reform.

It was not only in Ghana that the Ahmadiyya sect prospered but also elsewhere in West Africa. It was very active proselytizing along the coastal fringe of the Gulf of Guinea and in the subregion more generally after World War I. It arrived in Nigeria in 1916, before entering the Gold Coast (Ghana) and Sierra Leone (Nicholas 1981: 193). Indian missionaries spread the Ahmadi message, and one of them, Abd-ur-Rahim Nayyar, visited Accra, Lagos, Zaria and Kano in 1921. In 1933 a permanent Ahmadi mission was established in West Africa, with its headquarters at the Fante town of Saltpond, Ghana. In the north of the colony an Ahmadi mosque was built at Wa in 1936. In 1939 a permanent Ahmadi mission was started at Baomahun, near Bo, in Sierra Leone. There, Ahmadiyya, supported by Lebanese merchants, formed a new, modernist Muslim group which aimed at substituting itself for the Creole elite. Until recently, Liberia had relatively few Ahmadis, although the sect now has over 2,000 followers in the country, with the majority in Monrovia (Gifford 1993: 287–8). In south-west Nigeria, Ahmadiyya considerably extended the spread of Islam. Ahmadi missionaries opened schools and formed a new generation of Muslims open to modernity after World War II (Nicholas 1981: 226). From south-west Nigeria, the sect spread east to Benin, where it came into conflict with Hausa marabouts. Nevertheless, here and elsewhere, the Ahmadis did not by any means have it all their own way: on the contrary, they were often to come up against the entrenched prejudices of legalistic Islam, just as Maitatsine was to do in Kano in the 1970s, and with as little success.

In East Africa Ahmadi missionaries appeared in 1934 at the request of local people of Indian descent. The first Ahmadi mosque was built at Tabora (Tanganyika) in 1942 and the movement flourished. Yet, Ahmadiyya found entrenched orthodox Islam on the coast and among newly converted Muslims inland. The latter were reliant upon links with Arab traders for their prosperity, and so, at least initially, few converts were made (Trimingham 1980: 80). Part of the reason for the lukewarm response in East Africa, where Arabist culture predominated amongst local Muslims, was that Ahmadi missionaries advocated teaching the Quran through English translation; this threatened the status and livelihood of the ulama trained in Arabic. Later, however, the sect became established in several towns on the East African coast and in the interior, recruiting especially among the 'detribalized' urban arrivals, who were generally unimpressed by orthodox Islam. Rather than Arabic, the Ahmadis use the local lingua franca, Swahili, to spread their message, finding a ready audience among those who regard Arabic as the language of slavers and imperialists. The local communities of the sect are grouped in an organization whose headquarters is in Nairobi. Its leader, the emir Mubarak Ahmad, is a lieutenant of the Khalifa of Rabwah (Nicholas 1981: 193). There are also Ahmadi converts among the Nyamwezi of west Tanzania.

Despite Ahmadiyya's success in both West and East Africa, once it was known that the sect was regarded as deviationist by most of the rest of the Muslim world there was little chance of mass conversions. Nevertheless, with some half a million converts in Africa, it could not properly be regarded as marginal. Followers of Ahmadiyya tend to play a disproportionately important social role in their communities because of their economic influence. The sect's modernist religious and cultural approach has led it into conflict with entrenched Muslim elites, although its pragmatism has enabled it eventually to get on good terms with governments. It prospered because of its stress upon Western education, its appeal to women, and the commercial possibilities offered to converts through their membership of a relatively small, yet wealthy, group. It was attractive as a result of its modernist Islamic interpretation, which got away from the Arab-hegemony aspects of conventional Islam; it was also anti-colonial and anti-Christian. Ahmadiyya helped to create a new form of ethno-religious solidarity, building on local traditions interwoven with modernist themes – a mixture of the old and the new, which has been a familiar feature of this chapter.

Conclusion

The religious groups I have examined in the current chapter have little in common except for two things. First, they are all more or less Africanized derivatives of either Islam or Christianity. Several of the syncretistic Christian groups are (or were) based exclusively in certain rural areas where there was a tradition of anti-colonial opposition, which sometimes continued through to the post-colonial era. Second, their *raison d'être* was not so much that they were anti-colonial as such but rather that they were formed in response to perceived attacks from outside forces – usually the state – which sought to undermine their community autonomy. The development of syncretistic religious ideologies as emblems of opposition reflected how certain communities employed their collective feeling of singularity in a struggle with outsiders who did not share their community values.

Predominantly urban new religious movements, including the revisionist Muslim sect the Ahmadiyya as well as the heavily syncretic Aladura churches, also developed, at least in part, in response to the effects of modernization and, especially in their case, urbanization. Ahmadiyya was the chosen religious vehicle of often marginalized people who joined together to create communities based on concerns of ethnicity and economic advance, as much as on the issue of religious interpretation. The Zion Christian Church of South Africa, the largest independent church in the country, also offered both spiritual and material benefits to many people who had been economically and socially marginalized during the development of the modern, relatively urbanized and industrialized South African state. The church, however, took a rather apolitical stance in relation to apartheid and to the position of non-whites in the society. This was because its leaders perceived that their role was predominantly religious and spiritual rather than political. It was, additionally, deemed irrational to get involved in the political struggle because it was largely seen as the concern of 'communist' groups like the ANC, with which the ZCC felt no affinity whatsoever (Schoffeleers 1991). In sum, the growth of various types of new religious movements in Sub-Saharan Africa since the colonial period indicates clearly how vehicles of religious belief develop over time, moulded by their socio-political and economic context. On this note, we move on to one of the most interesting of recent religious developments in black Africa: the growth of religious 'fundamentalism', which, in the eyes of several observers of both Islamic and Christian types, represents little more than a vehicle of foreign religious dogma. I want to argue, however, that the growth of Christian 'fundamentalism' and the relative lack of growth of its Islamic counterpart are due more to the fact that many Africans see within the former important elements of religious and social rejuvenation which they do not necessarily perceive in the latter.

7

Religious 'Fundamentalism' and Politics

In recent debates about the role of religion in politics in Sub-Saharan Africa, so-called religious 'fundamentalism' has usually received short shrift, often being regarded as the epitome of the religiously negative, defensive and backward-looking – a 'set of strategies by which beleaguered believers attempt to preserve their distinctive identity as a people or group' in response to real or imagined attacks from those who wish to draw them into a 'syncretistic, areligious or irreligious cultural milieu' (Marty and Scott Appleby 1993: 3). Some analyses seek to portray religious fundamentalism as appealing exclusively to poor, simple people, and especially to those disoriented by the stresses of modernization, who are easy prey for cynical, manipulative champions of religious dogma that promises spectacular improvements in people's lives but can only deliver them into the clutches of domestic or foreign religious charlatans with altogether different aims. According to Wignaraja (1993: 33), for example, 'vested interests and immature political leaders ... manipulate the people' by the use of religious fundamentalism. In a similar vein, Kothari (1993: 68) argues that such people are duped by the 'ruling class' to follow religious fundamentalism in order that they forget their 'true' class interests. There is also the issue of alleged foreign manipulation of religious 'fundamentalists'. Both Gifford (1993) and Pieterse (1992) see the hand of United States imperialism fairly unequivocally behind Christian fundamentalism in Africa, while Krauthammer (1993: 4) regards Islamic fundamentalism as a kind of global fifth column, a vehicle of Iran's hegemonic designs: 'Iran is the centre of the world's new Comintern', he believes.

I want to examine two claims in this chapter: (1) the assumption by Gifford and by Pieterse that religious fundamentalism in Sub-Saharan

Africa may be little more than a manifestation of the impact of foreign religious-ideological manipulation; and (2) the assumption by Wignaraja et al. that fundamentalism is no more than a highly negative reaction to modernization on the part of disoriented, manipulated individuals. I will argue that in Sub-Saharan Africa, Christian fundamentalism is an example of popular religion which, adopted by Africans in time-honoured fashion, serves increasingly as an indigenized vehicle of community solidarity. The fact that Islamic fundamentalism has not found a niche suggests that when religious dogmatists do seek to impose what many of their co-religionists perceive as anathema, their goals are not realized. In addition, while we may accept that foreign and domestic purveyors of religious fundamentalist dogma in Sub-Saharan Africa may have political goals in mind, this is not to say that those in receipt of their messages perceive them in the way they are intended. The following discussion is intended to show how religious fundamentalism may be used either by elites for their own self-advancement or by communities for their corporate spiritual and sometimes material gain. I begin with a theoretical discussion concerning the notion of religious fundamentalism. I then proceed to an examination of both Christian and Islamic fundamentalism, assessing their supposed merits and demerits as perceived by ordinary believers. I then turn to the issue of foreign interference in Africa, as expressed through attempts to instil fundamentalist dogma. I conclude by stressing how religious fundamentalist 'messages', in common with other religious dogma from external sources, are over time comprehensively Africanized to produce relevant bodies of belief of relevance to many people, especially in the modernizing milieus of the urban environment.

Theorizing Fundamentalism in Black Africa

The character and impact of fundamentalist doctrines are located within a nexus of moral and social issues revolving around state–society interactions. They may have a political impact; they may incorporate a critique of powerful elites; they may even involve a challenge to state power – but none of these is their primary function. The main role of such doctrines is to provide spiritual and moral support and guidance to their followers; sometimes, in addition, there will be more material benefits. Marshall (1993: 215) argues that analytically, it is inadvisable to regard African Christian fundamentalism as simply involving attempts to reduce state power from below, because this risks the error of accepting the 'relatively empty dichotomies of state–society, church–state, formal–informal, temporal–spiritual, assuming some sort of• necessary, structural opposition between relatively homogeneous categories'. Marshall's point is an important one; yet it would be unwise to view what she argues are essentially non-dichotomized categories – state–society, and so on – as merely seamless webs of social and political interaction, where no divisions can ever be drawn between one set of interests and another. I argued earlier that leaders of mainstream religious organizations and of the state in Sub-Saharan Africa share a vested interest in perpetuating their hegemony as far as possible. I also argued that popular religious groups are one of society's responses to such hegemonic designs, inasmuch as they aim to create communities committed to achieving as much independence as possible. Many members of Christian fundamentalist groups are strongly motivated by the desire to escape from the web of clientelist relations that often shapes their lives, and to form 'clean' communities of believers united by their religious beliefs. The Christian fundamentalist world-view and discourse are concerned with issues like the family, gender roles, sexuality, health and wealth, and social justice. These are not generally regarded as political issues per se, but they nevertheless shade into political concerns – the nature of government, the health of the economy, the best form of state, and so on. What this amounts to is that fundamentalist ideas may supply believers with a 'manifesto' for social change and a programme for reform of the status quo which sets them apart from the norm of state–society interactions, dominated as it is by clientelist concerns.

I follow Haddad (1985: 277) in perceiving religious fundamentalisms as scripturalist forms of religious piety which affirm the central relevance of a holy book for day-to-day activities and which insist on the regulation of all aspects of individual and social behaviour. Fundamentalists believe that because God's own words are written in the holy books, scriptural revelations are central to the religion. I use the term 'fundamentalist' in a broad sense: pertaining not only to individual beliefs but also to religious movements. I agree with Caplan (1987) when he argues that religious fundamentalism is quintessentially modern, offering a response to contemporary conditions and events, including perceived threats from rival religions. In the United States, for example, Christian fundamentalists react not only against old enemies – evolutionary theory and communism – but also against social change which threatens their ideas of morality. In Africa, on the other hand, contemporary religious fundamentalism has its roots and *raison d'être* in the failed promises of independence; it reacts against unwelcome manifestations of modernization – poverty, marginalization and attendant insecurity – in just the same way as other vehicles of popular religion. What sets the fundamentalist doctrines apart is their ideological world-view based on moral concerns inscribed in holy books. The background to the rise of fundamentalism is the *pace* of change over the last three decades: traditional habits, beliefs, cultures and communities have been placed under considerable pressure to adapt. In an increasingly materialist world one's individual worth is increasingly measured according to one's wealth and hence status. As we shall see, Christian fundamentalists often emphasize a materialist 'gospel of prosperity' that encourages personal economic success – which is perceived as a sign of God's favour.

The impact of religious fundamentalism upon politics in Africa may be approached as a conventional area of enquiry: is society most swayed by determinist structural forces or by self-interested voluntarism? (Hyden and Williams 1994: 69). In other words, what is of greatest significance in explaining the spread of religious fundamentalism in Africa: local or international factors? If it is the former then we ought to expect African religious fundamentalists to be greatly affected by foreign interests as motivations to action. As noted above, some see the imperialistic hand of the USA or Iran behind Africa's religious fundamentalists. If, however, self-interested voluntarism is the appropriate explanation, then the creation and consolidation of fundamentalist communities may best be understood in terms of a combination of individualistic and collective concerns regarding spiritual and material welfare. Hyden (1983: 8) notes how 'economies of affection' are often of considerable importance in Africa, influencing and sustaining 'networks of support, communications, and interactions among structurally defined groups connected by blood, kin, community, [and] other affinities such as religion'. The drawback to this argument is that Hyden sees the existence of communities of affection only in rural areas where 'social interactions occur within a context ... perceived as a legitimate and integral part of each person's existence' (Hyden and Williams 1994: 71). The affective nature of these interactions helps to shape moral intentions (mutual respect, trust, fairness) among individuals within the community. Yet, such moral concerns are also highly important to urban fundamentalist groups where communitarian orientations and interactions help to develop religious communities.

The concept of community has not been high on the agenda of political-science research because key theorists such as Marx, Weber and Polanyi suggested that the spread of capitalism during modernization would fundamentally marginalize community values, leading to a rise in self-interested individualism and organizational bureaucratization. In independent Africa, however, disinterested bureaucracies did not, by and large, develop; while traditional community concerns were often pursued via ethnic association. Some Christian fundamentalist groups, however, have been able to transcend ethnic divisions while producing important material benefits for members, who regard themselves as part of a religious community. This development has been encouraged by the widespread failure of governmental institutions to ameliorate the poor conditions of life that exist for many people. Fundamentalist groups often provide what the state does not, allowing members to cope better with prevailing economic and social conditions. This suggests that in those societies in Africa undergoing economic dislocation and social upheaval, where an absence of shared group identity gives rise to what Eckstein (1988) calls 'cultural discontinuity', it is likely that individuals will turn to religious fundamentalism. In what follows, I shall look first at Christian fundamentalism and then at the Islamic movements; finally, I consider the role of foreign influences on Africa's religious fundamentalists, Christian and Muslim.

Christian Fundamentalism and Politics in Africa

There are no definitive accounts (indeed, there are not even any well-informed estimates) of the numbers of Africans who would describe themselves as fundamentalist Christians. It has been estimated, however, that since the mid-1960s fundamentalist churches in both the United States and Britain have gained around a 50 per cent increase in followers, while the mainstream churches have lost around one-fifth of their active membership over the same period (Linden 1991: 118). It is certainly conceivable that a shift of similar magnitude from the mission to fundamentalist churches in Africa occurred over the same thirty-year period. It is reasonable to assume that many of the estimated 6 million a year Africans who become Christians join fundamentalist churches (Lamb 1985: 143). What is reasonably clear is that such churches have emerged as a clear alternative for those seeking a religious and social experience that the mission churches appear unable to offer. There are as many as 20,000 churches in Africa, of both native and foreign origin; many of them could be described as fundamentalist-oriented. Benson Idahosa alone has established more than 2,000 branches of his Church of God Mission throughout Nigeria, while crowds of up to half a million at a time were reported during the Christ for All Nations 'crusade' in Africa in 1986, which resulted in mass conversions (Ndibe 1985b; Gifford 1987: 63–4).

The growth of Protestant fundamentalism in Sub-Saharan Africa has been swift over the last two decades in a number of countries; these include Nigeria, Kenya, Ghana, Liberia, Malawi, Zimbabwe and South Africa. African fundamentalist Christians (sometimes referred to as 'born again', 'reborn' or 'charismatic') normally believe in experiential faith, the centrality of the Holy Spirit, the spiritual gifts of glossolalia and faith healing, and the efficacy of miracles. The fundamentalist world-view is informed by belief in the authority of the Bible in all matters of faith and practice; on personal conversion as a distinct experience of faith in Christ as Lord and Saviour (being 'born again' in the sense of having received a new spiritual life), and in helping others achieve a similar conversion experience. Rather than relying on foreign donations, as many of the former mission churches do, fundamentalist churches seem to be largely reliant upon donations from their members (Akakpo 1994; Ter Haar 1992; Deiros 1991). Millions of Africans have joined the fundamentalist churches because of the intensity of the prayer experi-ence they offer; the attraction of a simple and comprehensible message that seems to make sense out of the chaos which many followers perceive all around them; a moral code that offers guidance and the resusci-tation of community values; as well as a sense of group solidarity, exemplified in the way that individual followers call each other 'brother' and 'sister' (van Dijk 1992; Marshall 1991, 1993). In addition to such spiritual and social objectives, members of the fundamentalist churches also seek material goals. Indeed, the belief that membership may bring material prosperity forms one of the main attractions of the churches for some, leading to charges that their message of hope is little more than a mindless and self-centred appeal to personal material well-being (Akakpo 1994). Fundamentalist preachers, on the other hand, claim they offer their followers two interlinked benefits: worldly self-improvement and ultimate salvation. Some accounts suggest that members of such churches are politically conservative, and that they tend to submit willingly to those in authority (Moran and Schlemmer 1984; Roberts 1968). They are said, in addition, to reconcile themselves easily to the norms of consumer capitalism, which helpfully mitigates criticism of the social order (Martin 1990: 160).

It is difficult to determine whether members of fundamentalist churches are more conservative than those who do not join them; for it is debatable whether Western conceptions of political preferences have bearing on the situation in Africa, where people's view of politics and political change is coloured by experiences quite different from those in the West. What seems clear is that the fundamentalist churches create a kind of counter-society, which has several ramifications for a given social order. First, they often have rigid conceptions of morality: lying, cheating, stealing, bribing (or being bribed), adultery and fornication are all frowned upon (Marshall 1991: 23–4). In short, fundamentalist Christians usually have a strongly moralistic world-view; there exists a strong sense that the well-being of society is dependent upon the highest standards of personal morality (Shepard 1987: 364). Second, fundamentalist church members are also concerned to increase collective material benefits. Marshall (1991) notes how in Lagos fundamentalists run their own catering companies, hospitals, kindergartens and record companies. Employment is offered to co-religionists because they are considered to be honest and will work hard. Third, the nature of social interactions within the fundamentalist churches helps to reorientate traditional gender relations and, in the process, transform sexual politics. While some of the churches continue to promote a doctrine of female submissiveness, many do not. According to Marshall (1991: 29), this is one of the main attractions of the churches for young, urban women in south-west Nigeria: 'it is particularly in the spheres of marriage, family and sexuality that one finds born-again doctrines and practice transforming [gender relations] quite dramatically.' Fourth, because members of the churches conceive of a clear division between what is right and what is wrong, they tend to be opposed to public corruption.

Fundamentalist Christianity in Africa is a distinctive reinvention of an externally derived innovation. Just as orthodox Christianity and orthodox Islam have taken on African characteristics, so too is religious fundamentalism being transformed. The original (North American) religion is being indigenized, appropriated and reconstructed to serve popular aims and objectives. Fundamentalist Christianity is moulded and adapted to offer spiritual rebirth, potentialities for material improvement, and an urban community spirit. Yet to consider the movement in an undifferentiated manner is to ignore an important question: why has fundamentalist Christianity apparently grown much more rapidly in some states than in others? The answer is to be found in a combination of factors, some with domestic and some with foreign roots. Although no hard data is available, most accounts agree that the recent growth of fundamentalist churches is part of a wider trend which has resulted in many new religions being established. Several countries which have experienced particularly severe periods of political and economic upheaval – including Nigeria, Ghana, South Africa, Liberia and Zimbabwe – are areas of significant Christian fundamentalist growth (Marshall 1991, 1993; Ephson 1989; Akakpo 1994; Gifford 1991a, 1992a).

On the other hand, strong growth has also been noted in Malawi and Kenya, deemed to be countries that are relatively politically and economically stable (van Dijk 1992; Gifford 1992b), but not in equally stable Tanzania or Botswana (Molutsi and Holm 1990). We might have expected fairly similar growth patterns in the latter four (until recently) *de facto* or *de jure* one-party states. In both Malawi and Kenya Christian fundamentalist growth is partly attributable to the tight political and social control which single-party rule imposed: the growth of fundamentalist churches and sects was a social response; they were, in effect, counter-societies reminiscent of those formed in the colonial era when political organization was banned. In Tanzania (also a one-party state until 1992), on the other hand, government was skilful at creating a social consensus which regarded one-party rule in a context of ethnic and religious diversity as being, by and large, right and proper. More recently, however, the growth of ethno-religious groups which utilize Islam as a symbol of discontent have appeared in the country. Following the retirement of Julius Nyerere and the contemporaneous introduction of International Monetary Fund (IMF) structural adjustment programmes from the mid-1980s, growing dissatisfaction with the status quo emerged. In Botswana, on the other hand, where there is a high level of ethnic homogeneity, regular elections and fairly continuous economic growth contributed to a societal feeling of relative satisfaction with the status quo; this served to inhibit the growth of fundamentalist sects (Molutsi and Holm 1990).

As already suggested, followers of Christian fundamentalist churches generally believe that people's redemption and prosperity is in their own hands (or rather, in God's and the individual's hands), and that expectations that government could or should supply all people's needs is misplaced. What this implies is that followers of such churches believe they should 'keep out of politics', because what happens on earth is all part of the continuing battle between the Devil and God for dominance. Consequently, secular rulers are not really to blame for what goes wrong. Such a belief in the guidance of policy by God obviously lets political leaders escape attack which might otherwise result from deteriorating socio-economic conditions. In the words of a leader of Nigeria's Christian Students' Social Movement:

We must understand that quite a lot of the problems we face in the country today with relation to the politics, agriculture, weather, etc., may be due in part to the fact that certain things have been programmed by the forces of darkness through interference in the heavenly bodies ... The political, economic and social situations will be the result of what goes on in the spiritual realm ... Learn to DAILY pray and intercede for at least a prayer item concerning Nigeria (*sic*). (Christian Students' Social Movement of Nigeria 1983)

Despite this apparent belief that particular political outcomes result from the misalignment of the planets, Christian fundamentalists in Nigeria nevertheless seemed to welcome the Buhari coup of December 1983, which removed the corrupt Shagari government, as a sign of 'God's intervention par excellence' (ibid.). Benson Idahosa, leader of the Church of God Mission, welcomed Ronald Reagan's election as president of the United States in 1980 as a sign of God's power: 'The Holy Spirit can change the power of government in any nation. For many years America had weak presidents.' After American Christians gathered to pray for a change, Ronald Reagan was elected: 'After that election, things began to change.' Such remarks appear to suggest that Christian fundamentalist leaders are not so much apolitical as politically conservative, and indeed often supporters of 'strong' – authoritarian – government (Toulabor 1994). Yet, the relationship of fundamentalist churches to the state is not constant: it differs from country to country and from political issue to political issue. In Zambia and Ghana, Christian fundamentalist leaders strongly support the Chiluba and Rawlings regimes respectively; in South Africa, they may belong either to the conservative right wing or to the radical-reformist left; in Liberia, American-style fundamentalist churches are said to decry any political involvement; in Nigeria, Christian fundamentalists are in the forefront of anti-Islamization campaigns; while in Zimbabwe, fundamentalist churches are often regarded as seditious or subversive of the state and its socialist ideology. What this suggests is that there is no common political attribute that can easily be linked to the fundamentalist churches, although there may well be a general tendency towards political conservatism.

As we have already noted, fundamentalist groups may actually be in the forefront of endeavours to change social norms, concerned as they are with transforming established conceptions of correct moral and social behaviour. Linden (1991: 120) suggests that 'Dualism [the doctrine of two divine beings: one good, one evil] as a means of stopping critical evaluation and blocking insight and understanding of political causality may well be the most important function of extreme-right religion in the realm of political consciousness.' In fact, no such clear-cut political uniformity exists. Evidence from a number of regions, including the Americas, France, and both West and South Africa, suggests that Christian fundamentalism is not always politically quietist (Seguy 1975; Marshall 1991; Wald 1990). The political consequences of fundamentalism in Africa will vary from place to place and from circumstance to circumstance, contingent upon three factors: the numbers of fundamentalist Christians in the society; the degree to which the churches seek to dictate how society should behave; the extent to which the churches attempt to involve themselves directly in the political process – from such activities as public-resource allocation to the forging of a state in which religious laws are paramount. The closest that fundamentalist Christians have come to formulating a political ideology for a specific type of Christian polity is in Zambia and Nigeria, as we shall see shortly.

Followers of fundamentalist churches are neither inherently 'political' nor inherently 'apolitical'. Material resources and the organizational framework of a church will be utilized if there arises a political issue of sufficient importance to the fundamentalist community – a 'trigger' issue. A trigger issue is needed to galvanize political activity because the norm is for fundamentalists to eschew politics. Yet, as the involvement of Christian fundamentalists in politics in America shows, aspects of modernization that are perceived as undesirable – abortion, homosexuality, state education, public corruption and so on – lead Christian conservatives into the political arena to try to reverse such developments.

Trigger issues will differ from community to community, and from state to state. In Nigeria, it was the fear of Islamization which led to the involvement in politics of fundamentalist Christians at the national level; in Malawi the issue was elite corruption; while in South Africa it was the nature of the post-apartheid society. In the last example interpretations differ as to the political character of the (usually) white fundamentalist churches. De Haas (1986: 40), for example, sees the white minority attracted to the 'reborn' (that is, fundamentalist) churches because they offer 'assurance of worldly success as well as spiritual salvation, minimize the threat posed by possible future changes in the status quo, and divert attention from the uncomfortable realities of contemporary South Africa. Poewe (1987: 3), on the other hand, considering the same white churches, sees their followers going through an 'emotional turmoil of leaving the old [society] and embracing the new ... with repentance and hope, with victory and celebration'. According to her, what is happening is the beginning of the detribalization of the Afrikaner, a crossing of boundaries between them and other distinctive groups. The apparent ambiguity of the fundamentalists' response to political developments in South Africa seems to suggest that it is hazardous to expect a uniform response to political issues throughout Africa. I want now to illustrate the range of fundamentalist responses to important political developments by considering three countries: Malawi, Liberia and Zambia. It would seem that political responses are tied to both collective and individual self-interest, which will differ from case to case.

Malawi

I want to examine in this section the indigenous kubadwa mwatsopano ('Born Again') movement which has flourished in several urban centres in Malawi over the last twenty years (van Dijk 1992). It is a Christian fundamentalist initiative which began in about 1974 – that is, once the state had established its authoritarian ruling structures. It was influenced by the introduction into Malawian society of a specific type of evangelical Christianity which had its roots in American fundamentalism. The same type of development was also apparent in Nigeria. What this suggests is that American fundamentalist Christianity is appropriated by Africans and remoulded for local use, in the same way that mission church Christianity was adopted by Africans and then transformed in the independent churches into indigenized vehicles of Christianity.

Kubadwa mwatsopano preachers have a fundamentally moral message: they exhort their converts to demonstrate the strength of their Christian convictions by rejecting unwelcome symptoms of urban life, such as adultery, promiscuity, violence, and the consumption of alcohol, cigarettes and (narcotic) drugs such as marijuana and cocaine (van Dijk 1992: 159). Converts must hand over any stolen goods they might have, as well as tobacco and related products, knives, and magical amulets, which are commonly carried in Malawi as protection against evil spirits. In return they receive the inflowing of the Holy Spirit through the blessings given by the young preachers; they are then considered 'born again'. Followers reject traditional village culture, which is associated with paganism. A further aim of the movement is to develop individual assertiveness, and to achieve success in life and business (ibid.: 160).

Many of the first generation of 'born again' preachers later gained prominent positions as bank managers, lawyers, accountants and the like. Others became religious entrepreneurs, some with foreign backing (Mbembe 1988: 92–3). One of the main motivations for the second generation of Malawi's fundamentalist preachers was to emulate the material success of their predecessors. Such a conception of religion as a means to gain materialist success is by no means new in Malawi. According to a former British police intelligence officer in colonial Nyasaland: 'Religion in Central Africa was an alternative to politics. It provided an alternative structure of ambition' (Marishane 1992: 62).

Material prosperity, as Bayart notes (1993a: 242–3), is a significant, if not the most important, political virtue; it is not something that ordinary people see as reprehensible. Religious figures need to share this aura of prosperity if they wish to gain converts; the figure of the Indian ascetic, personified in Mahatma Gandhi, has no place in African cultures. Successful figures in whatever field, including religion, are of necessity materially prosperous. Amongst the young preachers of Malawi's kubadwa mwatsopano groups, as at large, there is a widespread belief that political success is due to the efficacy of magical amulets, which greatly aid a person's chances of material success (Van Dijk 1992: 166). The tendency of Malawi's post-colonial political society has been to throw up extremely powerful political operators; these have largely replaced traditional power-holders, including traditional religious figures. The experience of the Jehovah's Witnesses in Malawi, who refused to toe the line and were brutally treated as a result, led young preachers to learn from the Witnesses' experience: never to touch upon political issues during their teaching sessions (Bayart 1993a: 256). As a result, a working arrangement was reached with local party officials. The preachers' dictum is that 'religion and politics do not mix'. For them, 'politics posed a threat very similar to that posed by witchcraft: there could be no open discussion about it, there were few countermeasures available, and protection was usually hard to find (Van Dijk 1992: 173).

Liberia

The emergence of the fundamentalist preachers in Malawi showed one way of dealing with a situation in which most options for self-advance and group solidarity are closed off by the political straitjacket of single-party rule. Yet, for many socially progressive Western Christians it is the ideas of liberation theology that should offer their poor, oppressed, undereducated fellow religionists in the Third World a doctrine of self-growth and spiritual and political self-sufficiency based on unity, organization and local mobilization. One of the few detailed studies of the impact of fundamentalist Christianity in an African state, Liberia, is by Gifford (1993). He concludes that Liberia is being taken over by foreign (American) conservative evangelicals; from this he extrapolates that their impact throughout Africa is more or less the same. The problem with this view is that it supposes (from a study of a small, highly Americanized, West African country, as it slid into civil war in 1989) that throughout Africa people's religious – and thus political – choices are formulated, controlled and expressed by reference to a foreign *deus ex machina* alone. Whereas, in fact socio-political life in Liberia in the 1980s was an unfortunate example of the effects of brutal, self-serving government administered by a pack of ruthless men and women led by Samuel Doe. To suggest that Liberians were passive in the face of this onslaught because of the received ideas of American fundamentalist Christianity is problematic. Political oppression in Liberia under Doe was ubiquitous, sometimes casual, and always for purposes of social control. Historically, the socio-political situation in Liberia was forged by a unique set of circumstances. There was slavery in the country until the 1930s, orchestrated by the Americo-Liberian elite (Crowder 1959: 192). These black colonists ruled the country between 1877 and 1980, their True Whig Party governing by way of a well-developed authoritarianism. Following his *coup d'état*, Doe, after promising a revolution, allowed his regime to degenerate swiftly into a personalized predatory state reminiscent of the worst excesses of Mobutu, Amin or Macias Nguema. In this African-created heart of darkness, the concepts of community action and conscientization beloved of Freire, Gutierrez and others would find little sympathy.

Zambia

State president Frederick Chiluba is both a fundamentalist Christian and a former trade-union leader. The rise to power of his Movement for Multiparty Democracy (MMD) in October 1991 was aided and abetted by local fundamentalist individuals and churches. Three main political issues galvanized the fundamentalists at this time. First, thirty years of disappointing rule by Kenneth Kaunda's United National Independence Party (UNIP) government had seen the country fail to develop economically; second, during this period state-level corruption had increased; third, local fundamentalist Christians, adhering to the precepts of the 'gospel of prosperity' (whereby personal prosperity is adjudged a sign of God's favour), considered that the allocation of resources made available by an IMF-supported economic-reform programme should be weighted towards those who would make best use of them. As has usually been the case with recent IMF packages in Africa, resources were disproportionately extracted from the poor and less well off, and handed to the burgeoning middle classes, many of whom were fundamentalists. The economic reform programme of the MMD government was so stringent that the local World Bank representative counselled caution and urged that greater concern be given to the issue of social instability, which he judged to be a direct result of too fervent an application of adjustment policies (Hall 1993: 15). These latter included: the abrupt elimination of state subsidies on the staple food, maize flour, which led to a tenfold price increase; major reductions in governmental expenditure, especially the sacking of (low-ranking) state employees; the merging of the official and free-market rates of the national currency, the kwacha, which involved a 29 per cent devaluation. The reward was $1.1 billion in foreign aid. Domestically, the government's policies were less well received: less than 10 per cent of the electorate bothered to vote in the local elections of December 1992.

The zeal with which the MMD government adopted the austerity measures reflected, on the one hand, a convergence in the views of the Zambian regime and the IMF; on the other hand, the policy bore the mark of fundamentalists like Chiluba and his supporters among the country's business community. The latter stressed the need for harsh social policies to increase people's propensity for self-help. It was clear, however, that the new elite did not suffer from the effects of austerity: the term 'Nyu Kacha' (new culture) was coined to refer satirically to the sartorial elegance represented by the smart double-breasted suits (with matching tie and handkerchiefs) worn by President Chiluba, his ministers, and the new Christian elites (Hall 1993: 15).

Once the Christian fundamentalists had attained power in Zambia, they became gripped by the fear of Islamization. Whereas in Nigeria, a country polarized between large constituencies of Muslims and Christians, the issue of Islamization has contributed significantly to political tensions, in Zambia some three-quarters of the population are Christians. There is a growing number of fundamentalist churches; one of the biggest is the Church of God in Zambia, led by Bishop John Mambo, whose headquarters are in America (*Africa Confidential* 1991). Only 1 per cent of the population of 9 million (90,000 people) currently follows (Sunni) Islam. In recognition of the majority religious allegiance, Chiluba declared the country a 'Christian nation' soon after coming to power. Neverthelesss, notwithstanding the very small numbers of Muslims in Zambia, Chiluba warned of the danger of an attack from Islamic fundamentalists.

The MMD government's claim to have discovered an Iranian- and Iraqi-funded coup plot, involving the connivance of the former ruling UNIP party, led to a severing of diplomatic relations between Lusaka and Tehran and Baghdad in March 1993 (*Africa Confidential* 1993a). The Iranians admitted that they were working to sponsor national Muslim political parties in Africa through the Islam in Africa Organization. The national co-ordinator of Zambia's Islamic Youth and Students organization had received funds from an Iranian source, probably the Ministry of Culture and Islamic Guidance, headed by Hojatoleslam Sayed Muhammad Khatami (Shaikh 1992: 109). The Ministry's activities are wide-ranging and include the dissemination of religio-political publications through the cultural section of the country's embassies abroad; the holding of regular conferences on various aspects of Islam in Iran; as well as the previously mentioned funding of Muslim political groups in Africa and elsewhere. Iran's strategy was reminiscent of Libya's in Uganda, the Gambia, Chad and elsewhere in the 1970s and 1980s: to benefit from local socio-political instability both for reasons of national interest and to facilitate the spread of Islam.

The above account of the political significance of Christian fundamentalist activity in Malawi, Liberia and Zambia indicates that adhesion to fundamentalist doctrine was by no means coterminous with political quietism. In Malawi, followers of kubadwa mwatsopano used religious tenets to create and build a collective solidarity one of the concerns of which was the corrupt nature of rule in the country. In Liberia, on the other hand, adoption of American-style Christian fundamentalism seems to have been related to the extreme societal tensions that were developing in the 1980s as the country slid into civil war. Finally, Zambia's Christian rulers developed a philosophy of rule which dovetailed neatly with their fundamentalist beliefs. The apparently risible fear of Islamic fundamentalism in a country of so few Muslims should be regarded as a tactic by a government shaken by its inability to turn round the economic situation quickly: it needed to find an 'enemy' (previously it might have been 'communism') to justify authoritarian means of societal control.

Islamic Fundamentalism in Sub-Saharan Africa

The raising of the spectre of Islamic fundamentalism in Zambia opens onto the wider issue of its importance in Sub-Saharan Africa more generally. In the next section I want to focus upon Nigeria, one of the few countries in the region – notably one divided between Christian and Muslim communities – where Islamic fundamentalist ideas have made some progress, and to describe the nature of the two forms of fundamentalism present in the country. First, however, I should note some general points about Islamic fundamentalism in black Africa.

There are two types of Islamic fundamentalist organization to be found in Sub-Saharan Africa. On the one hand, there are the reforming groups, influenced by Iranian or Saudi Arabian conceptions of Islamic orthodoxy; these mostly attract the educated, who are intellectually convinced of the desirability of attaining an Islamically 'pure' society. On the other hand, another kind of Islamic fundamentalism has emerged, notably in Nigeria, in response to growing polarization between Christians and Muslims over the issue of which religion is to dominate in the country. This is an Islamic fundamentalism less concerned with the introduction and promulgation of orthodox Islamic purity than with championing the 'rights' of Muslims in relation to Christians.

Yet, generally speaking, Islamic fundamentalism has had little impact in much of Sub-Saharan Africa because its aim, the imposition of Islamic orthodoxy, is not welcomed by many of the region's Muslims, who are either followers of traditional Sufi Islam or live in small Muslim communities where local orthodoxies dominate. Around the fringes of the Sahara – where the Arabicized north meets the black African south – there are, however, widespread conflicts between reformist and traditional Islam. We have already noted the example of Sudan, where Islamic reform dovetails with Arabicization as a hegemonic project of domination. In Nigeria similar issues of religious reform and dominance are important political concerns.

Muslim–Christian conflict in Nigeria

Nigeria's 90 million or so people are divided mainly between Muslims and Christians, with a diminishing number of followers of traditional African religions. There are a number of groups which portray themselves as the standard-bearers of fundamentalist Islam. Their aim is twofold: to purge the country of 'corrupt' Sufism, and to diminish Christianity's influence. Their leaders portray themselves as the Islamically 'just' fighting to wrest the soul of Islam from the Sufi brotherhoods, including the Tijaniyya, the Qadiriyyah and the Shadhiliyyah. Thus they stand for a fundamental change of Islamic society. The reformist Islamic groups cannot really be called revolutionary as they lack blueprints to achieve an Islamic society; nor do they necessarily wish to see the end of secular rule. There are, in fact, a number of groups, which, as in Algeria, perceive the route to an Islamic society in a variety of ways.

Nigeria is home to some 45 million Muslims (50 per cent of the population), 30 million Christians (33 per cent), and 15 million followers of traditional religions (15 per cent). Figures are necessarily speculative because the only census since 1963 (that of 1991) failed to ask respondents about religious affiliation. Religious competition between Muslims and Christians is without doubt the single most significant political issue in the country. Antipathy between the religious communities was fuelled during the 1980s as many Christians came to believe that the predominantly Muslim north of the country enjoyed a disproportionate share of both political power and economic resources (Ibrahim 1991: 135). Tension was exacerbated by the government's secret decision in 1986 to join the 45-member Organization of Islamic Conference (OIC), within which Saudi Arabia and Iran – with their contending visions of Islamic society – strive for political dominance. Whereas the Nigerian government's motivation for joining the OIC was probably partially financial – aid was expected from rich Middle Eastern states – many Christians feared that Nigeria's membership of the organization would jeopardize the country's status as a secular state. Proponents of membership of the OIC countered that Nigeria was a member of the Commonwealth, a 'Christian' organization (because it is led by the British monarch, who, legally, must be a Protestant Christian). The issue was not settled before a further religious controversy ensued during 1987–88. The point of contention this time was whether a Sharia court of appeal would be allowed a place in the democratic regime which was scheduled (abortively, as it turned out) to accede to power in late 1992. Muslim members of the Constituent Assembly wanted Sharia law in the Nigerian constitution, while Christians would not countenance such a move. Negotiations on the issue broke down (and were to an extent superseded by other controversies), whilst President Babangida was forced to affirm in October 1988 that Nigeria would remain a secular state despite its membership of the OIC.

Tension between the two communities had already escalated into political violence. In early 1987, and again in May and October 1991, anti-Christian riots broke out in parts of northern Nigeria (Maier 1991). In total, over 3,000 people were killed in Christian–Muslim clashes between 1987 and 1993. The death toll included about one thousand killed in a series of pitched battles in May 1992 when Christian Katafs fought Muslim Hausa and Fulani. Churches were destroyed and both Christians and Muslims killed and injured. The political context of this religious violence was the continuation in power of the military government, which did not allow political debate. With political parties banned and with no legislature, the result was that anger and frustration among Muslims was channelled into religious issues. In effect, many ordinary Muslims were turned into 'fundamentalists' in the sense that they began to perceive their Christian countrymen and women as their chief foes; while many Christians, fearing what appeared to them to be a growing threat from Islam, retaliated.

Proponents of radical Islam, active in the north of the country particularly, were encouraged and aided by Iranian, Libyan and Saudi Arabian financial largesse (Abubakr 1986). Government fears of Libyan and Iranian-inspired subversion in Nigeria in the mid-1980s led to increasing suspicion of radical Islamic preachers and groups. As a result, the Gongola state government banned open-air religious preaching in early 1988, while later in the same year Bauchi and Kwara states acted to restrict the activities of Kungiyar yan Shia, an Islamic group inspired by Iran's example of an Islamic state.

Various explanations have been offered for the apparently increasing influence of both Islamic and Christian fundamentalism in Nigeria in recent times. One influential explanation for the increased salience of religion in politics in Nigeria is to be found in the Marxist-inspired 'manipulation theses'. In these interpretations, religious tensions between Muslims and Christians are manipulated by a local 'intermediary bourgeoisie' in an attempt to mystify the way in which they are exploiting the masses, and by the machinations of foreign countries, such as Libya, intent to use Islam as a tool of foreign policy (Usman 1979: 78–93). Such a thesis is not new: in the 1970s the 'manipulators' were deemed to be foreign 'neo-colonialists' rather than local exploiters. Those on the (secular) radical left argue that the Sharia debate in the 1980s was being used 'to sow the seeds of division and confusion among us [Nigerians] in order to divert attention from seeing the way they [the neo-colonialists] exploit us and carry away our resources' (Clarke 1982: 204). In other words, foreign capitalist forces used religious differences to divide and rule Nigeria for their own nefarious purposes. A variant of this is the argument that the outbreak of religious violence between Muslims and Christians in Kaduna State in 1987 was fomented by certain Kaduna politicians for their own ends (Ibrahim 1989). While it is the case that Nigerian politicians, like their counterparts almost everywhere else in the world, at times seek to use religious, ethnic and regional issues for political gain, this is not the same thing as understanding political conflict simply in terms of manipulation by scheming individuals, whether Nigerian or foreign. We need to look a little deeper than such manipulation theses do if we are to discover the roots of religio-political conflict.

The context of this religious conflict is the particular nature of Nigeria's state–society relations, its fragmented civil society, and the virtual absence of civic culture. Since independence in 1960, the military has ruled the country for all but ten years (1960–66 and 1979–83). During the post-independence period three, often interrelated, sources of socio-political tension have been apparent: ethnicity, regionalism and religion.

The relation of Islam to Christianity in Nigeria has been shaped by four developments since the colonial period: first, the independence political process itself was important because it served to pit the largely Muslim north against the mostly Christian south; second, Muslim–Christian friction, which involved the constitutional status of Sharia law, in the 1970s and 1980s; third, the role of Islamic fundamentalism, which has defined itself in relation to both Sufism and Christianity; finally, the forging of strong ties with radical North African and Middle Eastern Muslim groups by Nigeria's Muslim fundamentalist reformers.

Sklar argues (1987: 696) that 'federalism in Nigeria has helped to localize and contain the threat of such anti-democratic tides as Islamic fundamentalism'. It is debatable, however, whether the factor of federalism is any longer of especial weight in restraining Islamists, especially given that the number of states in Nigeria has been increased to thirty, primarily to create more states in the north of the country with a Christian majority (Birai 1993: 185). What is of interest in Sklar's observation, however, is his apparently casual reference to Islamic 'fundamentalists' and 'anti-democratic' tendencies. Because of the importance of the issue of the interaction of Islam and (liberal) democracy in Africa generally I want to address this issue in the context of Nigeria where it is especially topical.

Islamic fundamentalism and democracy in Nigeria

All religious fundamentalists seek to redefine their religions' basic tenets and ideals: to modernize, albeit by reference to traditional beliefs and activities. Nigeria's Islamic reformists are usually influenced by Muslim ideologues such as Hasan al-Banna and Sayyid Qutb. For them, it is necessary to effect a return to the Texts, beyond the tradition [that is, Sufism] which has dulled and deformed them ... The enemy is not modernity but tradition, or rather in the Muslim context, all that is not in the Tradition of the Prophet. It is really a question of reform. (Roy 1985: 12)

Because the Sharia, although of divine origin, is not a blueprint for running a modern society, contemporary Islamist radical reformists are free to use it as an ideological tabula rasa. Ideological formulations that claim the Sharia as their inspiration range across the political spectrum from the revolutionary right to the revolutionary left. On the right of the spectrum the call for an Islamic state might imply: general hostility to any innovations since the Prophet Muhammad's time; contacts with the West; strong opposition to women's rights; the imposition of 'Islamic education'; and discrimination against religious or ethnic minorities. A leftist vision might involve: the establishment of an egalitarian society; redistribution of wealth and land; 'honest', corruption-free government; and reform of the Islamic establishment (Mayer 1993: 111). In May 1990, the Centre for Islamic Legal Studies at Ahmadu Bello University established a Fatwa (authoritative ruling) Commission. The aim of the Commission was to come up with a workable Islamic political programme. Its plan for a 'just' state included: country-wide laws disallowing prostitution, gambling and alcohol sales and consumption; a zakat (poor tax) to be institutionalized and made compulsory; the confiscation of land from 'multinational corporations', to be given 'back to the peasants'; economic reform of an (as yet unspecified) appropriately Islamic variety; and Islamically based courses of instruction in 'economics, banking, political science, and so forth' in the country's higher-education establishments (Birai 1993: 193–4).

The doctrinal debate between the Nigerian Islamic groups is highly charged. Yet none of them appears to have a workable economic blueprint, beyond a universal faith that the introduction of Sharia law will produce a just society; or even a plan to replace the controversial IMF-approved economic reform programme. Nigerian Islamists tend to be split between those (for example, the radical Islamic Movement) who see Iran's theocratic state as a model for Nigeria, and those (for example, members of the pro-Saudi, conservative Izala) who see Sharia law as the first stage in a gradual process of building a more 'Nigerian' Islamic state. The first task in this process is a moral one: Islamic reform encompasses primarily individual religious behaviour as well as social change.

This failure to address the economic issue is rather ironic, given that Nigeria's Islamic renewal (*tajdid*) has at its root the country's serious and prolonged economic decline, which resulted in the virtual collapse of health and educational provision and a steep rise in violent crime and corruption. The impact of tapping into a wider Islamic network was reflected in 1978 by the formation of a Saudi Arabian-influenced movement, Izalatul-Bid'a wa Iqamat al Sunna (Izala: 'Those who reject innovation'), a loosely integrated reformist organization with headquarters in Kaduna, led by Shaikh Abubbakar Mahmud Gumi, a former Grand Kadi of northern Nigeria during the First Republic (1960–66). Izala enjoyed a decade of expansion, and 'succeeded ... at the price of fierce resistance, to implant itself in all the urban areas in northern Nigeria' (Kane 1990: 8). Izala aims to eradicate innovation (*bida*) and to promote an Islam based solely on the Quran and the Sunna. It is a Wahhabist-inspired movement, opposed to an Iranian-style Islamic state and the Sufi brotherhoods. Because Kano was also an important centre for several Sufi brotherhoods (the Niassist 'Reformed' Tijiniyya and a branch of the Qadiriyyah), there was conflict there between them and the reformers. The brotherhoods co-ordinated their efforts in a group known as Jundullahi (Soldiers of God), founded by Kamaluddeen Na Ma'aji, and Fityan al Islam (Young Muslims), founded by Mudi Salga. During the 1980s, virtually all-out war was fought between the reformists and the brotherhood traditionalists (ibid.: 9).

Izala is challenged by Mallam Ibrahim El-Zak Zaky's Islamic Movement, which is based in Zaria. The movement is renowned as being more radical than the 'gradualist' Izala. Zak Zaky rejects the idea of a secular state constitution for Nigeria, regards Iran's theocratic state favourably, argues that the battle for an Islamic state must start with the destruction of the secular state, and claims that *jihad* is necessary until Sharia becomes Nigeria's national law (Birai 1993: 197). Other Iranian-influenced groups include the Muslim Students' Society (MSS), formed in 1954, and an offshoot, Da'wa. The MSS wishes to see an Islamic state in Nigeria modelled along Iranian lines; its leaders are very close to Iran's government, distribute Iranian propaganda against the Nigerian secular state, and have been in the forefront of recent Muslim–Christian clashes in several Nigerian universities. Da'wa, led by Shaikh Aminudeen Abubbacar, is close to the governments of Kuwait and Saudi Arabia. Abubbacar persuaded benefactors from those countries to finance the construction of his centre (a very large modern mosque, a primary school, and educational facilities for adult courses) based in an exclusive residential area of Kano. Individuals associated with Abubbacar's Islamic centre allegedly became involved 'in money-lending and frequently attacked Imam Khomeini for being a demagogue (Kane 1990: 9).

Birai estimates that up to 65 per cent of Nigerian Muslims belong neither to a Sufi brotherhood nor to one of the fundamentalist groups such as Izala (Birai 1993: 195). Many of them would probably regard the conflict between Sufis and reformists, or between 'radicals' and 'gradualists', as both trivial and unnecessary. Many of these 'ordinary' Muslims have suffered through years of economic mismanagement and political ineptitude by their rulers. Their desire for a more just society necessarily assumes an Islamic dimension; many would argue that the five pillars of Islam need strengthening. In some parts of Nigeria, however, Islam became an overtly politicized religion of subordinate and lower-middle-class opposition to the dominant elites, especially in the context of the class polarization in Nigeria during the oil-boom years of the 1970s and early 1980s. Muslim religious and cultural ideals became a focus for concern about wage exploitation, inflation, and their result – a declining standard of living for many people. Social frustrations; unease over the pace and direction of change in the wake of Nigeria's petrodollar-fuelled bonanza; Libyan adventurism; and the Iranian Revolution's exemplary effect amongst Nigerian Muslims – these factors combined to produce an explosive situation in parts of Nigeria, which was exploited by the late Muhammadu Marwa in the northern city of Kano, as we saw in Chapter 6.

Christian and Islamic fundamentalists in contention

The growth of tension between Muslim 'have nots' and the state in Kano was paralleled by a more general increase in bad feeling between many Muslims and Christians in the 1980s and 1990s. Conflict between the religious communities led to the emergence of an organizational body for the country's fundamentalist Christians, the main purpose of which is to comment on both religious and political issues. The Pentecostal Fellowship of Nigeria (PFN) is an influential voice in the interdenominational Christian Association of Nigeria, which claims to represent the interests of the country's Christians at both federal and national levels. The PFN was formerly an avowedly apolitical organization; it re-evaluated its traditional stance of indifference to political issues in the mid-1980s because of its fear of creeping Islamization. Some influential figures in the PFN, including Benson Idahosa, founder of the international Church of God Mission, warned of religious war in the country if tensions between Muslims and Christians were not diminished. Somewhat ironically, religious tensions were exacerbated in northern Nigeria in the early 1990s, in part because of aggressive proselytizing by missionaries of several of the fundamentalist churches, including Idahosa's, which led to some conversions in the predominantly Muslim north. There, where socio-cultural norms dictate that Islam is an integral part of many people's lives, conversion to Christianity was facilitated by a modern variant of the colonial missionaries' 'gospel of prosperity' argument: Christianity brought medicine, education and wealth to the country, so it was quite sensible for those who wished to share these benefits to follow the Christian faith. 'Muslims in power know that they have nothing to offer the country', claimed Idahosa, alluding to the three decades of 'Muslim rule' of the country which had seen the living standards of most Nigerians plummet (Elliot 1993).

The fundamentalist churches consider themselves involved in a three-way conflict: not only with Muslims but also with mainstream Christians, whom they accuse of being apostates for having abandoned the fundamentals of the Christian faith while their leaders set themselves up as individuals whose power challenges that of God (Ibrahim 1991: 121), and with those who follow traditional religious beliefs. In short, all people of whatever religious faith outside the community of fundamentalists are not true believers and cannot be saved from hell unless they convert.

In addition to religious issues, the growth of fundamentalist churches in Nigeria has been encouraged by the socio-economic condition of the country. Over the last fifteen years or so – a period of increasing economic stringency – the number of new religious movements in general has grown appreciably. The volatility of the religious environment mirrors the unpredictability of the political arena: the battle for power between various ethnic groups, and between civilian politicians and military figures, corresponds to the fight for 'theological space' between traditional and *arriviste* religions. Interlinked economic, social and spiritual crises help to spread fears of the end of the world and an accompanying, increasingly desperate, striving for salvation (Adubofuor 1992). This combination of factors is good business for the plethora of emergent preachers, who capitalize on fear and a common desire for order, stability and community. Traditionally, politics, business and religion have been the three areas of endeavour from which individuals may expect financial reward. Politics in Nigeria is the domain of a homogeneous (northern military) elite; business success requires capital, contacts and a fair quota of luck, each of which may be in short supply; while religious success may only require a charismatic personality with the ability to attract disciples and followers. They, as a sign of their faith, will be willing to pay for the costs of running a church and the considerable expenses incurred by its leader.

The emergence and growth of Nigeria's fundamentalist churches should be seen in relation to a number of political, social and economic developments since the mid-1960s. The civil war (1967–70) resulted in more than a million dead, social upheaval and economic chaos. As a result of the massive growth in oil revenues, the 1970s was a period of rapid, yet uneven, economic expansion. The 1980s was a decade of reduced optimism: of decline in public morality and trust, in the state education system, in the numbers of jobs available for school-leavers and university graduates, cumulatively resulting in widespread fear and lack of confidence in the future. During this time price inflation grew swiftly. Previously lucrative avenues of patronage and access to external capital sharply contracted. Patron–client networks were less replete with funds and consequently shrunk; less money trickled down to lubricate the wheels of politics. The early 1990s was a time of political uncertainty as military rulers showed themselves quite unwilling to give up power to elected civilians; the economy declined further, and religious schisms widened.

As society appeared to fall apart, the hierarchies of the mainstream Christian churches conspicuously failed to speak up for ordinary people, or to criticize the inept political system and the accompanying corruption in public life. The fundamentalist churches offered, in contrast, a sense of solidarity between co-religionists, a code of behaviour, moral values, and, above all, a sense of stability in a world profoundly disrupted. The Christian revival involved a movement away from the crassly materialist ways of the established churches and an attempt to reconstruct a new type of socially responsive organization. It stressed a fundamentalist return to the tenets of the Bible, calling on Christians to experience spiritual rebirth.

This account of the conflict between Christian and Islamic fundamentalists in Nigeria has demonstrated clearly that each fears that the other wishes to impose a particular way of life on the other. The growth of fundamentalist Christian communities in the country was a result of its socio-economic upheavals, which were related to the rise and fall of the oil industry. Like fundamentalist churches elsewhere in Africa, those in Nigeria offered their followers new communities where solidarity between individuals was a function of religious belief. It does seem to be the case that the political concerns of Nigeria's Christian fundamentalists were largely forged by the fear of a growth in Islamic fundamentalism in the country. Both Iran and Saudi Arabia were important influences on the growth of Islamic reform groups, although it seems that many Nigerian Muslims were unimpressed by their religious arguments.

In the final section of the chapter, we turn to the wider issue of the influence of foreign religious actors on the growth of religious fundamentalism in Sub-Saharan Africa. The aim is to shed light upon the issue of whether religious fundamentalism in the region is anything more than the most recent example of external manipulation of peoples and governments.

Religious Fundamentalism and Foreign Manipulation in Africa

Islam and foreign manipulation

To what extent are Africa's religious fundamentalists manipulated by foreign interests for the latter's political ends? Where Islamic fundamentalism is concerned it does seem that both Iran and Saudi Arabia use part of their oil wealth to conduct a competition for influence in Africa which has both temporal and religious aspects. Post-revolutionary Iran has developed two particular foreign-policy objectives: to proselytize on behalf of Islam wherever possible and to compete with what the government perceives as a Western – especially American-dominated – international system. Since its revolution Iran has been linked with a number of radical Shiite groups – in Lebanon, Bahrain and Iraq. It has also sought to develop links with radical co-religionists in parts of Africa, including Nigeria. During 1985, Iran's diplomatic representatives in Lagos were accused of distributing posters of the late Ayatollah Khomeini and radical Islamic literature which the chief imam of Lagos Central mosque, Ibrahim Laidi, criticized as 'perilous for the religious peace of the country' (*Guardian* [Lagos] 1985). The Nigerian government also criticized the activities of some Iranian embassy staff, who, it claimed, tried to introduce what it referred to as 'fundamentalist and revolutionary doctrines' in order to 'corrupt' Nigerian Islamic culture and forms of worship (*Standard* [Lagos] 1985).

Iran's attempt to target Nigeria in order to help it achieve its foreign-policy objectives should be seen in the context of its rivalry with Saudi Arabia. The Iranian government wished to create pockets of influence in Sub-Saharan Africa as the first step in a campaign to achieve a much higher profile in the region than hitherto. In February 1986, Iran's spiritual leader, Sayyid Ali Khameini, stated that Iran 'will survive, defend and protect our revolution and help others in the same cause of Islam to establish the rule of God wherever they are in the

world (*Sunday Triumph* [Lagos] 1986, emphasis added). A symptom of
Iran's growing influence in Africa was exemplified by its close alliance
with the Islamic rulers of Sudan. Saudi Arabia – until the 1990–91
Gulf War Sudan's main ally – on the other hand, lost much of its
influence there following its friendship with the United States. Saudi
Arabia, like Iran, utilized Islam as a foreign-policy tool – when it
suited it. During Ethiopia's civil war, Saudi Arabia's support for the
Eritreans remained constant despite the leadership of the main
guerrilla groups passing from Muslims to Marxist-Leninists, and then
to Christians in the mid-1980s (Clapham 1989: 73). What this brief
discussion of the foreign policies of Iran and Saudi Arabia in Sub-
Saharan Africa has shown is that both states use religion to help them
to pursue national interest goals, targeting putative allies among local
Muslims to help them.

Christian fundamentalism and foreign exploitation

It is less clear whether the American religious right also has a wide-
ranging foreign policy that involves partnership with African conservative Christians. Once again the issue concerns the difficulty of clearly
separating political and religious issues. For example, was it a 'political'
goal (defeating communism) or a 'religious' objective (helping to defend
co-religionists from communist attack on their faith) which galvanized
some members of the American religious right to become concerned
with events in southern Africa in the 1980s and 1990s? Were such
individuals acting on their own behalf or at the behest of certain government agencies? It is well documented that US foreign-policy goals of
anti-communism in Latin America during the Reagan and Bush presi-
dencies dovetailed with those of American conservative Christians (for
details, see Haynes 1993a: 139–45). It is less clear whether the American
Religious Right pursued its anti-communist objectives so tenaciously
outside strategically important Latin America – with the exception of
southern Africa.

In southern Africa during the 1980s there are clear indications that
US fundamentalist groups sought to aid rebel movements like Renamo
and Unita whose conflicts with their governments were portrayed to
the outside world as a battle against 'communism'. American fundamentalist Christians also aided and abetted 'anti-communist' forces in
Latin America in the 1980s (d'Antonio 1990). During the Cold War the
United States was particularly concerned to control perceived Soviet
expansionism in Africa. Fundamentalists were concerned to confront

'Satan' (communism) and to 'win souls for Christ'. It is by no means certain, however, that their efforts were co-ordinated or funded by the US government or one of its agencies.

One of the clearest examples of the dual religious and anti-communist role of American fundamentalists was in southern Africa. In 1988, the Mugabe government curtailed proselytizing among Mozambican refugees in Zimbabwe by American groups such as Jimmy Swaggart Ministries, World Vision International and Compassion Ministries. All were suspected of close links with Renamo. These suspicions appeared to be confirmed when the South African Peter Hammond of Front Line Fellowship and six American missionaries of the Christian Emergency Relief Teams (CERT) were captured in Tete Province by Frelimo soldiers in late 1989 (*Southscan* 1989). Front Line Fellowship had been founded on a South African military base in Namibia, allegedly by soldiers who wanted to take Bibles into Angola when they were engaged in attacks; in other words, they were soldier-missionaries, virulently anti-communist, drawn from the (former Rhodesian) Selous Scouts and Five Recce, the South African Special Forces unit which ran Renamo (*Africa Confidential* 1987a). A local Zimbabwean church, Shekinah Ministries, associated with the American evangelist, Gordon Lindsay 'was discovered aiding the Renamo bandits in Mozambique in 1987'; while in neighbouring Angola the counterproductive nature of the MPLA government's anti-religion policy was evidenced in the Ovimbundu highlands and to the south-east, where 'a resistant Church of Christ in the Bush developed in tandem with UNITA' (Marcum 1987: 75; Gifford 1992a: 126, 132). It seems, then, that individuals took it upon themselves to aid their anti-communist allies in Mozambique and Angola during the civil wars; yet this does not seem to have been a campaign involving either the hierarchies of the churches themselves or the American government.

More significant for the development of fundamentalist Christianity in Africa were two waves of fundamentalist evangelicalism, both with their roots in the United States. The first wave took place between the 1920s and the 1950s, and comprised both European and North American pentecostalist groups (Hoekema 1966: 24–31). The Seventh Day Adventists were especially successful, with an estimated 2,000 missionaries in the field by the 1950s; while the American Assemblies of God had about 750 (Wilson 1985: 309). By the early 1960s the Full Gospel Businessmen's Fellowship International, founded in 1952 and with headquarters in Los Angeles, had established international chapters in Southern Africa (Hoekema 1966: 33). It aimed, along with other groups such as Campus Crusade, Youth With A Mission, and Christ for the Nations, to focus a fundamentalist message of redemption on higher-education campuses, particularly West African institutions, where mass conversions took place. A second wave of foreign evangelical penetration of Africa began in the 1970s, a result of the success of American television evangelists like Pat Robertson, Jim and Tammy Bakker, Jimmy Swaggart and Oral Roberts – who focused upon Africa as a benighted continent crying out to be saved (Gifford 1991a: 4).

The spread of American fundamentalist churches in several parts of Africa was greeted with understandable concern by leaders of the mainstream churches, who often saw their followers leaving for the foreign sects. Sponsored by the American television evangelists and local allies, thousands of fundamentalist foreign crusaders promoted American-style conservative Christianity. Ardently anti-communist, they worked to convert as many Africans as possible to their type of Christianity, and, in the process, it is argued, to promote American political ideology (d'Antonio 1990).

Pieterse (1992: 10–11) alleges that a new religio-political hegemony has emerged in Africa as the result of American fundamentalist ideas. The purveyors of these ideas were able to gain the cultural leadership of Christianity, he claims, because of their social prestige and personal persuasiveness. Norms, beliefs and morals favourable to American interests are disseminated among the believers as a fundamental aspect of the religious message. What this amounts to is a claim that Africans who convert to the American-style fundamentalist churches are victims of manipulation by the latest manifestation of neo-colonialism; the objective is not to spirit away the region's material resources, but rather to deflect popular political mobilization away from seeking structural change of the society and the economy, presumably in order to serve either American strategic interests and/or financial objectives of US transnational corporations.

Yet, as Mbembe (1988: 181) makes clear, successive waves of foreign Christian proselytization in Sub-Saharan Africa have resulted in the indigenization of that faith. He makes the point – one that was argued in Chapter 2 of this book – that colonial Christianity tried unsuccessfully to appropriate the richness of the autochthons' imagination and beliefs, in order better to convert and to dominate. Colonial and post-colonial anti-establishment religious entrepreneurs – including fundamentalists – related their message to the uncaptured store of paganism which existed side by side with orthodox Christian belief; their work resulted in the birth of African independent churches as well as Africanization of the former mission churches. Generally, they rehabilitated

certain central givens of orthodox Christianity and added to the
structure elements adapted from local traditions and beliefs. The same
process occurred in the post-colonial period in relation to Christian
fundamentalism: preachers attract followers in part because they offer
the same kinds of material benefits that the mission churches did 100
years ago. Physical well-being was derived from the missions' control of
health-care systems, while prosperity was believed to be a function of
the education which they also controlled.

In recent times, health and education facilities have faltered in many
African states, in part as a result of the effects of IMF-supported economic reform programmes which cut government expenditures. It has
been widely noted that alternative methods of achieving material
benefits may be found through membership of Christian fundamentalist
groups, the attractions of which may well be enhanced further by perceived links with wealthy foreign figures like the American Kenneth E.
Hagin, who heads the Rhema Bible Church, which has daughter
churches in South Africa, Zimbabwe, Swaziland and Malawi. Among
local proponents of the 'gospel of prosperity' are: Andrew Wutawun-
ashe's Family of God Church (Zimbabwe); Mensa Otabil's International
Central Gospel Church (Ghana and beyond); Bishop Duncan-Williams's
Action Faith Ministries (Ghana and beyond); and Benson Idahosa's
Church of God Mission International (Nigeria and elsewhere). Gifford
argues that the 'gospel of prosperity' serves to prevent the development
of a 'genuine African Christianity' as it becomes subsumed within
American fundamentalist beliefs (Gifford 1991b: 19).

According to the ideas associated with the 'gospel of prosperity', it
is only right and proper – indeed, it is God's will, that those who deserve
it achieve earthly prosperity. Poverty, illness, poor health, and other
misfortunes are sure signs of sin, of a lack of true Christian commitment, and God's signal that he is aware of an individual's personal
shortcomings. It follows, in this line of reasoning, that the most devoted
Christian is the most wealthy; the sight of a millionaire preacher
addressing a sermon to a prosperous congregation is a material justification of such beliefs (Marishane 1992: 84–5). As Benson Idahosa re-
marked: 'My God is not a poor God. God did not say you should
worship him in rags. My God is a living and kind God' (Ndibe 1985a:
9). The point is endorsed by Bishop Duncan-Williams of Ghana's Action
Faith Ministries: '[T]he problem of our people is poverty ... the only
thing that is going to bring us out from being a third world nation is
creativity, productivity, having a sense of achievement. These things
have to do with prosperity' (Akakpo 1994: 1111).

One tactic used by the American fundamentalists is the personal 'crusade', in tandem with radio and television dissemination of the religious message. Radio stations under their control transmit their messages throughout much of Africa. For example, the Sudan Interior Mission's radio station, known as ELWA, broadcasts from Monrovia, transmitting programmes in about forty languages across West Africa (Gifford 1993: 102–3), while Trinity Broadcasting Network transmits to an appreciative audience in South Africa. It also provides the Swazi television network with programmes, featuring American television evangelists such as Robert Schuller, James Kennedy, Kenneth Copeland and Jimmy Swaggart. In 1988 TBN hosted three evangelical rallies in Ciskei which attracted crowds of over 10,000 each; following these, TBN recorded '6,000 decisions for Christ' (a conversion rate of one in five of those attending) (CIIR 1991: 87). There is also the Christian Broadcasting Network, the fourth largest cable network in the United States, which broadcasts its programmes to some twenty-five African countries, including Egypt, Kenya, Uganda, Nigeria, Zimbabwe and South Africa.

Critics of the 'gospel of prosperity' preachers argue that their message is inappropriate in the current phase of economic and political upheaval in Africa. They cite three reasons, which have to do with the nature of the purveyors of the message, the social effects of the message, and the (not so) hidden agenda of the message. First, the preachers are 'spiritually fraudulent, little more than money-making machines taking advantage of the naivety of their followers' (Ephson 1989: 584). Second, they 'encourage a passive acceptance of disasters, misfortune and a lack of social responsibility, leading to the absence of any commitment to development' (Gifford 1991b: 9). What is needed, it is implied, to help Africa emerge from its problems is a commitment to fight for socio-economic and political change, and to work to develop individual self-determination, independence, political responsibility and social involvement. In short, the ideas and ideals of liberation theology would be beneficial to the mass of Africans. Finally, critics argue, American-promoted Christian fundamentalism has as its primary aim a decidedly non-spiritual concern: the promotion and pursuit of America's anti-communist foreign-policy goals. Abraham claims that

> [n]ew [Christian fundamentalist] sects have invaded Africa since the period of independence. These sects are imported products, cleverly introduced to perpetuate the dominance of Africa by foreign powers ... Pseudoreligious sects from Europe or mostly from America borrow a certain vocabulary from rituals in the Holy Bible or in Christian churches and use it in a distorted and bizarre way. Their commonalities are the fact that they exploit the

emptiness left in the African soul by the sudden suppression of most of the traditional secret societies during the colonial period. Basing themselves on the propensity of the African soul for esotericism, they offer it plenty of initiation rites, uses of incense, talismans, prohibitions, and fabulous promises of success here below and in the world to come (Abraham 1990: 29, 39).

Oduyoye argues, further, that

[t]he most devastating [religion in Africa] to my mind is the type of Christianity being promoted by certain Western countries. It can be substantiated that the very people who own the wealth of the multinationals also sponsor this type of Christianity that orientates Africans towards buying into the capitalist system so that they may serve as its labour force and cannon fodder for its militarism. This religion is nothing short of demonic (Oduyoye 1990: 100).

The alliance of capitalism and foreign fundamentalism work together, these authors suggest, to limit severely the impact of liberation theology in Africa. African speakers at the Oaxtepec meeting of the Ecumenical Association of Third World Theologians in December 1986 emphasized also the idea of 'anthropological poverty' to explain why liberation theology had not been more influential in Africa. The concept of anthropological poverty relates to the way that 'black people ... interiorized the patterns, values, and models' of the colonial powers (Bingemer 1990: x–xi). What is necessary to counteract the baleful influence of neo-colonial, fundamentalist Christianity is an African Christianity that is embedded in local culture, coupled with sustained, equitable socio-economic progress. Two questions suggest themselves in relation to these issues: first, is there a distinctively *African* Christianity?; and, second, if so, is it being subverted – and with what results – by the influence of the foreign fundamentalist preachers?

As argued above, it seems clear that Africans were never fully appropriated by orthodox mission Christianity, with its tendency, especially pronounced in Catholicism, to proclaim one narrow set of spiritual and theological concerns as the 'truth' (Mbembe 1988). The primary aim of many Africans who adopted Christianity was to benefit materially in some way (Horton 1993: 154–6). In the post-colonial era, Africans continued to regard Christianity as a means to attain both material and spiritual goals; many preachers emerged in response to social needs, as the material quality of life diminished for many, especially during the 1980s and 1990s, as economic adjustment programmes began to bite.

The assumption of those who regard themselves as socially progressive Christians is that it is foreign fundamentalists who prevent the development of appropriate religious vehicles of community advancement, and that the growth of their churches helps to explain the disappointing failure of the basic Christian communities to develop widely in Africa as they have done in Latin America. Yet, even in the latter region, the numbers and dynamism of the communities appears now to be diminishing, with hundreds of thousands of poor people converting to fundamentalist Protestantism (Burdick 1994). Progressive Catholicism, standing for solidarity and collective commitment, for a reading of the Bible through the eyes of the poor, and for the pursuit of the Kingdom of God on earth and in society rather than in heaven and in individual isolation, has been found lacking as an ideology of community development in many social environments. Given that the nature of African society has changed greatly as a result of urbanization over the last thirty years or so, then we might well expect that the types of church people want would reflect this development. African societies, riven as they are by ethnic schisms, are inherently unlikely to develop a set of religious beliefs which are orientated towards the amelioration of structural deficiencies. It is far more likely that people will be attracted to a religion which puts the individual and his or her family first. By giving money to the church the individual will become richer; conversion will solve the individual's problems and those of his or her family. Salvation comes through faith. Fundamentalist churches in Africa, as in Latin America, are largely urban phenomena: they are products of modernization. Their followers come both from the ranks of the poor and from the urban middle classes. Their churches reflect the social changes that accompany modernization, as well as the globalization of ideas whereby a faith concocted in one place – the United States – can be adopted and adapted elsewhere – Africa, Latin America – to satisfy the religious needs of millions of people.

The fundamentalist churches in Africa should be seen not as an indication of the negative impact of American cultural and spiritual hegemony, but as manifestations of both individual and community self-interest. They may acquire political interests and have an important role as mobilizing agents. Churches will interact with public authority when they seek to diversify into other activities: schools, hospitals, clinics, businesses will all be subject to governmental regulation. Given that the standard procedure for dealing with drawbacks, the bribe, is not (or not so readily) open to fundamentalist Christians, then it is necessary instead to mobilize the religious community as a whole to achieve desired results. What is needed to galvanize fundamentalists into wider political activity is the existence of a trigger issue – a concern of such commu-

nity interest that corporate efforts are focused to gain the desired results. If there is a trigger issue, members of fundamentalist churches
will become political actors. Because church members regularly (perhaps several times a day) communicate with each other, it is fairly easy
to develop a sense of purposive group solidarity. Obviously if political
action is contemplated the church's human and material resources will
be of immense value.

Conclusion

This chapter has been concerned broadly with three issues: one, the
reasons for the growth and political significance of Christian fundamentalism in Africa below the Sahara; two, the relative lack of advancement of its Islamic counterpart; and, three, the political attributes
of followers of fundamentalist religions in the context of foreign religious
influence in the region. A number of conclusions emerge. First, as far
as Nigeria is concerned, when Muslims and Christians see each other
as threats, this will enhance the political involvement of both constituencies in relation to each other. Second, an important catalyst in the
growth of Christian fundamentalism in Sub-Saharan Africa was the
involvement of foreign interests. In relation to Islam, Saudi Arabia,
Libya and Iran all pursued foreign-policy goals in Africa by seeking to
enlist the allegiances of different groups of self-styled Islamic fundamentalists. Finally, it appears that, in general, not many Africans were
impressed by the Islamic fundamentalist programme of reform, religious
purity, austerity and intolerance of 'unorthodox' versions of Islam. The
story was quite different for Christian fundamentalism.

As in Latin America, East Asia and parts of the Pacific, there has
been a swift growth of fundamentalist Christianity in parts of Sub-
Saharan Africa over the last two decades or so. During its growth,
however, American-style fundamentalism was increasingly indigenized
in a manner reminiscent of early periods when orthodox mission Christianity also underwent a process of Africanization. It was noted that
African Christian fundamentalists, like their Islamic counterparts, are
not necessarily apolitical: apprehension at real or putative Islamization
or Christianization, and, generally, corruption in public life were two
issues which led them to involve themselves in politics.

It seems clear that the increasing popularity of fundamentalist
Christianity in several parts of Africa can be accounted for by the
combined effects of social, economic and political disruptions associated

with the process of modernization. Such a development has a historical precedent: in Europe, the First World War was the progenitor of a plethora of new religious movements, and indeed, a return to witch-craft as an alternative religious philosophy, at a time when orthodox or mainstream Christianity was widely deemed to have failed to prevent international conflict. Many people felt lost in the vastness of a world over which they had no control and in which they were buffeted by forces beyond their comprehension. Paralleling the rise of new religious movements at the time was the growth of socialism as a secular form of redemption (Fulton 1987: 202).

In modern Africa, the loss of faith in orthodox Christianity was not resolved by a turn to secular ideologies of redemption, such as socialism, which was judged to have fundamentally failed when applied as a socio-political and economic palliative in the Soviet Union and elsewhere. Rather, it was fundamentalist Christianity which often supplied the philosophical underpinning and ideological substance of a new moral order. In Nigeria, the quarter century since the civil war was filled 'every day [by] the birth of a new "church"!' (Mbon 1987: 220). Nigeria's unfortunate post-colonial socio-political history was paralleled to a degree in most African states. The social, economic and political situation generally deteriorated from the period of relative optimism in the late 1960s and early 1970s. Many Africans found themselves 'SAPped' by the IMF and World Bank economic recovery programmes and by the eco-nomically debilitating effects of their country's foreign indebtedness.

Fundamentalist Christians as a group have had less impact upon the recent process of democratization in Africa (with the exception of Zambia) than have leaders of the former mission churches. This in itself demonstrates only that the former are less willing than the latter to become involved in pro-democracy campaigns; there is no especial trigger issue to stimulate their political entry. In addition, there is also the belief that religion and politics belong in distinct spheres. Matthew 22: 15–22 is the biblical reference and justification: 'Render to Caesar what belongs to Caesar and to God what belongs to God.' On the other hand, there is no concrete evidence to suggest that members of the fundamentalist churches vote for more conservative candidates than their counterparts in the mainstream churches, or that their members are indifferent to political or union activism. (Frederick Chiluba, president of Zambia, is both a fundamentalist Christian and a union activist, for instance.)

The question remains whether it is analytically necessary to make a spiritual, political, social, or economic distinction between the American-derived fundamentalist churches and those which have grown from indigenous roots. The answer is: no. The point is that many of the African fundamentalist church leaders seem to locate themselves towards that end of the Christian spectrum because that is what their devotees appear to want. Religion is big business; those with a product that no one wants will change their approach for better rewards. The nature and form of fundamentalist Christianity is the result of a demand-led revolution. All manner of religious figures act as religious leaders and scriptural interpreters, offering hope to those (especially in the urban centres) who are disaffected by what independence and modernization have brought. They function as 'healers' to a people suffering despair, disillusionment and pessimism (Mbembe 1988: 122). To succeed, preachers must render the current epoch intelligible to their followers. Their teaching must skilfully explain apparently disordered events as coherent and logical. The fact that fundamentalist Christianity has widened its appeal while its Muslim counterpart has generally failed to do so suggests that the former fulfils a need in many people which the latter does not.

8

Conclusion

In an earlier work on the relationship of religion and politics in the Third World (Haynes 1993a), I argued that analysis of the issue had to take into account the effects of modernization on Third World societies. With the focus primarily on Islam and Christianity, I concluded that over the last twenty years or so four developments were of significance to an understanding of how religion related to political developments in Third World regions. The first was that religion often serves as a vehicle of political opposition; second, religions sometimes interact with ethnicity and nationalism to produce a volatile and powerful ideological hybrid; third, contemporary interactions of religion and politics emphasize Third World societies' dynamism and propensity to change; fourth, several Muslim states – notably Iran and Saudi Arabia – pursue a type of 'Islamic foreign policy' with religious objectives which under-pin their national-interest goals. In some respects the current project aims to be a successor to the earlier volume. I wanted to develop my thesis in specific relation to Africa. In this book I have been concerned with two main issues: the relationship of religious institutions and their leaders to the state, and, the political role (if any) of popular religions.

In order to apply the conclusions of the earlier book to the African context, I set out in the current volume to examine the interactions between both mainstream and popular religious organizations and the state in Africa during the colonial and independence periods in the context of a general process of modernization. By the latter term I mean the collective process, with all the ramifications, of urbanization, governmental centralization, the spread of Western-style education, and the growth of modern economies. Yet, in peeling away the levels of interaction between African religious and political issues, each issue proved to have several dimensions. In short, the analytical precision of each of the terms 'religion', 'politics' and 'state' when viewed in the African context are fraught with hazards. For example, the state is obviously greater than the sum of its institutional parts, but how much greater and in what ways? I chose to regard the state largely as the sum of its leaders and institutions, though retaining an awareness that the boundary between public institutions and private interests in Africa is, to say the least, fuzzy (Bayart 1993a; Chabal 1992; Lemerchand 1992).

Further, it is clear that no consensus exists as to what, precisely, religion *is*. Anthropologists, for example, regard religion as one component of the cultural aspects of social life; sociologists seek its more general social import; theologians are interested primarily in its individual or collective spiritual significance; political scientists will look for signs of political activity when assessing religious groups and organizations. The concern of the political scientist will often be expressed in questions such as: How far is religious group X really a vehicle of political change, perhaps in disguise? (Buijtenhuis 1985). I chose to regard 'religion' in both a spiritual-material sense involving personal belief systems, and an ideology which can motivate individuals and groups in certain ways.

Finally, it is generally agreed that 'politics' involves the workings of formal political institutions (legislatures, executives, presidents, and so on), as well as relations of power in an organized setting, and focuses on issues involving authority, legitimacy, power and equity. I share this view.

Mainstream Religious Organizations and the State

I have argued that there are two key factors in an analysis of the relationship between politics and religion in Africa. The first is that the leaders of religious institutions are always products of their times and of the particular social class they come from (or grow into); as such, they have social and class positions and needs which exist independently of their spiritual and theological views. In my view, what such leaders believe their religious message to comprise in a spiritual sense is of interest but is primarily the concern of theologians; what they seek to gain from their personal position or for their religious institution in competition with others is, however, relevant to a study of African politics and religion.

Africa's generally declining economic position over the last two decades or so has been noted by just about everybody with a professional interest in the region. Many have commented on the way economic failure has produced (or exacerbated) significant levels of clientelism and corruption, involving both elites and ordinary people (see Bayart 1993a; Chabal 1992; and Joseph 1987 for the best accounts). I have suggested as implausible the belief that many religious professionals would somehow succeed in rising above the material concerns which energize most ordinary people. They may be concerned with spiritual development and moral issues, but they are still people with human needs and desires. It is surely rational for them in the circumstances in which Africa currently finds itself to seek to augment their personal well-being when possible; sometimes this involves using their professional positions for personal gain. Often religious professionals, encouraged by necessity to seek to augment often insufficient incomes by additional means in order to maintain or enhance their social positions, have found their concerns shaped by the imperatives of *la politique du ventre* (Bayart 1989a; Gifford 1993; Toulabor 1991; Ibrahim 1989b, 1991). Foreign NGOs supplied funds to churches; priests and bishops became entrepreneurs and businessmen; clientelism became a mode of dispersal of money and other material goods to family and friends. Togo's Catholic archbishop is especially notorious in this respect, accused of ethnic favouritism, empire-building and corruption (Toulabor 1991).

When it comes to the political relationship between Church and State, theologians and political scientists usually agree that both institutions are involved in different aspects of life. This seems to me to be reasonable (most of the time) if one is concerned with Christian religious institutions and the state in Western Europe and North America. Yet even in these regions religion and politics sometimes concern each other (Moyser 1991). In the United States, for example, Christian fundamentalists have plenty to say about a range of moral, social and political issues. In Britain, the Anglican Bishop of Durham was warned by government ministers in 1993 not to meddle in politics when he raised the issue of the links between poverty and crime; while in Germany the issue of racist attacks on Turks and other foreign immigrants has been condemned by a range of Christian figures. Clearly, when religious professionals comment on issues like these it is hard to argue that religion and politics are clearly, and invariably, distinct from each other. In short, the separation of Church and State in individual national contexts is usually one of theoretical degree rather than practical certainty; in other words, Christian professionals and activists comment upon, argue about, and attempt to affect political outcomes. Within the

Islamic universe, on the other hand, sacred and temporal issues are never, even theoretically, divorced from each other. When we turn to examine the relationship between African religious leaders and the state, it is by no means clear why their interactions should be qualitatively any different to those of their counterparts in other regions. Two such power centres are bound to affect each other a great deal given the nature of African politics, with its personalization of issues and the often close relationship between socio-economic elites.

Christianity has major spiritual centres in Western Europe, including Vatican City and Canterbury. Because the region's socio-political development was characterized by a clear-cut division between Church and State, it is sometimes assumed that the division was a universal characteristic of Christian institutions rather than one which evolved in the particularistic circumstances of Western Europe. These include the emergence of industrialized society and the evolution of associational groups which often developed into loci of political power outside the control of either Church or State. In Sub-Saharan Africa, on the other hand, the brief duration of colonialism and the way that European administrations were often tacked onto pre-existing political structures resulted in a form of state power which on the surface, and theoretically, resembled European institutions, but in practice was quite different. Alternative centres of independent power are rare. The acquisition and use of state power for personal purposes results in the holder(s) becoming rich (Bates 1993). Those associated with the state, including some senior religious figures, may use their positions to benefit themselves personally and their churches corporately. 'Certain members of the [Anglican] church at high level are very close to the [former] government', stated an Anglican Church official soon after the overthrow of Rwanda's Hutu-dominated government in August 1994 (McGreal 1994). While it would be false to claim that every senior church figure throughout Africa had a relationship such as the Anglican Archbishop of Kigali had with government (to the extent that he appeared to seek to justify the massacre of Tutsis [McGreal 1994]), it would be equally difficult to deny that senior church figures – as in colonial times – generally enjoy cordial relations with political authorities (Bayart 1989b, 1993; Hansen 1992; Ranger and Vaughan 1993; Mbembe 1988; Schatzberg 1988).

There were several additional factors which helped to produce particular relationships between Church and State. First, it was of course especially difficult for *any* manifestations of independent power to assert themselves for the first twenty or thirty years of the independence era, during which time the one-party or military regime was all but ubiquitous and invariably, it seemed, rather powerful. The state's security forces could quickly quell isolated manifestations of dissidence. Second, churches were usually slow to pronounce publicly on political issues because of the existence of the two realms, the temporal and the sacred, which often resulted in the church 'keeping its nose' out of the state's affairs (Boyle 1992). Third, mainstream religious institutions were also involved with the state inasmuch as political leaders expected them to be quiescent partners in the national-unity project. The former, by their control of educational and other welfare roles, were also of singular importance to many regimes, for their ability to replace the church in the provision of such goods was limited. As a result, even those regimes motivated by Marxist-Leninist ideology eventually arrived at working relationships with the main churches, whereby the latter would be tolerated, even encouraged, so long as they offered welfare services and did not proselytize too openly or too strongly.

Popular Religion and Politics in Africa

The second main area of concern in the book is the degree to which popular religions in Africa have political significance. I focused here on three categories of religion: community-oriented groups, often with clear political goals; Christian and Muslim fundamentalist groups; and new religious movements. The development of each type was linked to the stresses and strains occasioned by modernization, but their differing forms and responses were explained by a number of factors, involving a variety of issues.

I argued that both Christianity and Islam in Africa are adapted to local conditions and cultures to produce more or less indigenized faiths. When Benson Idahosa, leader of one of Nigeria's most popular fundamentalist churches, claimed that his God was not a god who wanted his believers to worship him in poverty, he was astutely tuning in to one of the most important roles of religious faith for many Africans: to offer not only individual and community spiritual benefits, but also material attractions, including social solidarity, healing, a sense of belonging, and, occasionally, financial rewards. Followers of the Zion Christian Church in South Africa wear distinctive khaki uniforms when job-hunting. The reason is that employers will note the uniforms and see in the job-hunter an honest person who will give his or her full commitment to their employment, however undistinguished (Tingle 1992). In Lagos, members of fundamentalist churches organize entrepreneurial and business opportunities which employ co-religionists (Marshall 1991). Such practices are not confined to those in the Christian churches. Senegalese marabouts control the groundnut trade and achieve high social standing and wealth. Their positions are further enhanced by their role as interlocutors between state and society. Iranian and Saudi Arabian money is passed to Muslim leaders in a number of African countries in order to increase their national and religious influence.

There are many variants of both Christianity and Islam in Africa. This is explained by Laitin (1979). He identifies three independent sources of religious influence on political life in differing national and cultural contexts. These are: the original, orthodox or 'pure' religious doctrine; the 'practical' religion, which emerges from the interaction of proclaimed religious orthodoxy with people's interpretations of it; and, finally, 'the practical religion of the converted' – the interaction of religious orthodoxy with the pre-existing spiritual beliefs of converts. Laitin's schema is instructive: it highlights the fact that forms of religious belief held in a community reflect both the physical distance of the believers from the birthplace of the religion, and the community's cultural characteristics. One might say that a set of religious beliefs travels rather like a snowball as it rolls, with one important difference: whereas a snowball gathers snow and other materials in its progress, increasing in mass as it does so, a set of religious beliefs, in contrast, gathers to itself bits and pieces of other religious and cultural matter without necessarily expanding in size overall. The result is a set of religious beliefs containing some aspects of the religious orthodoxy, but at the same time characteristics of other belief systems. In Africa below the Sahara, religious hybrids are the norm; there is no mere replication of the religious orthodoxies of the 'parent' religion.

Culturally specific Islam and Christianity – the first with its roots in Arab lands of the Middle East, the second with its focus for Catholics and Protestants in European Christian centres – were Africanized in the course of their penetration of the region. Sometimes Africanization involved ethnicization. In Tanzania and in Kenya, for example, one product of the tentative political liberalization of the early 1990s was in the emergence of popular Muslim groups which used Islam as a symbol both of solidarity and of opposition to a status quo which they perceived to operate for the benefit of other groups. The Diola of Casamance are also mobilized to resist what they perceive as encroachment on their economic position by outsiders. Not all Diola are by any means Christians – indeed, about half are Muslims – yet their opposition

centres upon a movement the *raison d'être* of which is its distinctiveness
vis-à-vis Senegal's Muslims.

Another example of anti-centrist, popular opposition that uses
religious ideas and concerns is those feminist groups which have appeared in, among other countries, Nigeria and Senegal in recent times.
Groups such as the Federation of Muslim Women's Association of
Nigeria are concerned to increase their members' social and political
standing by seeking to mobilize them in support of more liberal interpretations of Islamic teaching than those propounded by members of the
ulama (Callaway and Creevey 1994: 156).

The mobilization of popular religious groups around issues of community interest, in order to resist what they regard as unacceptable
pressures, was also exemplified by the basic Christian communities.
These were established in Africa from the 1960s in order that groups
of Christians, predominantly in urban areas and without the services of
a priest, would continue to exist as such – as *Christian* groups. The
communities try to hold forms of religious service as well as involving
themselves in community self-improvement projects.

Popularly oriented Protestant fundamentalist churches grew swiftly
in Africa, especially from the 1970s, offering both spiritual and community benefits to their members. Islamic fundamentalism, on the other
hand, did not progress in the same manner that it did in parts of the
Middle East and Southeast Asia. I explained this fact by reference to
the *type* of Islam the fundamentalist groups champion: in North Africa,
Arabic culture predominates; this is not the case in Africa below the
Sahara. Thus the bulk of African Muslims adhere to their own, often
culturally distinct, versions of the faith (Last 1988; Bernal 1994; Ali
Ibrahim 1989).

Muslim reformists in the ulama, on the other hand, often work
closely with their governments, with the aim of achieving control of
national Muslim organizations. They do not seek to impose their
leadership upon popular Islam, including Sufism, only to ensure
spiritual purity, but also because they recognize that their own power
would be enhanced by control of the organizations. The Sufi 'folk'
religion – to the purists a culturally 'debased' form of Islam – has to
be controlled because Sufism is seen as a serious challenge to those
wishing to impose their religious orthodoxies on ordinary Muslims
(Bromley 1994: 42).

Given the generally poor, and declining, economic position of many
ordinary Muslims in Africa, it is perhaps surprising that there have
not been more outbreaks of millenarian violence like that associated

with Muhammadu Marwa and the Maitatsine movement in Kano some fifteen years ago. It seems less surprising, though, when we consider that many ordinary Muslims in the area actually regarded Marwa as an apostate, a false prophet who was in reality a 'devil', one who condemned and attacked local Muslims of whatever social category if they chose not to follow his teachings (Clarke 1988). It is equally clear, however, that the social and economic circumstances which produced the Maitatsine movement were not unique to Kano. Perhaps they were merely more focused there than in many other African towns and cities: a particular catalyst for the Marwa-led violence appears to have been the social changes brought about by a decade of rapidly expanding oil revenues flowing into the city, the effects of which were dramatic, including the rise of a small class of *nouveaux riches* and a much larger stratum of increasingly poverty-stricken young men, Islamically educated and increasingly alienated (Clarke 1988; Lubeck 1985).

The Role of Foreign Interests in the Growth of Fundamentalist Religious Groups in Africa

The role of *agents provocateurs* in the eruption of Islamically inspired social protest is a complex one. On the one hand, there are often localized reasons behind the outbreak of Islamic opposition, perhaps economic or ethnic inspired; yet, on the other, there are also often foreign interests at work among the already disaffected. Such interests include the Iranian, Saudi Arabian and Libyan governments, which seem to regard Sub-Saharan Africa as a region where they can pursue their foreign-policy goals by stirring up Islamically oriented discontent (Bernal 1994; Shaikh 1992; Haynes 1993a: ch. 5). Two decades of oil revenues gave such states the financial resources to prosecute aggressive foreign policies in which the separation of political, diplomatic and religious goals was impossible. Iran's biggest handicap – that it is predominantly a Shiite country, when most African Muslims are Sunni – was partially offset for some African Muslim radicals (for example, in Nigeria) by its bona fide revolutionary credentials. Some ambitious African Muslim radicals allowed themselves to be seduced by Iran's revolutionary message for two reasons: it gave them an immediately recognizable radical programme for their own societies; and it offered Muslim radicals a political platform from which to launch attacks on incumbent Muslim elites – especially members of the ulama – associated by many people with the championing of an often welcome religious orthodoxy and social conservatism. Saudi Arabia's concerns, on the other hand, were less revolutionary in orientation: they were to encourage alternative groups of Muslims to work towards the building of a Saudi-style Islamic state (Haynes 1993a: ch. 5).

A second manifestation of foreign religious interest in Africa is that of American-style Christian fundamentalist churches. On the surface they could not be more different from Muslim fundamentalist groups. Where radical Islam was a vehicle of popular opposition to the status quo, Christian fundamentalist churches often appeared to be supporters of 'strong', sometimes authoritarian, government. Where radical Islam thrives on ethnic rivalries, the fundamentalist churches often appear to seek to overcome them (Marshall 1991, 1993). Where fundamentalist Islam works towards installation of Sharia law, the fundamentalist churches claim as far as possible not to involve themselves with political controversies, preferring instead to seek the creation of a just moral realm on earth in preparation for Judgement Day. Yet, despite the dissimilarities between Christian and Muslim fundamentalist groups, they have several features in common: each is rather intolerant of the other; each regards the successes of its rival to be detrimental to its own position; each perceives religious conflict as highly likely because of an incompatibility of goals.

The 'invasion' of the American-style fundamentalist churches in Africa was seen by some, and not only Muslims, as the 'Trojan horse' of US foreign policy in the region (Pieterse 1992; Gifford 1991a, 1992a, 1993). The argument was that the fundamentalist churches often associated with American evangelical preachers work towards a dampening down of political opposition by spreading a 'gospel of prosperity'. Self-interest is paramount; the more one prays and gives financially to God, the more one will receive earthly (and later heavenly) reward. Now, there is nothing unusual about Africans moving from one faith to another, dependent on where they perceive their best self-interest to lie. Many, for example, moved from belief in traditional deities to either Islam or Christianity because the old gods had failed to protect them from invasion by Europeans (Horton 1993). The appeal of American-style fundamentalist churches should be seen in the same way: they offer a clear and simple message which suggests that faith is all that matters. There is little clear indication that Africans have been 'brainwashed' into a political conservatism by the message of these churches. Their appeal is straightforward: if you have enough faith, everything you want will come to you. Many Africans move from the mainstream

Christian churches because they are not being fulfilled spiritually. It follows that the current popularity of the fundamentalist churches will probably only last for as long as they are delivering what they claim to offer: enhanced spiritual help to those who feel they need it.

Bibliography

Abraham, K. C. (1990) 'Regional Report: Africa' in Abraham (ed.), *Third World Theologies. Commonalities and Divergences*, Orbis Books, London, pp. 28–56.

Abubakr, M. (1986) 'BUK Mosque and Divisive Sermons', *The Triumph* (Lagos), 5 May.

Adubofuor, S. (1992) 'Parachurch Church Movements and Christian Order in Ghana: A Review of Past and Present Developments', paper presented at the African Studies Association of the UK conference, University of Stirling, September.

Africa Confidential (1987a) 'Mozambique/South Africa: The Special Forces behind RENAMO', vol. XXVIII, no. 24, 2 December.

———— (1987b) 'The Men of Power', vol. XXVIII, no. 24, 2 December.

———— (1991) 'Zambia: Turbulent Priests', vol. XXXII, no. 3, 8 February.

———— (1992) 'Malawi: Referring to the Opposition', vol. XXXIII, no. 22, 6 November.

———— (1993a) 'Zambia: The Model Democracy Loses its Shine', vol. XXXIV, no. 10, 14 May.

———— (1993b) 'Algeria: Generals in the Firing Line', vol. XXXIV, no. 13, 2 July.

———— (1993c) 'Kenya: A Murderous Majimboism', vol. XXXIV, no. 21, 22 October.

———— (1993d) 'Sudan: Turabi's Unconvincing Transition', vol. XXXIV, no. 21, 22 October.

———— (1993e) 'Sudan: God and Caesar', vol. XXXIV, no. 22, 5 November.

———— (1994) 'Tanzania: Threatening Mwalimu's Ghosts, vol. XXXV, no. 13, 1 July.

Africa Watch (1991) *Kenya. Taking Liberties*, Africa Watch, New York.

Akakpo, B. (1994) 'Save and Prosper', *West Africa*, 20–26 June, p. 1111.

Allen, T. (1991) 'Understanding Alice: Uganda's Holy Spirit Movement in Context, *Africa*, vol. LI, no. 3, pp. 370–99.

Ali Ibrahim, A. (1989) 'Popular Islam: The Religion of the Barbarous Throng', *North-East African Studies*, vol. XI, no. 2, pp. 25–40.

Amin, S. (1993) 'Social Movements at the Periphery', in P. Wignaraja (ed.), *New*

Social Movements in the South, Zed Books, London, pp. 76–100.

Anderson, J. N. D. (1969) 'The Legal Tradition', in J. Kritzek and W. Lewis (eds), *Islam in Africa*, Van Nostrand Rheinhold, New York, pp. 35–53.

Antoun, R. (1989) *Muslim Preacher in the Modern World*, Princeton University Press, Princeton.

Ashe, R. (1890) *Two Kings of Uganda; or, Life by the Shores of Victoria Nyanza*, Sampson, Low, Marston and Company, London.

Baeta, C. G. (1962) *Prophetism in Ghana*, SCM, London.

———— (ed.) (1968) *Christianity in Tropical Africa*, Oxford University Press, London.

Balandier, G. (1955) *Sociologie Actuelle de l'Afrique Noire*, Presses Universitaires de France, Paris.

Barkan, J. (1992) 'The Rise and Fall of a Governance Realm in Kenya', in G. Hyden and M. Bratton (eds), *Governance and Politics in Africa*, Lynne Rienner Publishers, Boulder, Colo. and London, pp. 167–93.

Barrett, D. (1982) *World Christian Encyclopedia*, Oxford University Press, Nairobi.

Bates, R. (1993) 'The Politics of Economic Policy Reform: A Review Article', *Journal of African Economies*, vol. II, no. 3, pp. 417–33.

Bavarel, M. (1983) *New Communities, New Ministries*, Orbis Books, New York.

Bax, M. (1987) 'Religious Regimes and State Formation', *Anthropological Quarterly*, vol. LX, no. 1, pp. 1–11.

Bayart, J.-F. (1979) *L'Etat au Cameroun*, Presses de la Fondation Nationale des Sciences Politiques, Paris.

———— (1986) 'Civil Society in Africa', in P. Chabal (ed.), *Political Domination in Africa*, Cambridge University Press, Cambridge, pp. 109–25.

———— (1989a) *L'Etat en Afrique*, Fayard, Paris.

———— (1989b) 'Les Eglises Chretiennes et la Politique du Ventre', *Politique Africaine*, no. 35, pp. 3–26.

———— (1993a) *The State in Africa*, Longman, London.

———— (ed.) (1993b) *Religion et Modernité Politique en Afrique Noire*, Karthala, Paris.

Beeley, B. (1992) 'Islam as a Global Political Force', in A. McGrew and P. Lewis (eds), *Global Politics. Globalization and the Nation State*, Polity Press, Cambridge, pp. 293–311.

Behrend, H. (1991) 'Is Alice Lakwena a Witch? The Holy Spirit Movement and its Fight against Evil in the North', in H. B. Hansen and M. Twaddle (eds), *Changing Uganda. The Dilemmas of Structural Adjustment and Revolutionary Change*, James Currey, London, pp. 162–77.

Beresford, D. (1993) 'Brotherhood of Man Sundered by Broederbond and Race', *Guardian*, 20 February.

Bernal, V. (1994) 'Gender, Culture and Capitalism', *Comparative Studies in Society and History*, vol. XXXVI, no. 1, pp. 36–67.

Berryman, P. (1994) 'The Coming of the Age of Evangelical Protestantism', *NACLA Report on the Americas*, vol. XXVI, no. 6, pp. 6–10.

Bingemer, M. (1990) 'Preface – Third World Theologies: Conversion to Others', in K. C. Abraham (ed.), *Third World Theologies. Commonalities and Divergences*, Orbis Books, London, pp. vii–xiv.

Birai, U. M. (1993) 'Islamic Tajdid and the Political Process in Nigeria', in M. Marty and R. Scott Appleby (eds), *Fundamentalisms and the State. Remaking Poli-

tics, Economics and Militance, University of Chicago Press, Chicago, pp. 184–203.

Birch Freeman, T. (1968) *Journal of Various Visits to the Kingdoms of Ashanti, Aku, and Dahomi in Western Africa*, Frank Cass, London (first published 1844).

Boahen, A. Adu. (1987) *African Perspectives on Colonialism*, James Currey, London.

Boillot, F. (1994) 'Les Communautés Chrétiennes de Base en Afrique', paper presented at round table, 'Mouvements Religieux de Debats Democratiques en Afrique', University of Pau, December 5–7.

Bone, D. (1982) 'Islam in Malawi', *Journal of Religion in Africa*, vol. 13, no. 2, pp. 126–38.

Booth, J. and Seligson, M. (1993) 'Paths to Democracy and the Political Culture of Costa Rica, Mexico and Nicaragua', in L. Diamond (ed.), *Political Culture and Democracy in Developing Countries*, Lynne Rienner Publishers, Boulder, Colo., pp. 107–33.

Boserup, E. (1970) *Women's Role in Economic Development*, St Martin's Press, New York.

Bourg, C. (1981) 'Politics and Religion', *Sociological Analysis*, vol. XXXXI, no. 4, pp. 297–315.

Boyle, P. (1992) 'Beyond Self-Protection to Prophecy: The Catholic Church and Political Change in Zaire', *Africa Today*, vol. XXXIX, no. 3, pp. 49–66.

Bratton, M. (1994) ' International Versus Domestic Pressures for "Democratization" in Africa', paper presented to conference, 'The End of the Cold War: Effects and Prospects for Asia and Africa', School of Oriental and African Studies, London, October.

Bratton, M. and van der Walle, N. (1991) 'Towards Governance in Africa: Popular Demands and State Responses', in G. Hyden and M. Bratton (eds), *Governance and Politics in Africa*, Lynne Rienner Publishers, London, pp. 27–55.

Brittain, V. (1991) 'Drought, Death and Donor Fatigue', *Guardian*, 18 April.

Brittain, V. and Watkins, K. (1994) 'A Continent Driven to Economic Suicide', *Guardian*, 20 July.

Bromley, S. (1994) *Rethinking Middle East Politics*, Polity Press, Cambridge.

Buijtenhuis, R. (1985) 'Dini Ya Msambwa: Rural Rebellion or Counter-Society?', in W. van Binsbergen and M. Schoffeleers (eds), *Theoretical Explorations in African Religion*, KPI, London, pp. 322–42.

Burdick, J. (1994) *Looking for God in Brazil*, University of California Press, Berkeley.

Burns, A. C. (1929) *History of Nigeria*, George Allen & Unwin, London.

Cabral, V. (1989) 'Colonisation et Religion, Depuis la Première Evangelisation jusqu'à la Colonisation des Peuples de Guinée-Bissau', *Mondes et Developpement*, vol. XVII, no. 65, pp. 233–8.

Callaghy, T. (1987) 'Culture and Politics in Zaire', Department of State, Washington DC, quoted in N. Chazan, 'Between Liberalism and Statism: African Political Cultures and Democracy', in L. Diamond (ed.), *Political Culture and Democracy in Developing Countries*, Lynne Rienner Publishers, Boulder, Colo. and London, pp. 67–106, at p. 83.

Callaway, B. and Creevey, L. (1994) *The Heritage of Islam: Women, Religion and Politics in West Africa*, Lynne Rienner Publishers, Boulder, Colo. and London.

Caplan, L. (1987) 'Introduction', in L. Caplan (ed.), *Studies in Religious Fundamentalism*, Macmillan, London, pp. 1–24.

Chabal, P. (1992) *Power in Africa: An Essay in Political Interpretation*, Macmillan, London.

Channel 4 (1993) television film, 'Witness: Man, God and Africa', 12 August.

Charnay, J.-P. (1980) *Les Contres-orients, ou Comment Penser l'Autre selon Soi*, Sinbad, Paris.

Chazan, N. (1992) 'Africa's Democratic Challenge', *World Policy Journal*, Spring, pp. 279–307.

———— (1993) 'Between Liberalism and Statism: African Political Cultures and Democracy', in L. Diamond (ed.), *Political Culture and Democracy in Developing Countries*, Lynne Rienner Publishers, Boulder, Colo. and London, pp. 67–106.

Christian Students' Social Movement of Nigeria (1983) 'Post-prayer Conference Letter', quoted in M. Ojo, 'The Contextual Significance of the Charismatic Movements in Independent Nigeria', *Africa*, vol. LVIII, no. 2, pp. 175–92, at 190.

CIIR (1991) 'Evangelical Broadcasting', *Review of African Political Economy*, no. 52, pp. 87–8.

Clapham, C. (1982) 'The Politics of Failure: Clientelism, Political Instability and National Integration in Liberia and Sierra Leone', in Clapham (ed.), *Private Patronage and State Power. Political Clientelism in the Modern State*, Pinter Publishers, London, pp. 76–92.

———— (1989) 'Ethiopia', in S. Mews (ed.), *Religion in Politics. A World Guide*, Longman, London, p. 73.

———— (1993) 'Democratisation in Africa: Obstacles and Prospects', paper delivered at European Consortium for Political Research Leiden Joint Sessions, University of Leiden, April.

Clarke, P. (1982) *West Africa and Islam*, Edward Arnold, London.

———— (1987) 'Islam, Development and African Identity: The Case of West Africa', in K. Petersen (ed.), *Religion, Development and African Identity*, Scandinavian Institute of African Studies, Uppsala, pp. 127–46.

———— (1988) 'Islamic Reform in Contemporary Nigeria', *Third World Quarterly*, vol X, no. 2, pp. 519–38.

Clévenot, M. (1987) *L'Etat des Religions dans le Monde*, La Decouverte/Le Cerf, Paris.

Collins, C. (1992) 'Mobutu's Troops Massacre Church-organized Protesters', *National Catholic Reporter*, vol. XXVIII, no. 17, p. 8.

Connor, W. (1973) 'The Politics of Ethno-nationalism', *Journal of International Affairs*, vol. XXVII, pp. 1–21.

Conus, G. (1975) *L'Eglise d'Afrique au Concile Vatican II*, Nouvelle Revue de Science Missionaire, Immensee.

Cook, D. (1978) 'Church and State in Zambia: The Case of the African Methodist Episcopal Church', in E. Fashole-Luke, R. Gray and A. Hastings (eds), *Christianity in Independent Africa*, Rex Collings, London, pp. 285–303.

Coulon, C. (1979) 'Les Marabouts Senegalais et l'Etat', *Revue Françaises de Politique Africaines*, no. 158, pp. 15–42.

———— (1983) *Les Musulmans et le Pouvoir en Afrique Noire*, Karthala, Paris.

———— (1985) 'Prophets of God or of History? Muslim Messianic Movements and Anti-Colonialism in Senegal', in W. van Binsbergen and M. Schoffeleers (eds), *Theoretical Explorations in African Religion*, KPI, London, pp. 346–66.

Cox, R. (1993) 'Social Forces, States and World Orders: Beyond International Relations Theory', in H. Williams, M. Wright and T. Evans (eds), *International Relations and Political Theory*, Open University Press, Milton Keynes, pp. 274–308.

Crowder, M. (1959) *Pagans and Politicians*, Hutchinson, London.

———— (1984) 'Introduction', in Crowder (ed.), *The Cambridge History of Africa, Volume 8: From c. 1940 to c. 1975*, Cambridge University Press, Cambridge, pp. 1–7.

Cruise O' Brien, D. (1981) 'La Filière Musulmane: Confrèries Soufies et Politique en Afrique Noire', *Politique Africaine*, no. 4, pp. 7–30.

———— (1986) 'Wails and Whispers: The People's Voice in West African Muslim Politics', in P. Chabal (ed.), *Political Domination in Africa*, Cambridge University Press, Cambridge, pp. 71–84.

———— (1988) 'Introduction', in Cruise O' Brien and C. Coulon (eds), *Charisma and Brotherhood in African Islam*, Clarendon Press, Oxford.

———— (1993) 'The Byways of Democracy', *West Africa*, 15–21 February, pp. 238–9.

Daloz, J.-P. (1992) 'L'Itineraire du pionnier: Sur l'Evolution Politique Beninoise', *Politique Africaine*, no. 46, pp. 132–7.

d'Antonio, M. (1990) *Fall From Grace. The Failed Crusade of the Christian Right*, André Deutsch, London.

Deiros, P. (1991) 'Protestant Fundamentalism in Latin America', in M. Marty and R. Scott Appleby (eds), *Fundamentalisms Observed*, University of Chicago Press, Chicago, pp. 142–96.

Demerath III, N. (1991) 'Religious Capital and Capital Religions: Cross-cultural and Non-legal Factors in the Separation of Church and State', *Daedalus*, vol. CXX, no. 3, pp. 21–40.

Desanti, D. (1971) 'The Golden Anniversary of Kimbanguism', *Continent 2000*, April, pp. 7–19.

Diallo, T. (1988) 'Pouvoir et Marabouts en Afrique de l'Ouest', *Islam et Societés au Sud du Sahara*, no. 2, pp. 7–10.

Diamond, L. (1993a) 'The Globalization of Democracy' in R. Slater, B. Schutz and S. Dorr (eds), *Global Transformation and the Third World*, Lynne Rienner Publishers, Boulder, Colo. and London, pp. 31–70.

———— (1993b) 'Introduction: Political Culture and Democracy', in Diamond (ed.), *Political Culture and Democracy in Developing Countries*, Lynne Rienner Publishers, Boulder, Colo. and London, pp. 1–33.

Dirven, P. (1970) 'A Protest and a Challenge. The Maria Legio Breakaway Church in West Kenya', *African Ecclesiastical Review*, vol. XII, no. 2, pp. 127–36.

Doi, A. (1978) 'Islam in Nigeria: Changes since Independence', in E. Fasole-Luke, R. Gray and A. Hastings (eds), *Christianity in Independent Africa*, Rex Collings, London, pp. 334–53.

Dorr, S. (1993) 'Democratization in the Middle East', in R. Slater, B. Schutz and S. Dorr (eds), *Global Transformation and the Third World*, Lynne Rienner

Publishers, Boulder, Colo. and London, pp. 131–57.

Droogers, A. and Sieberg, H. (1991) 'Popular Religion and Power in Latin America: An Introduction', in Droogers, G. Huizer and H. Siebers (eds), *Popular Power in Latin American Religions*, Verlag Breitenbach, Fort Lauderdale/ Saarbrucken, pp. 1–25.

Eckstein, H. (1988) 'A Culturalist Theory of Political Change', *American Political Science Review*, vol. LXXXII, pp. 789–804.

The Economist (1992) 'Editorial', 4 January, p. 10.

Elliot, J. (1993) 'Fundamentalists Prepare for Holy War in Nigeria', *Guardian*, 14 April.

Encarnacion, T. and Tadem, E. (1993) 'Ethnicity and Separatist Movements in South-East Asia', in P. Wignaraja (ed.), *New Social Movements in the South*, Zed Books, London, pp. 153–73.

Ephson, B. (1989) 'Spiritual Onslaught', *West Africa*, 17–23 April, pp. 584–5.

Errasova, I. (1989) 'La Theologie de la Libération et la Theologie Africaine', *Mondes en Developpement*, vol. XVII, no. 65, pp. 219–24.

Etherington, N. (1983) 'Missionaries and the Intellectual History of Africa: A Historical Survey, *Itinerario*, vol. VII, no. 2, pp. 116–43.

Etienne, B. and Tozy, M. (1981) 'Le Glissement des Obligations Islamiques vers le Phenomene Associatif à Casablanca', in Centre de Recherches et d'Etudes sur les Societés Mediterranéennes, *Le Maghreb Musulman en 1979*, CNRS, Paris, p. 251, quoted in C. Coulon, *Les Musulmans et le Pouvoir en Afrique Noire*, Karthala, Paris, p. 48.

Eveques de l'Afrique de l'Est (AMECEA) (1976), 'Lettre pastorale', quoted in R. Luneau, *Laisse Aller mon Peuple! Eglises Africaines au-dela des Modeles*, Karthala, Paris, p. 154.

Fanon, F. (1968) *The Wretched of the Earth*, Grove Press, New York.

Fatton, R. (1987) *The Making of a Liberal Democracy. Senegal's Passive Revolution, 1975–1985*, Lynne Rienner Publishers, Boulder, Colo.

——— (1992) *Predatory Rule. State and Civil Society in Africa*, Lynne Rienner Publishers, Boulder, Colo. and London.

Femia, J. (1975) 'Hegemony and Consciousness in the Thought of Antonio Gramsci', *Political Studies*, vol. 23, no. 1, pp. 29–48.

Fields, K. (1982) 'Charismatic Religion as Popular Protest: The Ordinary and Extraordinary in Social Movements', *Theory and Society*, vol. XI, no. 3, pp. 321–62.

——— (1985) *Revival and Rebellion in Colonial Central Africa*, Princeton University Press, Princeton.

Fine, R. (1992) 'Civil Society and the Politics of Transition in South Africa, *Review of African Political Economy*, no. 55, pp. 71–83.

Flint, J. (1993a) 'Islam on the Warpath in North Africa', *Guardian*, 24 April.

——— (1993b) 'Sudan Cracks Down on Muslim Rivals', *Guardian*, 11 June.

Forrest, J. (1988) 'The Quest for State "Hardness" in Africa', *Comparative Politics*, vol. XX, no. 4, pp. 423–42.

Fossaert, R. (1978) *La Societés. Volume 5: Les Etats*, Le Seul, Paris.

Furlong, P. (1991) 'Azikiwe and the National Church of Nigeria and the Cameroons', *African Affairs*, vol. LXXXXI, pp. 433–52.

Fulton, J. (1987) 'Religion and Politics in Gramsci: An Introduction', *Sociological Analysis*, vol. XXXXVIII, no. 3, pp. 197–216.

Furedi, F. (1994) *Colonial Wars and the Politics of Third World Nationalism*, I.B. Tauris, London.

Gaben, L. (1989) 'Les Aides Exterieures', *Politique Africaines*, no. 35, pp. 66–7.

Gerteiny, A. (1971) 'Islamic Influences on Politics in Mauritania', in D. McCall and N. Bennett (eds), *Aspects of West African Islam*, Boston University Press, Boston, Mass.

Geschiere, P. and van der Klei, J. (1988) 'Popular Protest: The Diola of South Senegal', in P. Q. van Ufford and M. Schoffeleers (eds), *Religion and Development. Towards an Integrated Approach*, Free University Press, Amsterdam, pp. 209–30.

Giddens, A. (1971) *Capitalism and Social Theory*, Cambridge University Press, Cambridge.

Gifford, P. (1987) '"Africa Shall be Saved". An Appraisal of Reinhard Bonnke's Pan-African Crusade', *Journal of Religion in Africa*, vol. XVII, no. 1, pp. 63–92.

—— (1989) 'Mozambique', in S. Mews (ed.), *Religion in Politics: A World Guide*, Longman, London, p. 185.

—— (1990) 'Prosperity: A New and Foreign Element in African Christianity', *Religion*, vol. XX, no. 3, pp. 373–88.

—— (1991a) *The New Crusaders. Christianity and the New Right in Southern Africa*, Pluto Press, London.

—— (1991b) 'Christian Fundamentalism and Development in Africa', *Review of African Political Economy*, no. 52, pp. 9–20.

—— (1992a) 'American Evangelicalism in Zimbabwe', in J. Pieterse (ed.), *Christianity and Hegemony. Religion and Politics on the Frontiers of Social Change*, Berg, Oxford, pp. 121–46.

—— (1992b) 'Bishops for Reform', *The Tablet*, 30 May, pp. 672–3.

—— (1993) *Christianity and Politics in Doe's Liberia*, Cambridge University Press, Cambridge.

—— (1994) 'Some Recent Developments in African Christianity', *African Affairs*, vol. LXXXXIII, no. 373, pp. 513–34.

Gitari, D. (1988) 'The Church's Witness to the Living God: Seeking Just Political, Social and Economic Structures in Contemporary Africa', *Transformation*, vol V, no. 2, pp. 13–20.

Goba, B. (1986) 'The Black Consciousness Movement: Its Impact on Black Theology', in I. Mosala and B. Tlhagale (eds), *The Unquestionable Right to be Free: Essays in Black Theology*, Skotaville Publishers, Johannesburg, pp. 57–70.

Goldthorpe, T. (1984) *The Sociology of the Third World*, Cambridge University Press, Cambridge.

Gramsci, A. (1971) *Selections from the Prison Notebooks*, translated and edited by Q. Hoare and G. Nowell-Smith, Lawrence & Wishart, London.

Gray, R. (1978) 'Christianity and Religious Change in Africa', *African Affairs*, vol. LXXVII, no. 306, pp. 89–100.

—— (1986) 'Popular Theologies in Africa', *African Affairs*, vol. LXXXV, no. 338, pp. 49–54.

Grenet, Y. (1989) 'L'Eglise Catholique et la Decolonisation', *Mondes en*

Developpement, vol. XVII, no. 65, pp. 207–18.

Gruénais, M.-E. and Mayala, D. (1988) 'Comment se Debarraser de l'Efficacité Symbolique de la Medicine Traditionnelle', *Politique Africaine*, no. 31, pp. 51–61.

Guardian (London) (1993) 'Fundamentalist Ban', 30 April.

———— (London) (1994) 'Torture Pacts Honoured in Breach', 5 April.

Guardian (Lagos) (1985) 'Iran Embassy Admits Responsibility for Circulating Islamic Posters', 17 August.

de Haas, M. (1986) 'Is Millenarianism Alive and Well in South Africa?', *Religion in Southern Africa*, no. 7, pp. 37–45.

Hackett, R. (1987) 'Conclusion', in Hackett (ed.), *New Religious Movements in Nigeria*, Edwin Mellen Press, Lewiston, pp. 237–41.

Haddad, Y. (1985) 'Islam, Women and Revolution in Twentieth Century Arab Thought', in Haddad and E. Findly (eds), *Women, Religion and Social Change*, State University of New York, Albany, pp. 275–306.

Hall, M. (1993) 'Zambia: Special Report', *Guardian*, 2 April.

Hall, S. (1985) 'Religious Ideologies and Social Movements in Jamaica', in R. Bocock and K. Thompson (eds), *Religion and Ideology*, Manchester University Press, Manchester, pp. 269–96.

Hansen, H. B. (1986) 'Church and State in Early Colonial Uganda', *African Affairs*, vol. LXXXV, no. 1, pp. 55–74.

———— (1992) 'Church and State in a Colonial Context', in M. Twaddle (ed.), *Imperialism, the State and the Third World*, British Academic Press, London, pp. 95–123.

I. Harris, S. Mews, P. Morris and J. Shepherd (1992) *Contemporary Religions: A World Guide*, Longman, Harlow.

Hastings, A. (1977) 'Church–State Relations in Black Africa, 1959–66', in Commission Internationale d'Histoire Ecclesiastique Comparée (CIHEC), *The Church in a Changing Society*, CIHEC, Uppsala, pp. 25–57.

———— (1979) *A History of African Christianity, 1950–75*, Cambridge University Press, Cambridge.

———— (1989) *African Catholicism: Essays in Discovery*, SCM, London.

Haynes, J. (1989) 'Ghana', in S. Mews (ed.), *Religion in Politics*, Longman, London, p. 89.

———— (1992) "One-Party State, No-Party State, Multi-Party State? 35 Years of Democracy, Authoritarianism and Development in Ghana', *Journal of Communist Studies*, vol. VIII, no. 2, pp. 41–62.

———— (1993a) *Religion in Third World Politics*, Open University Press, Milton Keynes.

———— (1993b) 'Sustainable Democracy in Ghana? Problems and Prospects', *Third World Quarterly*, vol. XIV, no. 3, pp. 451–68.

———— (1994) 'Religion, Fundamentalism and Ethnicity: A Global Perspective', United Nations Research Institute for Social Development, Geneva, typescript.

Henry, P. (1986) 'Indigenous Religions and the Transformation of Peripheral Societies', in J. Hadden and A. Shupe (eds), *Prophetic Religions and Politics. Religion and the Political Order*, Paragon House, New York, pp. 139–52.

Hoekema, A. (1966) *What About Tongue-Speaking*, Paternoster Press, Exeter.

Horton, R. (1993) *Patterns of Thought in Africa and the West*, Cambridge University Press, Cambridge.

Huband, M. (1994) 'Rwandan Rebels Kill 13 Priests', *Guardian*, 10 June.

Huntington, S. (1991) *The Third Wave. Democratization in the Late Twentieth Century*, University of Oklahoma Press, Norman.

Hyden, G. (1983) *No Shortcuts to Progress. African Development Management in Perspective*, University of California Press, Berkeley.

Hyden, G. and Williams, D. (1994) 'A Community Model of African Politics: Illustrations from Nigeria and Tanzania, *Comparative Studies in Society and History*, vol. XXXVI, no. 1, pp. 68–96.

Ibrahim, J. (1989) 'The Politics of Religion in Nigeria', *Review of African Political Economy*, no. 45–6, pp. 65–82.

——— (1991) 'Religion and Political Turbulence in Nigeria', *Journal of Modern African Studies*, vol. XXIX, no. 1, pp. 115–36.

Ibrahim, Y. (1992) 'Islamic Plan for Algeria is on Display', *New York Times*, 7 January.

Inglehart, R. (1990) *Culture Shift in Advanced Industrial Society*, Princeton University Press, Princeton.

Jenkins, K. (1991) 'Christian Churches in Africa: Agents of Change or Supporters of the Status Quo?, *Geonomics*, vol. III, no. 5, pp. 6–10.

Johnston, H. and Figa, J. (1988) 'The Church and Political Opposition', *Journal for the Scientific Study of Religion*, vol. XXVII, no. 1, pp. 32–47.

Joseph, R. (1987) *Democracy and Prebendal Politics in Nigeria*, Cambridge University Press, Cambridge.

——— (1993) 'The Christian Churches and Democracy in Contemporary Africa', in J. Witte, Jr. (ed.), *Christianity and Democracy in Global Context*, Westview, Boulder, Colo., pp. 231–47.

Jules-Rosette, B. (1979) 'Symbols of Power and Change: An Introduction to New Perspectives on Contemporary African Religion', in Jules-Rosette (ed.), *The New Religions of Africa*, Ablex Publishing Corporation, Ablex, N.J., pp. 37–41.

Kaba, L. (1976) 'Islam's Advance in Tropical Africa', *Africa Report*, March, pp. 37–9.

Kabongo, I. (1982) 'Déroutante Afrique ou la Syncope d'un Discours', *Revue Candienne des Etudes Africaines*, vol. XVIII, no. 1, pp. 13–22.

Kane, O. (1990) 'Les Mouvements Religieux et le Champ Politique au Nigeria Septentrional', *Islam et Societés au Sud du Sahara*, no. 4, pp. 7–24.

Kastfelt, N. (1989) 'Rumours of Maitatsine: A Note on Political Culture in Northern Nigeria', *African Affairs*, vol. LXXXVIII, pp. 83–90.

Kelley, M. (1987) *A State in Disarray. Conditions of Chad's Survival*, Westview, Boulder, Colo.

Kofele-Kale, N. (1987) 'Class, Status and Power in Postreunification Cameroon: The Rise of an Anglophone Bourgeoisie, 1961–80', in I. Markowitz (ed.), *Studies in Power and Class in Africa*, Oxford University Press, New York, pp. 135–69.

Kothari, R. (1993) 'Masses, Classes and the State', in P. Wignaraja (ed.), *New Social Movements in the South*, Zed Books, London, pp. 59–75.

Krauthammer, C. (1993) 'Iran to Become New "Evil Empire"?', *Democrat and*

Chronicle, 4 January, cited in A. R. North, 'The Future of Civil Society in the Middle East', *Middle East Journal*, vol. XXXXVII, no. 2, p. 4.

Krislov, S. (1985) 'Alternatives to Separation of Church and State in Countries outside of the United States', in J. Wood, Jr. (ed.), *Religion and the State. Essays in Honor of Leo Pfeffer*, Baylor University Press, Waco, pp. 412–40.

Kunz, F. (1991) 'Liberalization in Africa – Some Preliminary Reflections', *African Affairs*, vol, XC, no. 2, pp. 223–35.

Laitin, D. (1979) 'Religion, Culture and the Weberian Tradition', *World Politics*, vol. XXX, no. 4, pp. 563–93.

—— (1986) *Hegemony and Culture. Politics and Religious Change among the Yoruba*, Chicago University Press, Chicago.

Lamb, D. (1985) *The Africans*, Methuen, London.

Lan, D. (1985) *Guns and Rain*, James Currey, London.

Lanternari, V. (1963) *The Religions of the Oppressed*, Knopf, New York.

—— (1985) 'Revolution and/or Integration in African Socio-Religious Movements', in B. Lincoln (ed.), *Religion, Rebellion, Revolution*, Macmillan, London, pp. 129–56.

Lapidus, I. (1988) *A History of Islamic Societies*, Cambridge University Press, Cambridge.

Lawyers Committee for Human Rights (1990) *Zaire. Repression as Policy*, Lawyers Committee for Human Rights, New York.

Last, M. (1988) 'Charisma and Medicine in Northern Nigeria', in D. Cruise O'Brien and C. Coulon (eds), *Charisma and Brotherhood in African Islam*, Clarendon Press, Oxford, pp. 183–204.

Le Vine, V. (1980) 'African Patrimonial Regimes in Comparative Perspective', *Journal of Modern African Studies*, vol. XVIII, no. 4, pp. 657–73.

Lemerchand, R. (1992) 'Uncivil States and Civil Societies: How Illusion Became Reality', *Journal of Modern African Studies*, vol. XXX, no. 2, pp. 177–91.

Levine, D. (1984) 'Religion and Politics: Dimensions of Renewal, *Renewal*, vol. LIX, no. 233, pp. 117–35.

Levtzion, N. (1971) 'Islam in West African Politics', *Cahiers d'Etudes Africaines*, vol. XVIII, no. 3, pp. 333–45.

Lewis, I. (1986) *Religion in Context. Cults and Charisma*, Cambridge University Press, Cambridge.

Lewis, P. (1992) 'Political Transition and the Dilemma of Civil Society in Africa, *Journal of International Affairs*, vol. XXXXVI, no. 1, pp. 31–54.

Linden, I. (1991) 'Review of Paul Gifford, *The New Crusaders. Christianity and the New Right in Southern Africa*', in *Review of African Political Economy*, no. 51, pp. 118–21.

Livingstone, W. (1917) *Mary Slessor of Calabar. Pioneer Missionary*, Hodder & Stoughton, London.

Lonsdale, J. (1978) 'The Emerging Pattern of Church and State Co-operation in Kenya', in E. Fashole-Luke, R. Gray and A. Hastings (eds), *Christianity in Independent Africa*, Rex Collings, London, pp. 121–39.

Lubeck, P. (1985) 'Islamic Protest under Semi-industrial Capitalism: Yan Tatsine Explained', *Africa*, vol. LV, no. 4, pp. 369–89.

Luneau, R. (1987) *Laisse Aller mon Peuple! Eglises Africaines Modèles au-delà?*, Karthala, Paris.

MacGaffey, J. (1991) *The Real Economy of Zaire*, James Currey/University of Penn-sylvania Press, London/Philadelphia.

MacGaffey, W. (1990) 'Religion, Class and Social Pluralism in Zaire', *Canadian Journal of African Studies*, vol. XXIV, no. 2, pp. 249–64.

Magassouba, M. (1985), *L'Islam au Sénégal: Demain les mullahs?*, Karthala, Paris.

Maier, K. (1991) 'Blood Flows in Kano Streets in Christian–Muslim Battles', *Independent*, 16 October.

Mamdani, M. (1988) 'Uganda in Transition', *Third World Quarterly*, vol. X, no. 3, pp. 1155–81.

Manor, J. (1991) 'Introduction' in Manor (ed.), *Rethinking Third World Politics*, Longman, London, pp. 1–10.

Marchés Tropicaux (1987) 'Les Sectes en Afrique Centrale', 27 April, p. 474.

Marcum, J. (1987) 'The People's Republic of Angola', in E. Keller and D. Rothchild (eds), *Afro-Marxist Regimes. Ideology and Public Policy*, Lynne Rienner Publishers, Boulder, Colo. and London, pp. 65–85.

Mardin, S. (1993) 'The "Venture" of Democracy in the Middle East', cited in S. Dorr, 'Democratization in the Middle East', in R. Slater, B. Schutz and S. Dorr (eds), *Global Transformation and the Third World*, Lynne Rienner Publish-ers, Boulder, Colo. and London, pp. 131–57, at p. 151.

Marishane, J. (1992) 'The Religious Right and Low-intensity Conflict in South-ern Africa', in J. Pieterse (ed.), *Christianity and Hegemony. Religion and Politics on the Frontiers of Social Change*, Berg, Oxford, pp. 59–120.

Markowitz, M. (1973) *Cross and Sword*, Hoover Institution Press, Stanford.

Marshall, R. (1991) 'Power in the Name of Jesus', *Review of African Political Economy*, no. 52, pp. 21–37.

——— (1993) '"Power in the Name of Jesus": Social Transformation and Pente-costalism in Western Nigeria', in T. Ranger and O. Vaughan (eds), *Legitimacy and the State in Twentieth Century Africa*, Macmillan, London, pp. 213–43.

Martin, D. (1990) *Tongues of Fire. The Explosion of Protestantism in Latin America*, Basil Blackwell, Oxford.

Marty, M. and Scott Appleby, R. (1993) 'Introduction', in Marty and Scott Appleby (eds), *Fundamentalism and the State. Remaking Polities, Economies, and Militance*, University of Chicago Press, Chicago, pp. 1–9.

Marx, K. and Engels, F. (1975) *Early Writings*, Penguin, Harmondsworth.

Mayer, A. (1993) 'The Fundamentalist Impact on Law, Politics and Constitutions in Iran, Pakistan, and the Sudan', in M. Marty and R. Scott Appleby (eds), *Fundamentalism and the State. Remaking Polities, Economies, and Militance*, Univer-sity of Chicago Press, Chicago, pp. 110–51.

Mazrui, A. (1974) 'Piety and Puritanism under a Military Theocracy: Uganda Soldiers as Apostolic Successors', in C. Kelleher (ed.), *Political–Military Sys-tems*, University of California Press, Berkeley, pp. 35–70.

Mbembe, A. (1988) *Afriques Indociles. Christianisme, Pouvoir et Etat en Societé Postcoloniale*, Karthala, Paris,

Mbiti, J. (1969) *African Religions and Philosophies*, Heinemann, London.

Mbon, F. (1987) 'Public Response to New Religious Movements in Contempo-rary Nigeria', in R. Hackett (ed.), *New Religious Movements in Nigeria*, Edwin Mellen Press, Lewiston, N.Y., pp. 209–36.

McCarus, C. (1993) 'Election Showdown', *West Africa*, 22–28 February, pp. 289–91.

McGreal, C. (1994) 'Church Fails to Sever Links with Killers', *Guardian*, 3 August.

Medhurst, K. (1981) 'Religion and Politics. A Typology', *Scottish Journal of Religious Studies*, vol. II, no. 2, pp. 115–34.

Mettelin, P. (1984) 'Activities Informelles et Economies Urbaine: Le Cas de l'Afrique Noire', *Le Mois en Afrique*, no. 223–4, pp. 57–71.

Mews. S. (1989) 'Angola', in Mews (ed.), *Religion in Politics. A World Guide*, Longman, London, p. 10.

—— (1989a) 'Mauritania', in S. Mews (ed.) *Religion in Politics: A World Guide*, Longman, London, p. 178.

Mfoulou, J. (1978) 'The Catholic Church and Camerounian Nationalism', in E. Fashole-Luke, R. Gray and A. Hastings (eds), *Christianity in Independent Africa*, Rex Collings, London, pp. 216–27.

Miliband, R. (1970) *The State in Capitalist Society*, Quadrant, London.

Milton Yinger J. (1970) *The Scientific Study of Religion*, Macmillan, New York.

Mitchell, T. (1991) 'The Limits of the State: Beyond Statist Approaches and their Critics', *American Political Science Review*, vol. LXXXV, no. 1, pp. 77–96.

Mitra, S. (1987) ' Desecularising the State in India', paper delivered to the Political Studies Association of the UK Annual Conference, University of Aberdeen, April.

Molutsi, P. and Holm, J. (1990) 'Developing Democracy when Civil Society is Weak: The Case of Botswana', *African Affairs*, vol. LXXXIX, pp. 323–40.

Moore, L. (1989) 'South Africa', in S. Mews (ed.) *Religion in Politics: A World Guide*, Longman, London, pp. 238–44.

Moran, E. and Schlemmer, L. (1984) *Faith for the Fearful?* Centre for Applied Social Studies, Durban.

Morgenthau, R. and Creevey Behrman, L. (1984) 'French-speaking Tropical Africa', in M. Crowder (ed.), *The Cambridge History of Africa. Volume 8: From c. 1940 to c. 1975*, Cambridge University Press, Cambridge, pp. 611–73.

Morris-Jones, W. (1992) 'Shaping the Post-imperial State: Nehru's Letters to Chief Ministers', in M. Twaddle (ed.), *Imperialism, the State and the Third World*, British Academic Press, London, pp. 220–41.

Mottu, H. (1987) 'The Theological Critique of Religion and Popular Religion', *Radical Religion*, vol. IIII, no. 1, pp. 4–15.

Moyser, G. (ed.) (1991) *Politics and Religion in the Modern World*, Routledge, London.

Murphree, M. (1969) *Christianity and the Shona*, Athlone Press, London.

Mutibwa, P. (1992) *Uganda Since Independence*, Hurst and Company, London.

Ndibe, O. (1985a) 'To Higher Heights', *Concord Weekly*, 18 February, p. 11.

—— (1985b) 'A Babel of Believers', *Concord Weekly*, 18 February, pp. 7–9.

Nettl, J. (1968) 'The State as Conceptual Variable', *World Politics*, vol. XX, no. 4, pp. 559–92.

Nicholas, G. (1981) *Dynamique de l'Islam au Sud du Sahara*, Publications Orientalists de France, Paris.

Nimtz, A. (1980) *Islam and Politics in East Africa. The Sufi Order in Tanzania*, University of Minnesota Press, Minneapolis.

Nkrumah, K. (1967) *Axioms of Kwame Nkrumah*, Thomas Nelson, London.

Northedge, F. (1976) *The International Political System*, Faber, London.

Nolan, A. and Broderick, R. (1987) *To Nourish Our Faith: The Theology of Liberation in Southern Africa*, Order of Preachers, Hilton.

Nordlinger, E. (1981) *On the Autonomy of the Democratic State*, Harvard University Press, Cambridge, Mass.

Obasi, N. (1985) 'The Campus Believers', *Concord Weekly*, 18 February, pp. 10–11.

Oduyoye, M. (1990) 'An African Perspective', in K. Abraham (ed.), *Third World Theologies. Commonalities and Divergences*, Orbis Books, London, pp. 100–105.

Okullu, J. (1978) 'Church–State Relations: The African Situation', in World Council of Churches, *Church and State. Opening a New Ecumenical Discussion*, World Council of Churches, Geneva, pp. 79–89.

Oliver, R. (1991) *The African Experience*, Weidenfield & Nicolson, London.

Omara-Otunnu, A. (1992) 'The Struggle for Democracy in Uganda', *Journal of Modern African Studies*, vol. XXX, no. 3, pp. 443–63.

Oosthuizen, G. (1985) 'The African Independent Churches Centenary', *Africa Insight*, vol. XV, no. 2, pp. 70–80.

Otayek, R. (1989) 'Burkina Faso', in D. Cruise O'Brien, J. Dunn, and R. Rathbone (eds), *Contemporary West African States*, Cambridge University Press, Cambridge, pp. 12–35.

Owusu, M. (1978) 'Akan', in R. Weekes (ed.), *Muslim Peoples. A World Ethnographic Survey*, Greenword, London, pp. 13–19.

Owusu-Ansah, D. (1987) 'The State and Islam in Nineteenth Century Africa: Buganda Absolutism Versus Constitutional Monarchy in Asante', *Journal of Muslim Minority Affairs*, vol. VIII, no. 1, pp. 132–43.

Paden, J. (1973) *Religion and Political Culture in Kano*, University of California Press, Berkeley.

di Palma, G. (1991) 'Legitimation from the Top to Civil Society. Politico-cultural Change in Eastern Europe', *World Politics*, vol. XXXXIV, no. 1, pp. 49–80.

Parks, M. (1993) 'Israel Sees Self Defending West Again', *Los Angeles Times*, 2 January.

Parpart, J. (1988) 'Women and the State in Africa', in D. Rothchild and N. Chazan (eds), *The Precarious Balance. State and Society in Africa*, Westview, Boulder, Colo., pp. 208–30.

Parrinder, G. (1976) *Africa's Three Religions*, Sheldon Press, London.

Parsons, T. (1960) *Structures and Process in Modern Societies*, University of Chicago Press, Chicago.

Peel, J. D. Y. (1968) *Aladura. A Religious Movement Amongst the Yoruba*, Oxford University Press, London.

——— (1984) 'Social and Cultural Change', in M. Crowder (ed.), *The Cambridge History of Africa. Volume 8: From c. 1940 to c. 1975*, Cambridge University Press, Cambridge, pp. 145–91.

——— (1993) 'An Africanist Revisits *Magic and the Millennium*', in E. Barker, J. Beckford and K. Dobbelaere (eds), *Secularization, Rationalism and Sectarianism*, Clarendon Press, Oxford, pp. 81–100.

Peil, M. (1984) *African Urban Society*, John Wiley, Chichester.

Pénekou, E. (1984) *Eglises d'Afrique. Propositions pour l'Avenir*, Karthala, Paris.

Pieterse, J. (1992) 'Christianity, Politics and Gramscism of the Right: Introduction', in Pieterse (ed.), *Christianity and Hegemony. Religion and Politics on the Frontiers of Social Change*, Berg, Oxford, pp. 1–31.

Pirouet, M. L. (1980) 'Religion in Uganda under Amin', *Journal of Religion in Africa*, vol. XI, no. 1, pp. 13–29.

Pobee, J. (1977) 'The Fish and the Cock in Ghana, 1949–1966. A Problem of Adjustment', in Commission Internationale d'Histoire Ecclesiastique Comparée (CIHEC), *The Church in a Changing Society*, CIHEC, Uppsala, pp. 390–96.

——— (1992) *Religion and Politics in Ghana*, Asempa Publishers, Accra.

Poewe, K. (1987) 'In the Eye of the Storm: Charismatics and Independent Churches in South Africa', University of Calgary, unpublished paper, quoted in D. Martin, *Tongues of Fire*, Blackwell, Oxford, pp. 157–8.

Pro Mundi Vita (1982) 'Africa's Opaque Reality: Marxism and Christianity', *Dossier 23*.

Ranger, T. (1967) *Revolt in Southern Rhodesia: 1896–7*, Heinemann, London.

——— (1985) *Peasant Consciousness and Guerilla War in Zimbabwe*, James Currey, London.

——— (1986) 'Religious Movements and Politics in Sub-Saharan Africa', *African Studies Review*, vol. XXXIX, no. 2, pp. 1–70.

Ranger, T. and Vaughan, O. (1993) 'Postscript', in Ranger and Vaughan (eds), *Legitimacy and the State in Twentieth Century Africa*, Macmillan, London, pp. 255–61.

Ray, B. (1976) *African Religions*, Prentice-Hall, Englewood Cliffs, N.J.

Reveyrand-Coulon, O. (1993) 'Les Enoncés Féminins de l'Islam', in J.-F. Bayart (ed.), *Religion and Modernité. Politique en Afrique Noire*, Karthala, Paris, pp. 63–100.

Roberts, B. (1968), 'Protestant Groups and Coping with Urban Life in Guatemala City', *American Journal of Sociology*, vol. LXXIII, pp. 753–67..

Rossiter, J. and Palmer, R. (1991) 'Northern NGOs: Some Heretical Thoughts', *Refugee Participation Network*, 10 May, quoted in T. Ranger and O. Vaughan, 'Postscript', in Ranger and Vaughan (eds), *Legitimacy and the State in Twentieth Century Africa*, Macmillan, London, p. 259.

Rothchild, D. and Foley, M. (1988) 'African States and the Politics of Inclusive Coalitions', in Rothchild and N. Chazan (eds), *The Precarious Balance. State and Society in Africa*, Lynne Rienner Publishers, Boulder, Colo., pp. 233–64

Rowlands, M. and Warnier, J.-P. (1988) 'Sorcery, Power and the Modern State in Cameroon', *Man* (New Series), vol. XXIII, no. 1, pp. 118–32.

Roy, O. (1985) *L'Afghanistan. Islam and Modernité Politique*, Seuil, Paris.

Rueschemeyer, D., Stephens, E. and Stephens, J. (1992) *Capitalist Development and Democracy*, Polity Press, Cambridge.

Ryall, D. (1994) 'The Roman Catholic Church and Socio-Political Change in South Africa, 1948–90', unpublished MS.

Sachikonye, L. (1992) 'Civil Society and the Political Struggles in South Africa', *Southern African Political and Economic Monthly*, vol. V, no. 5, pp. 37–8.

Sahliyeh, E. (ed.) (1990) *Religious Resurgence and Politics in the Contemporary World*, State University of New York Press, Albany.

Sanneh, L. (1991) 'Religion and Politics: Third World Perspectives on a Comparative Theme', *Daedalus*, vol. CXX, no. 3, pp. 203–18.

Schatzberg, M. (1988) *The Dialectics of Oppression in Zaire*, Indiana University Press, Bloomington.

Schoffeleers, M. (1988) 'Theological Styles and Revolutionary Elan: An African Discussion', in P. Q. van Ufford and Schoffeleers (eds), *Religion and Development. Towards an Integrated Approach*, Free University Press, Amsterdam, pp. 185–208.

——— (1991) 'Ritual Healing and Political Acquiescence: The Case of the Zionist Churches in Southern Africa', *Africa*, vol. LX, no. 1, pp. 1–25.

Seguy, J. (1975) 'Situation Socio-Historique du Pentecotisme', *Lumière et Vie*, no. 125, pp. 33–58.

Shaikh, F. (ed.) (1992) *Islam and Islamic Groups. A Worldwide Reference Guide*, Longman, Harlow.

Shapiro, I. (1993) 'Democratic Innovation: South Africa in Comparative Context', *World Politics*, vol. XXXXVI, no. 3, pp. 121–50.

Sheikh-Abdi, S. (1993) *Divine Madness: Mohammed Abdulle Hassan of Somalia (1856-1920)*, Zed Books, London.

Shepard, W. (1987) '"Fundamentalism" Christian and Islamic', *Religion*, no. 17, pp. 355–78.

Shepperson, G. (1954) 'The Politics of African Church Separatist Movements in British Central Africa, 1892–1916, *Africa*, vol. XXIV, no. 2, pp. 233–45.

Shils, E. (1991) 'The Virtue of Civil Society', *Government and Opposition*, vol. XXVI, no. 1, pp. 3–20.

Showstack Sassoon, A. (1982) 'Passive Revolution and the Politics of Reform', in Showstack Sassoon (ed.), *Approaches to Gramsci*, Writers and Readers Publishing Cooperative, London, pp. 127–48.

Simmons, M. (1992) 'Church Leaders Tell of Massacre Horrors in Kenya's Rift Valley', *Guardian*, 22 December.

Simon, R. (1982) *Gramsci's Political Thought*, Lawrence & Wishart, London.

Sklar, R. (1986) 'Democracy in Africa', in P. Chabal (ed.), *Political Domination in Africa*, Cambridge University Press, Cambridge, pp. 17–29.

——— (1987) 'Developmental Democracy', *Comparative Studies in Society and History*, vol. 29, no. 4, pp. 686–714.

Smith, N. G. (1993) 'Fresh Hopes for Peace', *West Africa*, 20–27 September, p. 1673.

Soudan, F. (1990) 'Zaire: Les Eveques Accusent', *Jeune Afrique*, 9 April, pp. 20–25.

Southscan (1989) 'Far-Right Military Church Group Captured – and Released – by Frelimo', vol. IV, no. 41, 3 November, p. 317.

Sparkes, A. (1993) '"Coloureds" Back their Ex-tormentor', *Observer*, 14 February.

Spencer, L. (1989) 'Church and State in Colonial Africa: Influences Governing the Political Activity of Christian Missions in Kenya', *Journal of Church and State*, vol. XXXI, no. 1, pp. 115–32.

Standard (Lagos) (1985) 'Subversive Elements Existing in Our Higher Institutions', 23 April.

Stewart, C. C. (1985) 'Introduction: Popular Islam in Twentieth-Century Africa', *Africa*, vol. LV, no. 4, pp. 363–8.

——— (1986) 'Islam', in A. Roberts (ed.), *The Cambridge History of Africa. Volume*

7: *From 1905 to 1940*, Cambridge University Press, Cambridge, pp. 191–222.

Strayer, R. (1976) 'Mission History in Africa: New Perspectives on an Encounter', *African Studies Review*, vol. XIX, no. 1, pp. 1–15.

Sundkler, B. (1961) *Bantu Prophets in South Africa*, Oxford University Press, London.

Ter Haar, G. (1992) *Spirit of Africa*, Hurst and Co., London.

Thomas A. (with Crow. B., Frenz, P., Hewitt, T., Kassam, S. and Treagust, S.) (1994) *Third World Atlas*, Open University Press, Milton Keynes.

Tingle, R. (1992) *Revolution or Reconciliation? The Struggle in the Church in South Africa*, Christian Studies Centre, London.

Toulabor, C. (1991) 'Temoignage sur le Diocese de Lomé', *Politique Africaine*, no. 43, pp. 123–5.

——— (1994) 'Nouvelles Eglises et Processus de Démocratisation au Ghana', paper presented at round table, 'Mouvements Religieux de Debats Democratiques en Afrique', University of Pau, December 5–7.

Triaud, J.-L. (1982) 'L'Islam et l'Etat en Republique du Niger', *Le Mois en Afrique*, no. 194–5, pp. 10–25, 35–48.

Trimingham, J. (1949) *Islam in the Sudan*, Oxford University Press, Oxford.

——— (1980) *The Influence of Islam upon Africa*, Longman, London.

Tripp, A. (1992) 'Local Organizations, Participation and the State in Urban Tanzania', in G. Hyden and M. Bratton (eds), *Governance and Politics in Africa*, Lynne Rienner Publishers, Boulder, Colo. and London.

Turner, H. (1988) 'Africa', in S. Sutherland, L. Holden, P. Clarke and H. Friedhelm (eds), *The World's Religions*, Routledge, London, pp. 945–52.

Turner, V. (1969) *The Ritual Process. Structure and Anti-Structure*, Cornell University Press, Ithaca.

Twaddle, M. (1988) 'The Emergence of Politico-Religious Groupings in Late Nineteenth Century Buganda', *Journal of African History*, vol. XXIX, pp. 81–92.

Usman, Y. (1979) *For the Liberation of Nigeria*, New Beacon Books, London.

Vaillancourt, J.-G. (1980) *Papal Power. A Study of Vatican Control over Lay Catholic Elites*, University of California Press, Berkeley.

van Dijk, R. (1992) 'Young Puritan Preachers in Post-Independent Malawi', *Africa*, vol. LXI, no. 2, pp. 159–81.

Villalón, L. (1995) *Islamic Society and State Power in Senegal*, Cambridge University Press, Cambridge.

Voll, J. (1991) 'Fundamentalism in the Sunni Arab World', in M. Marty and R. Scott Appleby (eds), *Fundamentalisms Observed*, University of Chicago Press, Chicago, pp. 345–402.

Wald. K. (1990) 'The New Christian Right in American Politics', in E. Sahliyeh (ed.), *Religious Resurgence and Politics in the Contemporary World*, State University of New York Press, Albany, pp. 49–66.

Wallace-Johnson, T. (1936), quoted in F. Furedi, *Colonial Wars and the Politics of Third World Nationalism*, I.B. Tauris, London, 1994, p. 33.

Wallis, R. (1984) *The Elementary Forms of the New Religious Life*, Routledge, London.

Wallis, R. and Bruce, S. (1992) 'Secularization: The Orthodox Model', in Bruce (ed.), *Religion and Modernization*, Clarendon Press, Oxford, pp. 8–30.

Walshe, P. (1991) 'South Africa: Prophetic Christianity and the Liberation Movement, *Journal of Modern African Studies*, vol. XXIX, no. 1, pp. 27–60.

Wang, M. (1992) 'Long War of Words Brings No Peace', *Guardian*, 28 February.
Weber, M. (1969) 'Major Features of the World Religions', in R. Robertson (ed.), *Sociology of Religion*, Penguin, Baltimore, pp. 19–41.
—— (1978) *Economy and Society*, University of California Press, Berkeley.
Webber, M. (1992) 'Angola: Continuity and Change', *Journal of Communist Studies*, vol. VIII, no. 2, pp. 317–33.
Weekes, R. (1978). 'Introduction' and 'Punjab', in Weekes (ed.), *Muslim Peoples. A World Ethnographic Survey*, Greenwood, London, pp. ix–xxxii and 314–23.
Weiner, M. (1992) 'Peoples and States in a New Ethnic Order?', *Third World Quarterly*, vol. XIII, no. 2, pp. 317–33.
Welbourne, F. (1968) 'A Note on Types of Religious Society', in C. Baeta (ed.), *Christianity in Tropical Africa*, Oxford University Press, London.
West Africa, (1993a) 'Editorial: Diouf's Delayed Victory', 22–28 March 1993, p. 455.
—— (1993b) 'Memorial Mass', 1–7 November 1993, p. 1987.
Wignaraja, P. (1993) 'Rethinking Development and Democracy', in Wignaraja (ed.), *New Social Movements in the South*, Zed Books, London, pp. 4–35.
Williams, G. (1960) '*Egemonia* in the Thought of Antonio Gramsci', *Journal of the History of Ideas*, October–December, p. 587, quoted in J. Femia, 'Hegemony and Consciousness in the Thought of Antonio Gramsci', *Political Studies*, vol. XXIII, no. 1, 1975, pp. 29–48, at pp. 30–31.
Williams, H. (1992) *International Relations in Political Theory*, Open University Press, Milton Keynes.
Wilson, B. (1985) 'A Typology of Sects', in R. Bocock and K. Thompson (eds), *Religion and Ideology*, Manchester University Press, Manchester.
Witte, J., Jr (1993) 'Introduction' in Witte, Jr. (ed.), *Christianity and Democracy in Global Context*, Westview, Boulder, Colo.
Wuthnow, R. (1991) 'Understanding Religion and Politics', *Daedalus*, vol. CXX, no. 3, pp. 1–20.
Young, C. (1976) *The Politics of Cultural Pluralism*, University of Wisconsin Press, Wisconsin.
—— (1988) 'The African Colonial State and its Political Legacy', in D. Rothchild and N. Chazan (eds), *The Precarious Balance. State and Society in Africa*, Westview, Boulder, Colo., pp. 25–66.

Index